The Scandal of
ULYSSES

The Scandal of
ULYSSES

The Sensational Life of a
Twentieth-Century Masterpiece

Bruce Arnold

St. Martin's Press
New York

Library of Congress Cataloging-in-Publication Data

Arnold, Bruce.
    The scandal of Ulysses: The sensational life of a twentieth-century masterpiece / Bruce Arnold.
        p.   cm.
    ISBN 0-312-08288-8
    1. Joyce, James, 1882–1941.   Ulysses.   I. Title.
PR6019.O9U57   1992
823'.912–dc20   92-13274
                                                                CIP

First published in Great Britain as *The Scandal of Ulysses* by Sinclair-Stevenson Limited.

First U.S. Edition: June 1992
10 9 8 7 6 5 4 3 2 1

Contents

Acknowledgements		vi
Foreword		xi
ONE	The Birth of the Hero	1
TWO	Ulysses Sets Out	26
THREE	The Trials of Ulysses	42
FOUR	Which Version is Copyright?	64
FIVE	The Coming of the Scholars	87
SIX	*Ulysses* for Everyone?	102
SEVEN	A New, Original *Ulysses*	127
EIGHT	Floundering On	140
NINE	'Is No One Awake At The Wheel?	172
TEN	The Committee That Never Met	192
ELEVEN	'What Sort of a Kip is This?'	210
TWELVE	Anthony Burgess Takes Back His Words	227
Afterword		249
A Chronology of Ulysses		257
Index		267

Acknowledgements

A S THE text of this book makes clear, my interest in Joyce as a writer goes back to the early 1950s, when I read *A Portrait of the Artist as a Young Man*, and was so influenced by it as to choose Trinity College, Dublin, to pursue my university studies, with at least some weighting towards Irish literature. While there I put on the first full-length production of Joyce's play, *Exiles*, encouraged in the venture by Padraic Colum. By the time the James Joyce Tower was first opened, in 1962, I was editing a Dublin literary magazine. In that capacity, as well as the fringe capacity of journalist reporting for the *Guardian* newspaper, then in Manchester, I attended that event, with its impressive crowd of Irish Joyceans and post-Joyceans, among them Louis MacNeice, Flann O'Brien, Donagh MacDonagh, Patrick Kavanagh, Sylvia Beach and various Joyce relations. I still have the 'literature', as it is called – the event had a tourist angle to it. This, together with the growing emphasis on 'Joyce-appeal' at future literary events, particularly the 1982 centenary of Joyce's birth, which provoked a great deal of activity in his native city, lessened my own enthusiasm.

Interest of a quite different kind was provoked by John Kidd's essay, called 'The Scandal of *Ulysses*', published in June 1988 in the *New York Review of Books*. The title comes from the *Sporting Times* poster of 1922, prominently displayed in Sylvia Beach's bookshop at the time of the book's publication, when the newspaper, which catered more or less exclusively for a racing readership, took it into its editorial head to launch a vituperative attack on Joyce and his writing for its obscenity. I am in John Kidd's debt for inspiring my own interest, and for a long and detailed interview in Boston in the summer of 1990. By then I had attended my first International James Joyce Symposium and had interviewed many of the participants. I am particularly grateful to Clive Hart, Anthony Burgess, Hans Walter Gabler, Hugh Kenner, Charles Rossman, Morris Beja, Fritz Senn, Brenda Maddox, Carole Shloss, David Norris and Augustine Martin, who took part in the making of a film called 'The Scandal of *Ulysses*'.

The Scandal of *'Ulysses'* is more than the book of the film, but it did grow out of my experiences in 1990, making a film which sought to present, in an enjoyable and informative way, the complicated story which is now set out here in much greater detail. This film would not have been possible without the involvement and help of the Principality of Monaco, which invited me to the conference in a dual capacity, both as journalist and filmmaker. I owe in particular my gratitude for this to George Sandulescu, Nadia Lacoste and Virginia Gallico.

In addition to his help and encouragement in Monaco, Charles Rossman later helped me with researches at the Harry Ransom Humanities Research Center, in Austin, Texas, and organised for me a swift and fruitful visit to the University of Tulsa, in Oklahoma, to see the Ellmann Papers. In the first of these two institutions I was given assistance by Thomas F. Staley, who made available the impressive and newly-restored final proofs of *Ulysses* for a very rewarding inspection. At Tulsa Sid Huttner helped me with the Ellmann papers and also gave me assistance on other questions. I was helped also by Philip Hemming, Catherine Henderson and by Bob Spoo, editor of *The James Joyce Quarterly*.

· ACKNOWLEDGEMENTS ·

Denis Donoghue took the trouble to read the penultimate draft of the book and had many helpful suggestions. Charles Rossman helped with checking the typescript and he also suggested important changes.

I was greatly helped in my researches in Dublin by Mary Brennan-Holahan, who pursued and located many obscure references, found books, read and advised on early drafts, and became increasingly committed to the story contained in these pages. Paddy Masterson, President of UCD, was kind enough to lend me his copy of the Rosenbach Manuscript, which was of considerable help during the work on the book. So, too, was that given by Gerald Goldberg. Additional research help came from Seamus Helferty, of the Archive Department in UCD, Robert Nicholson, David Webb and Ian Graham. My sister, Lena Shaw, did research for me in England and made several analyses of texts which were of great use. And my wife read the drafts of the book from its early stages, and offered much advice and encouragement.

No bibliography is given and footnotes have been kept to an absolute minimum. Joyce readers, understandably, fall into numerous categories as far as their knowledge of the man and the texts is concerned. Absolute beginners, as well as being urged to read *Ulysses*, swiftly, soon and without reference to scholarly guidance, are also pointed in the direction of Richard Ellmann's *James Joyce*, an excellent and thorough life of the writer, described by Anthony Burgess as 'the greatest literary biography of the century'. The other great joy, for those who admire the author, is reading his *Letters*, edited by Stuart Gilbert and Richard Ellmann, in two groupings some 20 years apart, but later made available in a three-volume edition. This is currently out of print, though a *Selected Letters* is available. The *Letters* show how subtle and witty Joyce was in his dealings with people.

As soon as one moves into criticism, advice becomes more complicated. The following books have been used, both for general background and for specific detail, on a chapter-by-chapter basis. Where relevant this is indicated in the text, together with some judgment about the value of the information and the quality of the writing. *Nora*, by Brenda Maddox (London, 1988) adds considerable detail to the affairs of the family, both at the time of Joyce's death (one of the weaker points in Ellmann's life) and later. Sylvia Beach wrote a memoir called *Shakespeare and Company* (London, 1960) which gives a vivid first-hand account of the publication in 1922 of *Ulysses*, as well as covering the later developments, including her sale of the proofs. A more detailed study of Sylvia Beach and the period is contained in Noel Riley Fitch's book, *Sylvia Beach and the Lost Generation* (London, 1984). *Dear Miss Weaver*, by Jane Lidderdale and Mary Nicholson (London, 1970) is a rich and valuable account of a life which touched repeatedly on Joyce and his family's affairs. Marvin Magalaner and Richard M. Kain, in *Joyce: The Man, the Work, the Reputation* (London 1990; first published New York, 1956), give a lively and useful account of critical reaction to *Ulysses* from *The Little Review* appearances up to the 1950s. Stuart Gilbert's *James Joyce's 'Ulysses'* (London 1930, revised 1952) remains one of the best introductions to the book. Frank Budgen's *James Joyce and the Making of 'Ulysses'* (London 1934, new edition 1960) is very readable, and is close to the events in Joyce's life and to the actual work on the book.

For the serious student of the controversy covered in the following pages there is already a substantial literature, though much of it is in literary journals and not readily accessible. A detailed bibliography was prepared by Charles Rossman and published in the summer 1990 issue of *Studies in the Novel*. It is an essential starting point and also includes several important essays cited in this book. John Kidd's long-awaited work of detailed investigation, 'An Inquiry into *Ulysses: The Corrected*

Text', is in book form, to be obtained from the James
Joyce Research Center at Boston University, which has
also made available, over the past few years, a portfolio
of selected articles on the controversy. *Assessing the 1984
'Ulysses'*, edited by George Sandulescu and Clive Hart
(Gerrards Cross, 1986) contains important essays directly
related to the controversy.

Foreword

J AMES JOYCE'S *Ulysses* has always been a source of
scandal. Throughout its history it has provoked controversy. It is Joyce's most famous work, and also his greatest. It is certainly the most famous work of fiction of the
twentieth century, and arguably the profoundest and best as
well. An army of Joyce scholars around the world will attest
to these assertions. They know that their livelihoods depend
on that perception being maintained and strengthened, that
Joyce is all of this and much more besides. Major world
publishers have benefited from these immodest claims about
the writer, and most notably about *Ulysses* itself, which
has huge sales each year. Variously priced, and yielding
profit to the publishers and a substantial royalty to the heirs
of Joyce, the sales of the book – indeed of all Joyce's books –
have represented, for decades, an important part of the Joyce
industry.

On the first of January 1992 this changed. On that date,
throughout much of the world, James Joyce's works, as they
had originally been published, came out of copyright. By
that date John Kidd had signed a $350,000 contract with an
American publisher to produce the Dublin Edition of the
Works of James Joyce, to be published in Dublin under the
imprint of the Lilliput Press, and beginning, in June 1992,
with *Ulysses* itself. The introductions for each of the works
are being written by Denis Donoghue, Henry James Professor
of English and American Letters at New York University. In
January 1992 also the first four of seven volumes from the

Penguin Group in London appeared, constituting, in part, a post-copyright edition of Joyce's works. This enterprise, as has been the case with so much of the publishing of James Joyce, has been a botched job. For *Ulysses* the Penguin Group went back to the 1960–61, Bodley Head–Random House version, unannotated, and not edited at all. For *Dubliners* the Robert Scholes, Walton Litz edition was used. This edition, when it first appeared, and also when it was subsequently revised and re-issued, carried a James Joyce Estate claim to copyright. No such claim is made with the 1992 Penguin printing. As for *A Portrait of the Artist as a Young Man*, the overall editor of the Penguin edition, Seamus Deane, Professor of Modern English and American Literature at University College, Dublin, who also claims to edit this volume, in fact uses the Chester Anderson edition of 1964. The extent of his own editing is covered by a single sentence: "Some obvious errors have been silently corrected." Again, no copyright claim is made on behalf of the James Joyce Estate.

Other publishers, both in Dublin and London, are producing James Joyce's works in further editions, with introductions written by writers and academics.

The James Joyce Estate no longer controls the copyright in Joyce's works, except in the United States. And, as readers will discover in the following pages, the situation even in the United States is unclear, particularly in respect to *Ulysses*. Gone is copyright on quotations for academic and general works, on the films and television programmes made from Joyce short stories or other works, the theatre royalties on Joyce's one play, *Exiles*, and on adaptations of other works for the stage. And it would seem that those new copyright claims made for versions of *Dubliners* and *A Portrait of the Artist as a Young Man* in the 1960s are not being respected by publishers. And of course the new copyright claim for *Ulysses*, based on the re-editing of the work carried out between 1977 and its publication in 1984, by Hans Walter Gabler – the principal subject of this book – has been made largely redundant by the discrediting of that enterprise. All of James Joyce's published work, in the versions as they appeared at the time of first publication, including those mentioned above, or indeed as re-printed up to Joyce's death, on January 12, 1941, have now fallen within the public domain, and no longer attract a royalty payment to the James Joyce Estate.

The Scandal of Ulysses largely concerns one book and its critical and editing history during the twentieth century. In 1977 a re-editing of *Ulysses* was begun. It appeared to conclude in 1984, when the results were published, together with a further copyright claim, reinforced in 1986, by the appearance of a commercial, or trade edition of the work, which for a time has sold worldwide. Academically, this achievement can be debated, argued over, criticised. But as a legal claim to a new copyright it carries weight by virtue of the large number of changes to the text deriving from a substantial variety of sources, many of them manuscript.

That *Ulysses* needed re-editing was inescapable. The difficulties of achieving an acceptable new edition were enormous. James Joyce himself was a major source of those difficulties. Immensely complex in his writing, endlessly fertile in his use of language, full of wit, puns, tricks, intentional errors, numerological devices, classical, scientific, medical, military, sexual, psychological allusions, and in the end wonderful treatment of character, atmosphere, emotion, and thought, he left a trail of dilemmas, paradoxes, questions behind him which armies of scholars have wrestled with for seventy years. He intended this. He claimed that he had put so many enigmas and puzzles into the book that they would keep the professors arguing over *Ulysses* for centuries. He regarded this as a way of insuring his immortality. But he was ambiguous as well. "The pity is," he said, "the public will demand and find a moral in my book, or worse they may take it in some serious way, and on the honour of a gentleman there is not one serious line in it." But then, Joyce was no gentleman. . . .

There is no end to the roundabout of Joyce's life and work.

Ulysses is a masterpiece, flawed by the vicissitudes of its early publication, mended by its creator, then by academics, worried at for all the reasons offered by Joyce himself, unresolved in its final form, and probably unresolvable. But let us see.

This book is a life of *Ulysses*, giving some detail of generation and birth, infancy, growth, maturity. Recorded here are the expectations, which were prolonged and ecstatic, the judgments, which were mixed and extensive, the development, which was more prodigious than that of any other book of our time, the discovery of imperfections and faults, and the eventual decision to remedy these.

Well before it appeared in book form, *Ulysses* had acquired worldwide notoriety. It was condemned as obscene. It was banned in the United States of America and in Britain. It was prosecuted before publication, when portions appeared in serial form, and was found by the courts to be obscene. It *is* obscene, of course, and it *is* a dirty book. But brilliantly and profoundly so. That is its appeal. But the very experiences which its author, its eventual publisher, its printer, and its subsequent supporters and publishers in other countries went through as a result of this set of difficulties, meant that the book's history became part of the reason for the corruption of the book's text.

The 1977 decision to re-edit led to a major revival of controversy about the book which has raged, privately and publicly, for ten years, and is far from resolved. The Scandal of *Ulysses*, which revolved around the book at the time of its first publication, is with us all again. And it promises to stay, and to grow – more power to Joyce's elbow, that he could leave us with such a legacy.

ONE

The Birth of the Hero

'Would you let Shakespeare and Company have the
honour of bringing out your *Ulysses?*'
Sylvia Beach to James Joyce, 1921

J AMES JOYCE'S novel, *Ulysses*, is an obscene book.
It is also a very dirty book. It is obscene not today in
the accepted legal sense of the term but in the much
simpler form in which the word has a precise Latin
meaning, that it deals frankly with behaviour, habits and
actions which in life are generally private. It enters the
mind, for example, of a man sitting in a privy at the back
of his house in Eccles Street, Dublin, defecating. Joyce's
description is not simply of the episode as a passing event,
briefly noted; it is a detailed delineation of the whole
physical cycle of the action, from entering the privy and
looking up at the windows of neighbouring houses to see
if his duties are being witnessed to his coming forth again
from the gloom into the air. Leopold Bloom decides he
can take his time, hold onto it a bit. He retains his stool
until he is quite ready and then eases his bowels with
the sense of it being just the right size, not so big as to en-
courage piles, and clearly providing him, in terms of the
weight and girth and consistency of the matter, with evidence that the constipation he was suffering from the
previous day has passed. He is reading the newspaper as
he sits in the privy and goes on doing so, with his own

smell rising to his nostrils. He then relieves his bladder as well. He wipes his fundament with a portion of the paper he has been reading, pulls up his trousers, fixes his braces, does up his fly-buttons and leaves the jakes to set out on his day's journey through Dublin.

This is obscene literature, welcomed today as such and justly celebrated for the breakthrough in creative writing which in part it represented, in this and other sections. It is not, in the words of the judge in New York who eventually found in favour of the book and released it from the entirely undeserved ban under which it had suffered for the first ten years after publication, obscene in the legal sense as it was then defined, a book 'tending to stir the sex impulses or to lead to sexually impure and lustful thoughts'. On that score the judge in question, whose name was John M. Woolsey, thought the book to be quite the reverse, certainly when read in its entirety.

Other episodes are obscene in much the same way, though perhaps less obviously than the brilliant presentation, in the fourth episode, of Bloom's excretory performance. There is, for example, the much more subtle description, in the 'Nausicaa' episode, of Bloom masturbating at the sight of Gerty MacDowell's underclothes and thighs, up to her knickers. Then there is Molly Bloom's soliloquy, with its many references to sexual activity, menstruation and the same more frequent physical functions already referred to in the section involving her husband. Joyce treats all of them with artistic respect and incomparable literary skill.

He actually creates for us, perhaps for the first time in literature, what it feels like, in the mind and the gut, to be sitting on a lavatory having a shit, or, as might be more usual in Dublin, a shite. (Neither word, it should be pointed out, is used at that particular point in the book.) 'Shit' and 'shite' are dirty words. Judge Woolsey said of the words in *Ulysses* criticised as being dirty that they were 'old Saxon words known to almost all men and, I venture, to many women, and are such words as would be naturally and habitually used, I believe, by the types of folk whose life, physical and mental, Joyce is seeking to describe'. As American writers would in due course show, this was a somewhat refined and narrow view of the limitations upon the use of Saxon words in life and literature. But it was a matter at issue with Joyce and *Ulysses* – though not his other works – from the beginning. That in a sense brings us to the dirty aspect of the book. It is hardly obscene to use dirty words, which we hear and use ourselves regularly. Nevertheless, 'shit', 'cunt', 'fuck', 'bugger', 'shite', 'arse', 'prick', 'arsehole' – all of which appear, quite naturally deployed, in the text – are dirty words and make *Ulysses* technically a dirty book. Though we think we are more enlightened now, more liberal in our interpretation of what is permissible in writing, these are still words which we do not regularly find in newspapers and journals, used in no matter which way. Even in novels and stories, where descriptions involving such words abound, they are often replaced with euphemisms because of the continuing view that they are somehow in bad taste. In Joyce, they shock in a way in which so many similarly worded works fail to shock. This is because Joyce uses the language with absolute precision and masterly intent. There is a density and penetration in his writing which seems almost to leave behind it an odour, a stain on the emotions. But it is also because he is quite uninhibited in his interest in that which is obscene. It is equal with the other material he requires for his writing. He is determined to express it with the full range of language available to him, even if that range embraces words which shock and disturb.

The masterly and uninhibited use of ideas and language to express himself does not lessen, in the traditional sense of the term, the 'dirtiness' of Joyce's writing. Posterity has, quite properly, come to appreciate and admire both the obscenity and the use of dirty words.

But if one sought to explain the dilemma of *Ulysses*, its abiding scandalousness, indeed the very problems which have dogged the work from its inception, then it is its actual obscenity and its use of dirty language which will explain a great deal of what follows. In forcing upon its author the strange course he took in order to bring the completed work eventually to the eyes of an international reading public, the very real problems of obscenity in thought and the use of dirty words lie at the root of Joyce's later problems with the book. The book is infinitely more, of course. But at least part of its magic derives from Joyce's penetration into the deepest and most secret recesses of the human mind, particularly with his two immortal characters, Leopold and Molly Bloom.

Ulysses was published on James Joyce's 40th birthday, 2 February 1922. It had taken him eight years to write. It was already notorious. Its appearance with an American publisher had been blocked by prosecution for obscenity in New York in 1920. It had been appearing there in serial form, in the bi-monthly magazine, *The Little Review*, since 1918.

Its publication in England had also run into trouble. There, through the good offices of Ezra Pound, Joyce had earlier been introduced to Harriet Shaw Weaver, who had been principal editor of *The Egoist* since June 1914 and had been instrumental in persuading the magazine to publish *A Portrait of the Artist as a Young Man*. This book, Joyce's first novel, appeared in serial form during the latter half of 1914 and into the following year, being then published in book form in 1916. Her plan now was to publish the new novel, *Ulysses*, in the same way and in January 1918 she had offered Joyce the sum of £50 on the strength of the first three chapters, shown to her by Pound. When these had been read by Ezra Pound, he told Joyce, 'I recon' your a damn fine writer, that's what I recon'. An' I recon' this here work o' yourn is some concarn'd literature.' Five instalments of *Ulysses* appeared in *The Egoist* during 1919, but Weaver ran into trouble with her printers and there were objections from subscribers to the book appearing in a periodical. Some went so far as to cancel subscriptions.

Pound, who was also acting as go-between with American publications and publishers, was shifting his interest at the time from *Poetry*, edited by Harriet Monroe, and exclusively concerned with the publication of verse, to *The Little Review*, which was edited by Margaret Anderson and Jane Heap. Pound was instrumental in that introduction as well, though he obstructed any direct contact between the two American women editors and Joyce. They later complained that he treated Joyce as a private possession. But they were immensely impressed by the first episodes of *Ulysses*. Margaret Anderson read the opening lines of the 'Proteus' episode and exclaimed: 'This is the most beautiful thing we'll ever have. We'll print it if it's the last effort of our lives.' Print it they did, setting inexorably in motion the process which would lead to prosecution for obscenity and the start of all the book's subsequent tribulations.

During that period, between 1918 and the actual New York prosecution of *The Little Review* in December 1920, Harriet Shaw Weaver made further attempts to achieve publication. By March of 1918 she was telling Joyce that she wanted to publish in book form, which pleased him, though he replied by suggesting that the book – in more senses than one – might turn out to be 'a Greek gift'. But she needed to find an avant-garde printer with some courage. At Roger Fry's suggestion, Harriet Weaver went to see Leonard and Virginia Woolf. They found her an incongruous figure, as indeed she was, a fierce feminist, but at the same time a severely correct Quaker, whom Virginia Woolf described in her diary as 'buttoned-up' and 'a wool-gloved missionary'. Twenty years later, when Joyce died, the memory of that occasion was still vivid and Virginia wrote in her diary on 15 January 1941:

'Then Joyce is dead: Joyce about a fortnight younger than I am. I remember Miss Weaver, in wool gloves, bringing *Ulysses* in typescript to our tea table at Hogarth House.' The Woolfs' main problem about printing the book, quite apart from whether they would publish, was its length. Handsetting it at the Hogarth Press would take two years, though the book could have been set elsewhere and published under the Hogarth imprint. But Virginia Woolf had other reservations as well. She described the book as 'reeling with indecency'. In a later review, in the form of a general survey of her contemporaries which appeared after the publication of *Ulysses*, she described the book as 'a memorable catastrophe – immense in daring, terrific in disaster'. She modified this view, but remained ambivalent towards Joyce and his writing. In 1941, a few weeks before her suicide and shortly after James Joyce's death, she wrote: 'He was about the place, but I never saw him. I bought the blue paper book, and read it here one summer I think with spasms of wonder, of discovery, and then again with long lapses of intense boredom. This goes back to a pre-historic world. And now all the gents are furbishing up opinions, and the books, I suppose, take their place in the long procession.'

As Joyce continued to write, so he continued to distribute versions of the text of his masterpiece, with no clear idea of its future destiny. Not only did he send them to Ezra Pound, in duplicate, who in turn was sending them to two publishers in England and America; he also sent them to people for entirely different reasons. One example of this manuscript prodigality illuminates deviousness on Joyce's part, unsuccessful though it was.

One of the bountiful women who eased the erratic progress of James Joyce's life was Mrs Harold McCormick, who also managed to amuse Nora at the same time. Mrs McCormick, who was reputed to be the wealthiest woman in Zurich – a distinct possibility, since she was the daughter of John D. Rockefeller – and was in any case a splendid creature, with her *'embonpoint*, dresses, furs and diamonds', had bestowed money on Joyce. She had first wanted to do this anonymously and communicated to Joyce through a bank in Zurich that a credit balance of 12,000 francs was lodged there as a fellowship for him, with payments of 1,000 francs a month coming to him from 1 March 1918. He found out the identity of his benefactress quickly enough through the Zurich Opera House soprano, Charlotte Sauermann, who knew and was unable to keep the confidence to herself; and when he called on Mrs McCormick she told him 'I know you are a great artist'.

She was also a patroness of Carl Jung and was annoyed when Joyce repeatedly declined to submit to analysis. He attributed to this the cutting off of his allowance, which was done quite without warning. The rude shock was announced to him when he called in person at the bank on 1 October 1919 in dire need of cash, only to be told that his credit had been cut off. He blamed the treachery of friends – as he often did – though it seems much more likely that Mrs McCormick simply came to the belief that Joyce, in the calmer post-war atmosphere could, and should, make his own way. In an effort to restore her financial help he sent her a manuscript of part of *Ulysses* – probably 'Scylla and Charybdis', episode nine, which he later recovered and sold to John Quinn – but it had no other effect than to elicit a gracious note thanking him, telling him the reason for her decision – 'you will find publishers and will come forward yourself' – and offering to return the manuscript should he ever need it.

It seems reasonably certain that Mrs McCormick, who was a fine horsewoman, contributed to the character of Mrs Mervyn Tallboys, in her Amazon costume, hard hat, jackboots 'cockspurred', vermilion waistcoat and fawn gauntlets, appearing as a fantasy figure representing the society woman with a horsewhip who terrorises Leopold Bloom in 'Circe', the brothel episode from *Ulysses*. She gets a wonderful squirm out of Bloom when she threatens to flay him alive and goes on: 'You have lashed the dormant tigress in my nature into fury' – and she orders him to take down his trousers without further delay. 'Come here, sir! Quick! Ready?' This lively caricature by Joyce is not inconsistent with the quite generous feelings he expressed on her death, more than ten years later, nor with the amused tolerance Nora felt towards her, quietly speculating to her silent husband about the kind of underwear the rich American woman wore.

In due course this manuscript was to go to John Quinn, the New York lawyer, patron of artists and collector of writers' manuscripts. But it took time. Quinn was another of those who took an interest in Joyce and who were introduced to him by Ezra Pound, and Quinn first sent Joyce money as early as March 1917, in return for the manuscript of Joyce's only play, *Exiles*. At the time Quinn also offered to buy 'the corrected proof sheets' of *A Portrait of the Artist as a Young Man*, which Joyce apparently accepted.

Quinn's relationship with Joyce was always rather prickly. Quinn himself was a choleric man, abrupt and self-willed in his behaviour, impatient with the subtleties of normal friendship and wealthy enough to be able to behave much as he pleased. He was at first faint-hearted in his admiration and Joyce was quite mocking of him, composing a limerick which suggested that the lawyer took a long time to understand the purpose and meaning of the play. Quinn was later shocked by the language of the first episode from *Ulysses* published in *The Little Review*. But he had an eye for a literary 'find' and saw the potential of Joyce's writing from the collector's viewpoint. By the end of 1919, as Joyce records in a letter to Frank Budgen, negotiations were going on with Quinn for the purchase of the full manuscript of *Ulysses*, which of course was still far from finished. Quinn offered 700 francs on account and increased this offer to 1,500 francs, but with no mention of the final sum which would be paid. In 1920 what Quinn actually paid, altogether, was $503.85, and by the summer of that year an agreement had been reached between writer and patron. Quinn was sending these instalments, not exactly regularly, and Joyce was corresponding with him, telling him, among other things, of the overall design of the book, and that he was rewriting the 'Circe' episode *for the sixth time*. One manuscript sent by Joyce never arrived, as he recorded in a letter to his friend Frank Budgen in September 1920.

By then, John Quinn had become involved in Joyce's affairs in quite a different capacity. In that same month the secretary of the New York Society for the Prevention of Vice, John Sumner, had lodged an official complaint against the 'Nausicaa' episode, which had appeared in the July–August issue of *The Little Review*. Quinn, liking neither the magazine nor its two women editors, who reciprocated his distaste, agreed to take on the defence without fee. He had already been involved, trying to sanitise the episode slightly. 'Nausicaa' takes place at twilight, on the rocks on Sandymount Strand, where Gerty MacDowell, Cissie Caffrey and Edy Boardman (all of whom are to appear later in the book), with Cissie's two boys and Baby Boardman in his pushchair, gather to enjoy the warm June evening and to watch the bazaar fireworks. The lonely figure of Leopold Bloom sits nearby, staring at Gerty. They are drawn to each other, indeed sexually attracted, and silently, at a distance, they make love. Gerty, who wishes with increasing frustration that everyone else would vanish and leave her with the increasingly appealing gentleman who is exciting her, pulls up and by degrees lifts her skirt to show her legs above the knee, leans back ever further to watch the Roman candles, blushes, trembles and feels his eyes caressing her skin through the white nainsook knickers. Bloom, in his sad concentration upon her beauty, quietly masturbates. His climax and orgasm coincide with the climax of the firework display, a long Roman candle bursting up above the trees, and he makes his shirt wet. Later, he has to recompose it 'with careful hand'. On its way to *The Little Review*, the equally careful and fastidious John Quinn felt that this went too far and indulged in minor censorship: 'I did myself dry Bloom's shirt.' His real aim was to avoid the episodic appearance of the book prejudicing its eventual publication in its complete form. He was not successful.

There was a preliminary hearing in October 1920, followed by further attempts by Quinn to get the trial postponed long enough to have the whole book published. Quinn's strategy, aimed at getting a General Sessions trial before a judge and jury, would have delayed things for a year or more, and would possibly have allowed for the writing of the book to be completed and a private edition published, thus securing Joyce's copyright and making the case in the courts essentially academic. He pleaded the large issues at stake, including Joyce's copyright and American rights in the book. But he was tripped up by his own ingenuity, since the judge ruled in favour of an early trial, in Special Sessions, without a jury, before three judges, for exactly the same arguments which were being used by Quinn – that much was at stake. For this trial, with the prosecution's case based on the 'Nausicaa' episode, Quinn's line of defence was simple enough; people would either understand the passage complained of, or not. If they understood it, then it would either amuse or bore them, but would hardly corrupt. The magistrate, J. E. Corrigan, was unconvinced. He thought the passage 'where the man went off in his pants' unmistakable in meaning, and smutty and filthy in intent, and he ordered the case to go to trial. In February 1921, the trial took place and on 21 February the three judges, although two of them had found the allegedly obscene passages quite incomprehensible, convicted Margaret Anderson and Jane Heap of publishing obscenity, and fined them $50 each. Joyce told Bennett Cerf, of Random House, that he believed the two editors had their fingerprints taken.

Leaving the courtroom, and a bit humiliated at not being sent to prison and at having received so small a fine, the editors were told by Quinn: 'And now, for God's sake, don't publish any more obscene literature.' Margaret Anderson was totally bewildered. 'How am I to know when it's obscene?' Quinn replied: 'I'm sure *I* don't know, but don't do it.' The court decision effectively meant that no American publisher would risk bringing out the book. Joyce was close to despair and went to see his friend, Sylvia Beach, who ran Shakespeare and Company, the Left Bank bookshop which catered for expatriates in Paris. 'My book will never come out now,' he told her, and she recalled later how he always pronounced 'boo-ok' with a long, mock-Irish vowel sound, making the sad announcement even more plaintive. She startled even herself by replying to him: 'Would you let Shakespeare and Company have the honour of bringing out your *Ulysses*?'

This slightly diffident young American girl had only met Joyce in the summer of 1920, when her bookshop was in its first year. She had started it out of a love of literature and was inspired by Adrienne Monnier. Monnier was a bookseller who ran an establishment called La Maison des Amis des Livres, known as 'the Monnier Chapel' at 7 rue de l'Odéon, round the corner from Sylvia Beach's shop, which was in the steep little rue Dupuytren. Both women were to remain friends of Joyce's for the next twenty years. They had searched together for a vacant shop near to the 'Monnier Chapel', eventually finding what had once been a laundry. It had the words '*fin*' and '*gros*' on either side of the door, meaning that its services were offered for sheets as well as fine linen. Adrienne Monnier, who was a plump woman, placed herself on the *gros* side of the door, Sylvia on the other side. 'That's you and me,' she said. Sylvia Beach cabled her mother in Princeton: 'Opening bookshop in Paris. Please send money.' Her mother sent her all her savings.

When Sylvia Beach met Joyce, at a party to which her bookseller friend and mentor had brought her, he was drooping in a corner. He extended his limp, boneless hand and asked her what she did. He became intrigued with the name of her bookshop and promised to visit her, which he did the next day. Her interest was well-informed. She had read him and admired him as a writer, rather than as the literary celebrity he had already become. On that first visit to the shop they discussed his method of writing and the progress he was making with *Ulysses*. She learned then that Joyce, because of his money difficulties, was already selling the manuscript portions of the book, as he completed them, to John Quinn, but she claimed that as soon as he finished an instalment (the word is hers) he made *a fair copy* and sent it off.

It will be readily apparent that the physical fortunes of the manuscript were unusual, by any standards, and that Joyce himself played a material part in creating the textual and editorial problems which have haunted his book ever since. He did so because he needed money. He always needed money, spent it with prodigality and seemed quite prepared to furnish versions of his own manuscripts for the collectors who emerged – as we have seen – before the books themselves were complete. By the time he was rescued from despair, through the startling intervention of Sylvia Beach, he had published, sold and given away episodes, chapters, versions or drafts of his books and his play, in the United States and elsewhere, had distributed a variety of manuscript and typescript versions of parts of *Ulysses*, had been steadily selling further versions of the text to John Quinn, and had meanwhile been correcting either second or third copies of these sections, as his fertile mind continued to apply itself to the late transcripts.

In the light of this unusual process of gestation, a brief account should be given of Joyce's method of composition. There are many versions. They include that of Frank Budgen, who assisted Joyce during the writing of *Ulysses* and published *James Joyce and the Making of 'Ulysses'* in 1934. Budgen also corresponded with Joyce, notably about such issues as the manuscript sales he made and his general money affairs. Then there is Ellmann's detailed analysis in the pages of his great biography.

The writing of *Ulysses* goes back at least to the early years of the century and possibly earlier still. (Joyce claimed that the character of Ulysses had always fascinated him, even as a boy.) It was first conceived as an additional short story, to be added to *Dubliners*, but this was never written. It represented an idea during the period from 1907 to 1914, when Joyce was writing *A Portrait of the Artist as a Young Man*. For three years, from 1914 to 1917, his work on the book is unclear, since no manuscript material has come down to us and very few references are made to it before about 1916. In September of that year he wrote to W. B. Yeats to say that he was writing 'a book *Ulysses* which however will not be published for some years'. Two months later, in a letter to Harriet Shaw Weaver, he claimed that he began *Ulysses* in Rome either six or seven years earlier, in 1909 or 1910, and that he hoped to complete it in 1918. In a letter to Ezra Pound, written on 9 April 1917, he acknowledged having sufficient material to be able to send him just one excerpt, what Joyce called the Hamlet chapter. This was probably Episode 9, 'Scylla and Charybdis'. But in the same letter the author is evasive about offering anything else in the near future from *Ulysses* and suggests instead 'a simple translation or review', notwithstanding the fact that he not only did not wish to give time to other writing, but felt he was bad at it. He deplored his own capacities as a critic and gave Pound the example of a two-volume work given to him by a friend to read; Joyce found he had been concentrating for some days on the second volume without having looked at the first, possibly without realising that it wasn't the first. He described himself at the time as writing *Ulysses* by different means and in different parts. In a letter on 22 April to Harriet Shaw Weaver he described his writing of *Ulysses* as going at the usual snail's pace.

But it then began to speed up. In September 1917, he sent to Claud Sykes further parts of what he described then as the 'Telemachia', the first three episodes. This is earlier than Richard Ellmann records in his biography (which is December), since from the first days of that month Joyce was sending corrections and changes to the manuscript versions which Sykes had already had for some weeks.

Between then and 29 October 1921, when Joyce announced that the book was finished (though it was not, of course), he worked steadily, giving it virtually all his time and, as we have seen, distributing evidence of his work in all directions. The earliest manuscripts to have survived are fair copies of the opening chapters sent to Claud Sykes in late 1917. By March 1918, Pound had entered the picture and was receiving episodes as they were completed. They came to him in duplicate, so that he could send them on to the two magazines which were attempting to serialise the book.

By this stage Joyce had established a routine which involved his various typists doing a top copy with at least two carbons. The typists, as is generally the case with writers everywhere, were 'amateur' and some more so than others, so that there were usually slight revisions when the three copies came back to Joyce. It was his habit to correct two of them extensively, but to leave the third aside with only its initial revisions. The idea in Joyce's mind seems to have been that the book, in its *final* form, would be published by either, or both, of the publishers of it in *serial* form, or by close associates. It would therefore be set from one or other of the two revised typescripts which had passed through Pound's hands on their way to Harriet Shaw Weaver in England, and to Margaret Anderson and Jane Heap in New York.

Of course it was not to work out like that at all. In the nature of both printing and publishing, typescripts get lost, quite often irretrievably. When seas and oceans are put between them the situation becomes even more complicated. When it came about that *Ulysses*, instead of first appearing in book form in England and America, was to be published first in Paris by Sylvia Beach, there was no copy to send to the printer except the remaining, uncorrected carbon, which had been held back by Joyce in reserve. This copy did not carry the changes which had been made after the typing and before the scripts were sent off to Ezra Pound. Joyce was thus faced with a situation in which later corrected versions of parts of his book had already been published in serial form in New York, while he was offering to the printer in France an earlier, uncorrected version, or at least uncorrected in the sense of the changes made to the two distributed copies of each episode. This was in the spring of 1921. He of course set to work all over again, revising and correcting the unrevised, third typescript version, working, we must assume, from memory, from copies of *The Little Review* in his possession, or borrowed from Shakespeare and Company. He now regularly visited the shop and used it shamelessly when he needed to consult books, and also borrowed money pretty shamelessly, too; in return, he informed its owner about progress. What we know is that his correcting of *Ulysses* for actual publication was certainly not done from his own typescript version of the book.

Though the episodes of *Ulysses* which had appeared in *The Little Review* had been sent in what was then their final form, they still contained some errors. At the same time the episodes were, at that point in composition, authentic and up to date – more so than the uncorrected third typescript, which now should have been brought up to the same level of correction. But this could not be, since Joyce, by his very nature, was both a bad corrector of his own work and an inventive rewriter of the same material. It is as absurd to imagine that he could deal objectively with the existing third typescript, in terms of making it identical with the earlier two copies, as it is to imagine that Turner could arrive at a varnishing day at the Royal Academy and not bring out his paints and brushes and do more work on his allegedly finished canvases. James Joyce had become doubly the victim of his own impetuous and highly creative nature, and was faced with the problem of an opportunity not to be missed: that of reworking his novel.

This dilemma created just one of the many problems of later editing of *Ulysses* and it is peculiar to Joyce. It led to a situation where a question of the authenticity of the earlier, rather than the later corrected version, became part of the problem. In general, a writer writes in expectation of being published. He either does this without any clear idea of who will publish, or when, or he works directly for a publisher with whom he has an established relationship. The process has a harmony and rhythm to it which is detached from the intensity of preparing copy for a publisher, or working towards a series of deadlines for serial publication, long before the complete work can be seen as a whole. This may have been normal for 19th-century novelists like Dickens, whose ability to cope with serial publication was to some extent in keeping with his approach to fiction and his general style. But by the end of the 19th century this was unusual. It still prevailed, but it was in no sense the norm. With Joyce it was rather different. Longing, as he did, to see his work in print, he was nevertheless determined not to capitulate on content, even when the charges of obscenity had been proved in court and had frightened off his potential

American publishers. At the same time he was constantly prepared to change what he had written for the purer reason of getting it right, within the absolute limits of his own creativity. He therefore operated as a writer towards the target of serial publication, a condition greatly complicated by the fact that his work was seen as obscene and therefore handicapped in a way that Dickens's, for example, was not.

Both aspects affected Joyce. The writer who sent typescripts to Pound in 1918 and 1919 was altered by the experiences of 1920 and 1921, if by no other consideration than that of further writing. When he came to address the book all over again for a French printer and his new, inexperienced Paris publisher, we cannot make categorical statements about the earlier versions being closer to what Joyce wanted, simply because they were corrected in a sequence which was, at the time, more logical. The fact is that James Joyce was faced with a fair and positive offer from Sylvia Beach in 1921, having seen that his book would not succeed elsewhere, and he had to address the unusual problem for a renowned writer – as he was then becoming – of having a publisher but of not having the book, at least in corrected form and complete. The third typescript on which he worked then became the version of *Ulysses* which he sent to the printer. Even that did not suffice.

Joyce's agreement with Sylvia Beach was for an edition of 1,000 copies. She would find as many subscribers in advance of publication as she could. Joyce would get the handsome-sounding royalty of 66 per cent of the net profits. The prospectus for the book announced that it would be published 'complete as written' and that this event would take place 'in the autumn of 1921'. It gave details of the different versions, 100 on Dutch paper, and signed, at 350 francs; 150 on *vergé-d'arches*, at 250 francs; 750 on plain paper at 150 francs. Compared with the prices for French books at the time, this was specialist, book-collector pricing and it reflected the celebrity status of the author. Sylvia Beach knew virtually nothing about fine printing and limited editions. She had learnt the rules from Adrienne, who also helped her with the prospectus, ensuring that it looked professional. It had a small illustration of the author, a photograph taken in Zurich showing him bearded.

Joyce's women now rallied to his support. Sylvia Beach got on with the book and the problems of getting it printed. Adrienne Monnier had come up with the name of Maurice Darantiere, a printer in Dijon. He gave Sylvia Beach advice about paper, binding and typefaces. At that time she also took on an assistant, a Greek girl called Myrsine Moschos, who was to stay with her for nine years and who came from a large family of girls who could be called on to help when the pressure was intense. Joyce regarded her nationality as a good omen for his book.

Maurice Darantiere, who is often blamed for printer's errors in the first editions of *Ulysses* as though his Frenchness were a major stumbling block, was an intellectual. He lived in a fine house in Dijon with a younger companion who was also a printer, and was fond of cooking and of the fine Burgundy wines of the region. He possessed art treasures, a valuable library and a collection of ancient pottery. He enjoyed the association with La Maison des Amis des Livres, a bookshop already frequented by readers interested in modern French literature, and had printed for Adrienne the *Cahiers des Amis des Livres*. He was to be an heroic figure in the months ahead.

The third woman to come forward with real help was Harriet Shaw Weaver. She promised Sylvia Beach all the names she could think of to add to the list of potential subscribers. She sent Joyce an advance of £200 and undertook to publish the 'English Edition' under the imprint of *The Egoist*, but using the same plates as the French edition. Her royalty terms were more generous than Sylvia

Beach's; and the actual subscriptions began to come in, from Ernest Hemingway, from André Gide, from W. B. Yeats. Bernard Shaw refused to subscribe. He admired Joyce's picture of Dublin, thought it accurate and felt that every male Irishman should be forced to read this description of his own city, which was, to judge from Joyce's picture of it, as full as ever of 'slackjawed blackguardism'. But he did not need a book to tell him any more about the city of his own birth and childhood; economically, Shaw had read the book in *The Little Review*.

Joyce pushed on with the writing. He was working on the 'Circe' episode, the 15th of 18, and was having trouble with typists. Sylvia Beach actually had to supply him with a succession of them, since many dropped out, possibly on occasions scandalised by the content. The husband of one of his typists, who worked in the British Embassy, read over part of the manuscript and was so shocked that he threw it into the fire. She rescued most of it, but missing portions had to be filled in from a copy of an earlier draft sent to Joyce by John Quinn in New York.

It was at this time that the faintly bleak encounter took place between Proust and Joyce. Had either known of the excruciating trouble they were both to give to their printers and of the huge percentage of set type they each changed at the proof stage, they might have conversed to more point about their technical approaches to the physical and mental strains of writing. As it was Marcel Proust asked Joyce if he liked truffles and Joyce replied, 'Yes, I do.' Later he commented on how extraordinary it was that, when the two greatest figures in modern literature met, they talked of truffles.

Joyce calculated, and recorded the fact in a letter to Harriet Shaw Weaver, that he had spent nearly 10,000 hours in writing *Ulysses*. He had at this stage become enormously adept at creating and fostering legends about himself. He encouraged journalists to write outrageous things. His morning swim in the River Seine, the mirrors which surrounded him as he wrote, the black gloves he was alleged to wear when he went to bed, all of these legendary inventions – which to some extent parallel the stories about Marcel Proust – appeared in newspaper accounts, and were both resented and enjoyed by Joyce.

In the middle of the summer of 1921 the Joyce family moved flats again. He was working on the final two sections in the book, the 'Ithaca' and 'Penelope' episodes, and on 10 June he received the first galley proofs from Darantiere. If his life had been difficult before, with the trials of producing from uncorrected typescripts the version of the book which was to be printed and published, it now became vastly more complicated. As Richard Ellmann pointed out in his life of Joyce, 'the reading of proofs was a creative act; he insisted on five sets, and made innumerable changes, almost always additions, in the text, complicating the interior monologue with more and more interconnecting details. The book grew by one third in proof.' Sylvia Beach claims that the lives of the printers in Dijon, like those of everyone else involved in the book, had become invaded by *Ulysses*. Far from becoming resigned to this, they entered into the spirit of perpetual change which was induced by her instruction that Joyce was to be supplied with 'as many proofs as he wanted, and he was insatiable'. He covered the proof pages 'with Joycean rockets and myriads of stars guiding the printers to words and phrases all around the margins'. Darantiere developed a classic French gesture of mock despair, throwing his hands in the air, but taking away the changed versions and resetting the type. Sylvia Beach, who paid for the luxury of these inexhaustible additions and modifications to the book, remonstrated with her author, but he insisted and usually won.

The promised date for publication passed, and subscribers became restless. Through adroit handling of the press, Sylvia Beach and other friends of the author managed to maintain, at times at fever pitch, the sense of the book's publication being a world event. Then difficulties arose about the binding. Joyce had insisted on the blue and white colours of the Greek flag, which was kept flying in the bookshop in honour of Odysseus. Despite repeated visits to Paris, with colour samples, which were compared with the flag itself so that even looking at the cloth gave the owner of the bookshop a headache, the printer could not come up with the correct shade of blue. He eventually found printers' ink in the right colour in Germany and then had to lithograph the background colour onto thick white paper to get the lettering pure white.

For the final 'Penelope' episode, Joyce had no typist. It was probably the most complicated section of the manuscript and Robert McAlmon offered to help by typing it himself. He was a writer of short stories and a poet as well, an American, married to another writer, Winifred Ellerman, who used the pseudonym 'Bryher' and who was the daughter of Sir John Ellerman, an English shipping magnate of considerable wealth. McAlmon enjoyed spending his wife's money, using at least some of it to provide Joyce with a monthly stipend for which he received the writer's notes in hand, though he failed to cash them with Joyce later and they turned up in his papers as a further record of Joyce's cavalier attitude to debt. McAlmon muddled some of the text and was surprised when Joyce retained his changes. When McAlmon asked about this, Joyce told him he agreed with what he had done.

The problems with the last two episodes, 'Ithaca' and 'Penelope', which were written at the same time, are numerous and stem from the pressures under which Joyce was now labouring as he rushed to honour the last of the many broken commitments about when the book would actually appear. He was handing out sections for typing to Robert McAlmon, and getting them back as he continued to work on the episodes. He actually did this with ı episodes at the same time. This is not as curious as it sounds. 'Ithaca' concludes the main thread of the story, the parting in the garden at the back of the house in Eccles Street, of Bloom and Stephen, while 'Penelope' is devoted purely to Molly's soliloquy. They are collateral conclusions, deeply felt and deeply moving, and hurried under amazingly diverse and powerful pressures at a time when Joyce might have been expected to want a slightly more leisurely atmosphere in which to bring things to an end. Once again he announced that he had finished *Ulysses*, by completing the writing of 'Ithaca'. Once again he embarked on heavy revisions and additions, both in typescript and at proof stage. He added no less than 34 per cent of additional material to 'Ithaca' *after* his announcement about completing the 'episode' and therefore the book. Half of these additions were done on the typescript. So extensive were some of these that one typescript page turned into two or three replacement typescript pages which were then inserted in the original sequence. Unlike the earlier portions of the book, which in general had enjoyed periods of reflection and calm revision, the final two episodes were produced and completed in a period of unrelenting work which produced a collapse at the end of the summer.

Joyce had one other quandary facing him. 'Penelope' was not amenable to extraneous matter. The simple, direct trajectory of Molly's mind, even if its content is anything but simple and direct, was an exclusive creative phenomenon. 'Ithaca' was quite different. Joyce, with virtually all other options for the insertion of new matter closed off, or closing off, was still producing new material and wanted to include it. The repository became the penultimate episode and this further complicated his work during those final weeks of composition.

He turned his blue copy book upside down to write in parts of 'Ithaca' on the reverse sides of pages bearing 'Penelope' sections. At the same time also he was receiving proofs of earlier portions of the book, which had been set and sent back for correction by Darantiere in Dijon. A further constraint was the fact that he needed to get 'Penelope' typed up so that it could be translated into French in order to allow Larbaud to read it at the *séance* planned for 7 December. With some passion, Joyce told McAlmon that he was working like a lunatic, revising, improving, correcting, continuing and creating 'all at the one time'.

Joyce had told Harriet Shaw Weaver, in a letter dated 7 August 1921, that he had written the first sentence of the 'Penelope' episode, the Molly Bloom soliloquy. Since this, the first of the eight great sentences of that towering monument to feminine self-revelation, is some 2,500 words long, it was no mean feat. Exactly two months later he wrote to tell her that 'Penelope' was finished and had gone to the printer, that 'Aeolus' had been recast, 'Hades' and 'The Lotus Eaters' amplified, but that the 'Telemachia' – the first three books – was not much changed. At about the same time, seized with further inspiration about Molly, he wrote to a friend in Dublin with more questions about Major Powell (the model for Molly's father), Matt Dillon and their daughters. A month after that, on 6 November, he wrote to Frank Budgen, '*Ulysses* is finished'. But it was not finished. On 21 November he wrote to Dublin again, with questions about Eccles Street and whether or not it was possible to climb over the area railings of Number 7. At the theatre, late in November, Myron Nutting, a close friend with whom Joyce was to celebrate the publication of his 'boo-ok' the following year, came up to him and politely inquired, 'How is your corporosity sagaciating?' Joyce was so amused that he put the phrase into the 'Oxen of the Sun' episode the next day.

In further letters to Harriet Shaw Weaver – he wrote two on the same day, 6 November – he expressed his extreme irritation over the printer's errors and wondered whether these would be perpetuated in future editions. But he never complained about the overall text of the book. Despite the vicissitudes through which he had gone, regarding the abortive efforts to be published in book form in England and America, and the havoc this had played with the overall burden of correction, there is no sense in which he viewed what he was currently doing, at the time of these 1921 letters, as other than finalising the version of *Ulysses* which he wanted to see in print. This view is greatly reinforced by the extent of the changes which he made on the proofs. Indeed, at the time of the 6 November letters to Harriet Shaw Weaver he held back from sending her the fourth proof of 'Penelope' because it had been rendered illegible by interlineations. His eyes had been giving him a great deal of trouble, much more of course with the proofs than with the original writing.

In *The New York Herald*, the Paris-based American newspaper which was to become *The New York Herald Tribune*, there appeared a parody of the book, called *Ulysses Junior*, and Joyce complained that they might have waited until its senior relation was home from the sea before launching this attack. The latest bundle of proofs to arrive included three very different episodes, 'Circe', 'Eumaeus' and 'Penelope', two of which were in proof before he had completed them, and he set to work, correcting all of them. He likened himself to a musician playing several instruments with different parts of the body.

It was not Joyce's intention to end the book with the word 'Yes'. It was only as a result of a translation being done of parts of *Ulysses*, for the purpose of a reading organised by Sylvia Beach and Adrienne Monnier, that the translator, a young man called Jacques Benoîst-Méchin, made the change. He did so because of the weakness of the French; neither '*je veux*', nor '*je veux bien*' seemed quite right, so he simply tacked on the word '*oui*'.

Joyce told him that he did not write that and that the last word of a book was very important, 'a big question'. Benoîst-Méchin simply said, 'It sounds better that way.' Joyce appeared to cogitate a good deal, but in his mind had already accepted the proposed alteration and was then pleased with the great affirmative. It had to end, he felt, with the most positive word in the English language.

TWO

Ulysses Sets Out

'Sure, why would I bother? It's enough he talks about
that book, and he's at it all the time. I'd like a bit
of life of my own.'

Nora, on being asked whether she had read Ulysses

T O SAY that *Ulysses* was published on Joyce's 40th
birthday is to stretch a point. Legally, to denote
publication, the availability of more than three
copies of a book would be required. On the eve of publication Darantiere wrote to Joyce promising that three
copies would be put in the mail that day and would surely
arrive by noon the following day. But this was not good
enough. Joyce, who said he was in a state of 'energetic
prostration', persuaded his publisher that the printer
would have to do better and Darantiere undertook to
deposit copies of the book with the conductor on the
overnight Dijon to Paris express which arrived at seven
in the morning. Sylvia Beach met the train, found the
conductor and received from his hands the precious par-
cel. It contained only *two* copies. She took them in a taxi
direct to Joyce's flat, where she left one of them and then
went on to her bookshop to put the other on display.
From nine o'clock until closing time that evening people
crowded in to see it.

The book was a handsome sight. Like all French books
at the time, and indeed later, a paperback, it was large

in format and heavy. It ran to 732 pages and weighed exactly 1.55 kilogrammes. It had been bound in the blue lithographed colouring which had caused so much trouble, the title and the author's name only on the front, in white. Darantiere had to rectify a minor mistake with the cover, which further delayed copies. On 8 February Joyce wrote to Harriet Shaw Weaver to tell her that the edition de luxe, of which she was to receive copy number one, would not be ready before the following Saturday, so she would not receive hers until the Tuesday after that.

Of the first four copies he said that three had gone to subscribers who were leaving for different parts of the world. These first four were numbers 251, 252, 901 and 902. This is slightly in conflict with Richard Ellmann's claim that the first copy from Dijon was inscribed by Joyce and given to Nora, in the presence of his friend from Dublin, the painter, Arthur Power, to whom Nora promptly offered to sell the book. Nora was indifferent about it. Despite being urged on many occasions to read it, she declined. She affected not to know the significance of the date, 16 June, when, that summer of 1922, they were invited out to the ballet to celebrate the day in 1904 on which the events in *Ulysses* all take place. On another occasion, when Joyce and she met the American writer, William Carlos Williams, at Les Trianons, Nora was asked if she read her husband's work. 'Sure, why would I bother? It's enough he talks about that book, and he's at it all the time. I'd like a bit of life of my own.'

Joyce went in to Shakespeare and Company each day to help Sylvia Beach pack up the copies of the book which were to be sent to subscribers, and gave a somewhat hair-raising picture of 'packing parcels in a way they have never been packed before'. A copy had to go to the British Museum, a copy to *The Times*. Garret FitzGerald's father, Desmond FitzGerald, who was then in charge of publicity – Joyce called it propaganda – for the Irish Government, called on him to find out if he intended to return to Ireland. He had been following the fortunes of *Ulysses* in its serial publication and was going to propose Joyce for the Nobel Prize. The idea appalled the writer, who felt he had not the faintest chance of being awarded the prize and believed, furthermore, that if FitzGerald did not change his mind on seeing the complete text he would undoubtedly lose his position as a member of the Cabinet. (In fact FitzGerald was a minister outside the Cabinet at that time.) Though Joyce wrote about this after the publication of the book, it seems that the meeting between the two men took place in January, when Fitz-Gerald was in Paris to organise publicity for the World Congress of the Irish Race (*Congrès Mondial Irlandais*). A quite serious attempt by the Anti-Treaty side, involving Harry Boland and Sean T. O'Kelly, to hijack the congress on behalf of their leader, Eamon de Valera, was producing serious problems for FitzGerald. He seems, nevertheless, to have found time to meet Joyce.

Joyce advised his friend and helper, Robert McAlmon that, with all this activity, the Last Judgment could not be far away and he should go to confession. He also begged McAlmon, who was in Cannes, to send him a nice necktie if he was thinking of throwing any into the winedark sea. Joyce imagined that this American writer-friend, whose wife was very rich, travelled with a trunkful of them and threw out a few dozen each week. He was then embarrassed at having asked, because Mc-Almon went to Cannes and bought new ties for Joyce, sending him a ring as well, 'very nice and episcopal', which Joyce then wore on his forefinger.

In all his correspondence at this time Joyce referred frequently to the errors in *Ulysses* and was clearly frustrated by their number. Yet there is never any question of there being deeper textual problems. If there are other problems they are straightforwardly those of the writer, produced in the full flood of composition, who seeks throughout the process of composition to rectify or clarify points of fact or understanding. A precise example can be given, in a letter he wrote to Harriet Shaw Weaver two months before publication, where he told her that in the 'Ithaca' episode the problem was not the printer's errors but the need he had for a reader who had the combined skills of physician, mathematician and astronomer. This is not the complaint of someone still searching around for missing parts of a manuscript, but of a writer in the midst of composition and in control of his material, merely needing confirmation on detail from the kind of miraculous experts writers believe the world is there to provide.

Joyce did not refer to a recasting of any parts of the book, nor to the recovery of earlier, lost versions. His preoccupation was a straightforward one, with the errors in the version on which he was working. He must have been acutely aware that the majority of these were the result of his own continuous process of revision, alteration and addition, which had gone on through the final months before publication. This is borne out by the plans which had been made, quite some time before, with Harriet Shaw Weaver for the edition(s) which were to follow the first edition of 1,000 copies and notably for the second edition of 2,000 copies, which was set in train in the summer of 1922, as the stocks of the first began to run out. Harriet Shaw Weaver, according to Richard Ellmann, told James Joyce's bibliographer, John Slocum, that her publishing firm, the Egoist Press, bought from Sylvia Beach printers' plates of the book which had been made up by Darantiere from the type of the first edition and then printed with him, in Dijon, the new edition, though with a different imprint on the verso of the title page, reading: 'Published for The Egoist Press, London, by John Rodker, Paris'.

John Rodker, who was later to become a publisher in his own right, was then an associate of Harriet Shaw

Weaver and the Egoist Press. But as early as the winter of 1919–20 he had met Joyce. Indeed, his first encounter had been with the whole Joyce family, when he and his wife had taken the Joyces, who were particularly hard up, out to dinner. He had been dazzled by Joyce's brilliant presentation of his own genius. The plan he had then suggested to Joyce for *Ulysses* was that he would make the arrangements for the printing in France of the second edition, with the backing of the Egoist Press, but under his imprint, in which way it would be launched in England.

The course of events proved otherwise. According to Harriet Shaw Weaver's account, supplied to Slocum, Rodker took a room in Paris where the edition was delivered and from where he then dispatched copies to different parts of the world. They went out in various ways, some through the mail, some in packing cases which were stored in the offices of the Egoist Press in London, or at Harriet Shaw Weaver's private address. She was conscious of the possibility of police raids and needed to dispose of the edition in small parcels in different places. Distribution of this edition, from the beginning, was more or less clandestine, all the time. Harriet Shaw Weaver herself would take individual copies which had been ordered by bookshops direct to the owners or managers, who would surreptitiously store them under the counter for their customers.

Individual copies sent in the mail to the United States eventually began to arouse customs suspicions. They were held up and, eventually, when more than 400 copies had accumulated, they were confiscated and burnt. A further edition, or impression, of 500 copies was printed to replace the copies destroyed, but not for the United States. In this case a single copy was posted to London, the remaining 499, when they arrived at Folkestone, were seized by customs. No one subsequently knew what happened to these copies. Confirmation of their destruction was never given and Harriet Shaw Weaver suspected that the officials might have made away with the copies for their own amusement. But she did refer to them going up in smoke, and said they had been destroyed in what was known as 'the King's Chimney'. Harriet Shaw Weaver's recollections are at odds with those of John Rodker, who thought that he had sold 150 copies to Galignani, the bookseller in Paris, and that 800 copies had gone to an English bookseller called Jackson who cut them up to conceal the bulky and increasingly familiar form of *Ulysses* as it was at that time, and then sent them by mail to America to be rebound and sold.

In summary, the situation was as follows: *Ulysses* was first published in an edition of 1,000 copies on 22 February 1922. In October the second edition was published in a run of 2,000 copies, the title page bearing the Egoist Press imprint. Of this edition some 500 copies were impounded by the United States Postal Services and destroyed. A replacement order for these, of a further 500 copies, was printed in January 1923 and, after one copy had been dispatched by post to Harriet Shaw Weaver in London, the remaining 499 were shipped through Folkestone, where they were seized by British customs and, as suggested above, apparently destroyed, though there is no formal record of this. One year later, in January 1924, Shakespeare and Company published an unlimited edition which was then reset in 1926 and went on being sold by Sylvia Beach.

Throughout this same period Joyce, understandably, remained intensely interested in every aspect of the book. Unlike most writers, who see a complete manuscript or typescript go to the publisher and then, after a holiday, a rest, a pause for reflection and regeneration, begin something new, Joyce's involvement in his book right up to a month before publication left him physically prostrated after its appearance. This condition was aggravated by problems with his eyes, with his family and with his accommodation in Paris. He jokes in one letter about being asked by a journalist what he is now writing. It is not until mid-March of 1923, more than a year after the appearance of *Ulysses*, that he takes up his pen again and writes two pages. Such is the state of his eyesight that he has to make a fair copy, in large handwriting on a double sheet of foolscap so that he could read what he had written!

It would be very mistaken to suggest that Joyce was other than deeply concerned with the mistakes in the early editions of the book. While his first rage with the printer, Darantiere, was over the delivery of copies, it was swiftly followed by worry over misprints, heaps of which he found in the last two episodes of the book; the blunders and omissions which disfigured 'Ithaca' were especially lamentable, he told Harriet Shaw Weaver. But correcting in the text was not possible for the reprint made in 1922. This carried an errata slip. Joyce was even difficult about this, which he felt depreciated the printer. It was drafted by several hands, including Joyce himself, John Rodker and Harriet Shaw Weaver.

For whatever edition was then to follow Darantiere made clear that corrections would cost money. He put it at approximately one franc for each *opération*, in other words each change of letter, word or line. Joyce thought the word an 'agreeable' one. As to the cost, it was not his concern. It meant, however, that work would need to begin 'at once' and Joyce set out on this task in October 1922, managing about 30 pages a day. Darantiere had been making actual changes in the type, in implementation of the errata lists he had received by November 1922, but then laughed and threw his hands in the air, in a gesture already familiar to Joyce, when the author told him of the limited progress which he himself was making with corrections, adding that he had over 500 pages more to get through.

Most writers are aware of their own limitations when

it comes to proofreading. They are understandably reluctant, as regrettably are professional proofreaders, to get into the business of detailed, line-by-line, word-by-word comparison between the text from which the printer worked and the galley or page-proof stage of a book. It is a chore and a tedious one. What the author adds, Joyce more than most, can be a highly dangerous rewrite of the book. This has already been discussed. Once it was out and Joyce saw how many errors there were in it, a different problem arose which was never properly tackled. Because of the nature of the writing, particularly of the final episodes, the book was in existence with the basic proof-correcting work not done. Joyce then undertook it, admittedly with some help from others, who told him of errors they had found. He was not up to the task. It is as simple as that.

On what was essentially an *author's* read through the book, Joyce found what a later critic of the whole process referred to as 'a coupla hundred typos' and tried to put them right. His first effort had to be an errata slip, since few, if any, printing changes were possible, other than by accident, between February and October 1922, and even after that, between October 1922 and January 1923, when he had begun the arduous process of correcting, the achievement remained a limited one. Nor was this just a question of Joyce's difficulties with his eyes, with communicating with Dijon, with collecting together other peoples' proposals for change. Essentially, Joyce was working at the level of errors which disfigured the text. But we simply do not know and will never know where the dividing line runs, throughout the book, between intentional and accidental errors which persisted.

Joyce was obsessively interested in the very thing that he was least able to control: the physical appearance of the book. He exercised much more power than most authors, because of the curious and highly personal relationship established between himself and Sylvia

Beach, and with Darantiere as well. But he was no printer, he was an ineffective proofreader, he was half-blind and he was intentionally trying to perform two quite distinct tasks much of the time – to write the book, and to correct it, through the specialised activity of proof-reading.

Though he did not consciously go on with the process of writing *Ulysses* after it had appeared in February 1922, unconsciously the attitude of the writer – which includes natural doubt about what he intended with a particular sentence construction, the use of a particular word, the repeat of words, the italicising and spelling of them, and a host of other attitudinal positions – may be said to have prejudiced his overall capacity in the simple, straightforward correcting of the text, which remained a necessary task after February 1922.

There is no easy summary of this very complex argument. Joyce's keen interest in the physical appearance and presentation of his work encompassed decided views on such things as hyphens (he hated them and eventually expunged them from his writing almost totally), quotation marks (which he always tried to avoid), the indentation of the dashes which precede speech, the use of special, bold typefaces in particular parts of the book and of heavier punctuation in the 'Eumaeus' episode, and his concern, already mentioned, for the exact Greek national flag blue for the cover. At the same time he failed to see many misprints and it is this which raises the problem. Is it a misprint? Or is it an example of silent, unrecorded, authorial approval? And who is to decide? The relationship between the practical approach Joyce adopted, from the start, concerning his text and certain other events surrounding the book have some relationship to the longer-term aspects of editing, and even cast their shadow over the distant period following Joyce's death.

The most significant of all was the fate of the manuscript of *Ulysses* with which Joyce had been happily parting company. During the time that John Quinn had been acquiring the manuscript piecemeal from Joyce, their relationship, though somewhat inhibited by the well-defined characters of both men, had flourished. When all the tribulations in America and England had led finally to Sylvia Beach's decision to publish, Quinn had ordered a princely ten copies, five of them the most expensive version, on Dutch hand-made paper, three on *vergé-d'arches* paper and two of the ordinary version. He later increased this order further to 14 copies.

When the book appeared, Quinn was much affected by the coincidence of its doing so on the day on which John Butler Yeats died in New York, aged 83. He saw the old generation passing away and described *Ulysses* as the child of the new age. Knowing John Butler Yeats probably better than any other Irishman, Quinn had no hesitation in suggesting, in a letter to Sylvia Beach, how much the old man would have laughed and chuckled over it. Though Quinn was in correspondence with many figures in the Irish literary revival, he seems to have had poor responses from most of them about Joyce's new novel. George Russell told him he did not like the mood of it and felt that, like Nietzsche, Joyce had gone 'beyond good and evil'. Lady Gregory was non-committal. James Stephens was perplexed by the difficulty of getting hold of it, since it was too expensive and 'too difficult' to borrow, too difficult even to talk about. As for Shane Leslie, his severe Catholic morality made him wince at the studied disrespect towards, and perversion of, sacred things.

For someone so sensitive about the feelings of one Irishman, the father of the Yeats family, Quinn was curiously obtuse about Joyce over the matter of the manuscript of *Ulysses*. No sooner had he acquired the final parts of this and had confirmed with Joyce that he did indeed have the complete book than he decided to sell it at auction. He had already warned Joyce, during a visit to Paris, that this was what he intended to do and had noticed no particular reaction against this. He told Joyce that he would give him half the profit on the sale. Joyce seems to have been none too pleased. He hoped the price would be enormous and he referred thankfully to the 'Blooms of the Bourse' for creating a favourable international monetary situation in unstable times. The manuscript sold on 16 January 1924 for $1,975. Joyce was irked, among other things by the fact that Quinn, at the same sale, spent either $1,400 or $1,500 on some 70 pages of manuscript of George Meredith's 'not very meritorious verse'.

The *Ulysses* manuscript sale was in reality a fiasco. Quinn had sold off virtually the whole of his library over a period of many months. The star items had been his Conrad manuscripts, presentation copies and first editions. An investment of $10,000 now yielded a return of $111,000, with the highest price for the work in manuscript of a living author being the $8,100 for *Victory* paid by A. S. W. Rosenbach, 'terror of the auction rooms', who also bought *eleven* other Conrad manuscripts for a total of $45,900. He was not really a terror. Quinn liked him and described him to Joyce as 'an amusing cuss, sardonic and witty'. When it came to the manuscript of *Ulysses* the price was rather humiliating. When Quinn set it against what he had paid and after deducting the auction commission, the author was due $239.37. Joyce refused this share of the proceeds, and wondered whether his letter telling Quinn of his decision would, in turn, be put up for auction. He thought not. He described the sale by Quinn as a grossly stupid act and an alienation of valuable property, a half-share of which had, in Joyce's opinion, been given to him before the sale. This was how he interpreted the offer of a half-share in the profits. He was careful to recognise, in his own letter to the New York lawyer, that Quinn was entirely free, as owner of the material, to sell it if he thought fit, and he balanced against it the generosity he had been shown in Quinn's original purchase and also in the defence of *The Little Review*, which Quinn had undertaken without any fee. Joyce asked him to find out whether the purchaser would sell back the manuscript and he confessed that there had been moves before the sale to send a cable suggesting that it be withdrawn, followed by indignation at the outcome.

The name of the American book dealer, Dr A. S. W. Rosenbach, has since become both famous and notorious as a result of his association with Joyce texts. Rosenbach declined to sell what was clearly a bargain, even in those days, and countered by asking Joyce what his price would be for the corrected proofs of the book. Joyce in his turn declined to sell. This was in May 1924. At the beginning of August John Quinn died. Whatever Joyce's feelings may have been about the manuscript fiasco, he was genuinely saddened by the death and by what he learned of the events leading up to it, which suggested that Quinn had acted irrationally at the end over the sale of the manuscript, either as a result of business worries or physical suffering.

It is not known at what stage Rosenbach compared the manuscript with published versions of the book, but the dealer obviously realised early on just how important the proofs were. He must also have been conscious of the fact that the low price paid for the *Ulysses* manuscript from Quinn's collection set a precedent favourable to himself in offering for the proofs. But Joyce had other ideas. Outraged anyway at the manuscript fiasco, he had no intentions of dealing with Rosenbach, whom he variously dubbed 'Rosy Brook' and 'Rosenfelt'. Instead, the complete set of proofs of *Ulysses* were kept by Sylvia Beach as part of her archive.

Reluctantly, much later, in the 1930s, Sylvia Beach decided to sell a number of her bibliographic treasures. Initially, she approached a London book dealer, who was intensely interested in what she was offering, but then, when the possibility of Joyce and *Ulysses* items being seized by customs came up, ideas of a sale were abandoned. She next tried to sell them through a catalogue which she herself brought out, but the response was indifferent. Most inquiries were about Hemingway items and she disposed of her precious inscribed first editions of his works. She travelled to the United States and there she disposed of the proofs of *Ulysses* to Marian Willard of the Willard Gallery, in New York. She became Marian Willard Johnson, on her marriage to Dan Johnson, and the proofs were eventually deposited in Yale University Library, where they are now.

Despite the publicity, perhaps because of the price, certainly because the book was restricted from all but clandestine circulation in England and the United States, the sales of *Ulysses* remained relatively small. We witness in the early 1920s an elitist, literary event, with heightened critical acclaim and with the book itself falling into the category of a collector's item while it was still not published in an unlimited edition. Joyce was intensely interested in all of this, though not without still yearning for the greater fame and the greater wealth which might have derived from a more conventional destiny for his 'boo-ok'.

Something of the strange atmosphere surrounding the earliest editions of *Ulysses* may be gauged from the situation which developed in the autumn of 1922 over the Harriet Shaw Weaver–Egoist Press edition – the second. The involvement of John Rodker in Paris, as Harriet Shaw Weaver's agent, squeezed out Sylvia Beach. She felt she had been misinformed or misled, or perhaps just kept in the dark, and at this stage decided not to have anything to do with a third edition. Her problem was that she had to take public responsibility for *Ulysses*. She was its first publisher, and held such rights in it as had been agreed between herself and the author. This meant that buyers, book dealers, publishers and collectors came to her, often with angry complaints, about the proliferation of editions which seemed to be going on in an erratic way which could damage their investment in such choice items as the first, limited, signed edition. The complaints being made to her were based on the perception that the second edition, though it bore the Egoist Press imprint, had been got up to look exactly like the first and would undermine the value established by the initial publishing event.

She reported to Joyce the threats by booksellers that they would boycott the new edition, or bring her up in a French court for what she had done. Sylvia Beach, of course, had done nothing. Yet she felt responsible and she also felt a bit out of her depth. It needed the combined persuasion of Joyce and of Darantiere to clarify that, with the agreement of all parties, the second edition had been produced from plates made from the first edition and that no bookseller or dealer had the right to threaten or impose on her or them. The second edition was clearly a second edition, plainly marked, in Joyce's view, in two places. Philosophically, he remarked that no boycott could possibly work when there was a strong demand for the book. To prove his point he sent his 17-year-old son, Giorgio, 'with a couple of sinister-looking friends', on a surreptitious tour of certain Paris bookshops. They reported back that copies of the first edition, in the unsigned, ordinary version, were selling at Brentano's for 850 francs and at Galignani's at 650 francs (respectively £6 5s and £4 15s). Galignani's – although, according to Rodker, they had bought 150 copies – said that they did not have copies of the second edition, but if they did they would sell them for the same price. The second edition was published at 136 francs (or £2). The only place they visited which did have the second edition, Terquem, another bookshop, was selling it at 200 francs, a third above the published price. In each of the shops there were only a couple of copies. The youths detected no animosity towards the second edition.

According to Joyce, Sylvia Beach believed that any fresh 'hustling to boom the book' should now be undertaken by those newly involved in its republication. And Joyce surmised that John Rodker was responsible for this cooling off in her enthusiasm, but himself sympathised with Rodker, who was busy trying to ensure that the police would not descend on copies of the book during their transit and seize them. This in fact is what happened within the month, the report of the 499 copies being seized at Folkestone coming to him from Harriet Shaw Weaver in a letter that December of 1922. Joyce shows at length to her just how masterly he could be in handling his women. Detecting a huffiness in Sylvia Beach's reactions to the second edition and suspecting that this would have a bad effect in the two bookshops in the rue de l'Odéon, where he reckoned about 100 influential literary figures, French, English and American, visited each week, he went in to have a short interview and to ensure that nothing was being said or implied that might damage or discredit him. His inexhaustible charm clearly worked to his advantage. At one point he had obviously thought that Sylvia Beach was trying to manipulate a breach between them and he wished that such letters as hers were not written. We can assume that he presented himself to her in his usual baleful light: with his eye problems, his 'mute expectant' family needing money and assistance, his 'troublesome boo-ok', and himself, 'howling dismally for aid'.

It worked. Sylvia Beach, who emerges always from the colourful and exotic events in her life as a warm-hearted and generous woman, regarded the interregnum as a test carried out to see if *Ulysses* could be published in England. With the seizure at Folkestone this was clearly shown to be impossible and would remain so for the present, just as it would in her own country until someone suppressed the Society for the Suppression of Vice, which had been responsible for the original prosecution in New York. *Ulysses*, her 'lost one', returned to the rue de l'Odéon and she repossessed herself of the greatest prize in her life. Her hero, after many vicissitudes, came home to her again.

It was now time to go public in a more down-to-earth way and produce the book for a far wider readership. That readership had been created by critical acclaim. The timing was perfect for the next phase in her activities on Joyce's behalf. It also coincided with the fact that Joyce himself, increasingly preoccupied with the opening salvoes of *Finnegans Wake*, was beginning to lose interest in *Ulysses*.

THREE

The Trials of Ulysses

'The foullest book that has ever found its way into print.'

Alfred Noyes on Ulysses

'Enough to make a hottentot sick.'

Review in the Sporting Times

NOTHING WAS normal about *Ulysses*, least of all its critical reception. Sylvia Beach spoke shrewdly when she said how fortunate a thing it was that *Ulysses* was banned. She claimed that it brought Joyce to public attention in a most compelling way, when the book he had written was, in her opinion, of appeal to a comparatively small group. She also felt it gave him the excuse to feel persecuted: 'I wonder if he was ever that.'

But it had more profound consequences as well, one of which was the extensive critical attention given. Since it was never properly published, it was never properly reviewed. The normal 20th-century process, by which a book is published as a single item, sent out in advance to daily and weekly newspapers, literary journals and other magazines, and reviewed, as strictly as publishers can maintain, on or after the day of publication, was a meaningless concept with *Ulysses*. But if Joyce saw this as a disadvantage, his friends and supporters did everything they could to compensate for the irregular emergence of the book by repeatedly getting it reviewed and written about, and they were generally successful beyond the wildest dreams of a more conventional author. The book was constantly reviewed throughout the 1920s, into the 1930s, and in a sense has never stopped being reviewed. Reviewing, after the first couple of decades, simply changed in character and became scholarly critical attention, delivered on a variety of different levels.

As we have seen, normal reviewing for quite another reason could not have happened with the first edition. Apart from anything else, there were no review copies. With the delay, the main priority was to satisfy patient and impatient subscribers alike. And since the copies of the book came up from Dijon in irregular parcels and at erratic intervals, no sensible point emerged at which a critical assessment could be invited. Perhaps in an even more bizarre fashion, in addition to the continuous process of reviewing *after* publication there had actually been a fair amount of reviewing *before*, based on the serialised episodes. This attention from other writers was achieved primarily through the good offices of Ezra Pound.

Ezra Pound promoted the idea of James Joyce as the literary genius of the 20th century on the evidence of Joyce's writings as they came to hand and from a relatively early point in their association. Pound was a literary explorer and discoverer. He needed to find writers and to be proved right in what he found. He needed to go on promoting them, in order to continue to be right. Some would say his gift to literature is more in that than it is in his own writing.

He had first approached Joyce, on the advice of Yeats, in December 1913. More interested at that point in verse than in prose, since he was operating then in a vaguely editorial capacity for about four different publications which were themselves more likely to print poems by unknown writers than works of fiction, he was simply looking to see if Joyce had any work on hand. Since Joyce had by then only published *Chamber Music*, Pound was probably somewhat surprised by Joyce's response. He was sent *Dubliners* and the first chapter of *A Portrait of the Artist as a Young Man*. From that point until Joyce was engaged fully on *Finnegans Wake* Pound's espousal of the Irish writer's literary claims never really faltered. Though he thought the short stories uneven, he valued *A Portrait* highly and admired Joyce for being totally uncorrupted by commercialism. He compared Joyce, in 1915, with Flaubert and Stendhal.

He was unrelenting from then on. He corralled support, he orchestrated publicity, he cajoled new critics and commentators, and to a substantial degree Joyce played into his hands. Pound was largely responsible for the first phase, which resulted in there being a huge body of writing about Joyce with which the critics of the second phase could then disagree. It was inevitable that the major part of this writing should have concentrated on *Ulysses*. In any case, worldwide, a number of notable writers had already come to grips with fair portions of the book on its serial publication and had often given their critical views, eagerly seized upon, of course, by Joyce and the close circle of friends and promoters of the book. A more conscientious approach to getting the book reviewed was mildly attempted, by Joyce and Harriet Shaw Weaver, when the second edition was directed at an essentially English readership, mainly London, but also including New York. The publication, however, was outside the British Isles and the United States, and was handled, from a reviewer's point of view, in an amateur fashion.

There is something quite appealing in Joyce's elaborate instructions about the book. Harriet Shaw Weaver was to prepare two rubber stamps, to be applied sideways across the title-page of the book, if it was to be a normal copy. If a signed and numbered version was to be sent, then it would have 'UNNUMBERED PRESS COPY' where the numbering would normally be. He listed the critics whose words, or names, were to be used in publicity material and advertisements. It was his view that *The Times* should *not* get a second copy; and because he was old-fashioned enough to admire George Saintsbury he wanted him to have a copy. He felt that the aging critic and wine enthusiast might well throw it through the window of the Egoist Press, particularly if the 1922 Bordeaux vintage was not to his liking. Saintsbury did no such unmannerly thing, despite the fact that the 1922 vintage was fairly appalling, and he was by then probably too old to appreciate Joyce.

At this stage – the letter to Harriet Shaw Weaver about review copies is dated 17 November 1922 – *Ulysses* had been the subject of keen critical attention for four years. From its first instalment in *The Little Review*, in March 1918, hailed in advance as a 'prose masterpiece' by Margaret Anderson, it had been serially addressed by writers, critics and ordinary readers. By the time prosecution for obscenity brought this form of publication to a conclusion, 23 instalments, comprising almost half the book, had appeared. This covered the first 13 episodes and part of the 14th. Serial publication concluded with part of 'Oxen of the Sun'.

Writers as diverse as Virginia Woolf, Hart Crane, T. S. Eliot and Richard Aldington had all written about it, and their comments were available for publicity purposes when the first edition came out. Quotations from what they had said, with the addition of remarks from many new literary figures who had seen the complete *Ulysses*, were then available for the publicity which followed, rather than preceded the second, 'English' edition of October 1922. Though Marvin Magalaner and Richard M. Kain, in their analysis of this period (*Joyce: The Man, the Work, the Reputation*, published in 1956), suggest that 'the book was an immediate sensation', this cannot easily be sustained. It was a sensation, but one that was orchestrated by a variety of different people, beginning with Ezra Pound, continuing with Padraic Colum and T. S. Eliot, and then burgeoning into a collective pro-gramme of acclamation which went on and on, well before there was an actual book to discuss. Though the intense interest did create a fever of speculation about the author, which prompted Galsworthy rather belatedly to suggest that the changing tides of taste had caused Joyce to 'replace the Deity', this was hardly reflected in the early sales. Between 2 February 1922, and the appear-ance of the unlimited Shakespeare and Company edition of January 1924, if we allow that the confiscations are accurately recorded, well under 2,000 copies actually sold. In a period of almost two years, this is a pitiful figure for a masterpiece so widely and relentlessly proclaimed.

As a measure of this one could compare with it the fortunes of another large and expensive book published slightly later in the 1920s, *Seven Pillars of Wisdom*, by T. E. Lawrence. He shared with Joyce some of the mystery and appeal which derives from an eccentric life, and which benefited from friends acting on his behalf. Even with the early, limited editions there were some simi-larities. But Lawrence was published conventionally enough in March 1927 and by midsummer 30,000 copies of his book, at the then high price of £1 10s, had sold, totally transforming the fortunes of Jonathan Cape, the publishers, who built a five-room extension in Bedford Square, raised salaries, introduced a profit-sharing scheme, restructured their accounting system and put £15,000 into War Loans against future needs – all based on the success of Lawrence's book about the war in Palestine.

It can be argued, as it was by Joyce and his friends at the time, that the failure to obtain publication in Britain or the United States prejudiced a fair distribution among normal readers. But it could also be argued that the enormous publicity, which operated on a world scale, and attracted both literary and prurient purchasers for the book, counteracted any disadvantages which might have resulted from a more conventional treatment of Joyce and his literary endeavours. Sylvia Beach was emphatic on the point, as we have seen; and hers is a dispassionate voice. Others, less dispassionate, gave vent to powerful negative reactions which take on fiercely moral overtones. 'The foullest book that has ever found its way into print', was the judgment of the English Catholic poet, Alfred Noyes, famous for the wonderful narrative poem, 'The Highwayman'. 'An Odyssey of the sewer', was Shane Leslie's description. Arnold Bennett wrote that he put down the book with the feelings of a general who had just put down an insurrection. Katherine Mansfield tried hard, but found she could not overcome the feeling of 'wet linoleum and empty pails'. A. E. Housman thought D. H. Lawrence 'more wholesome' than Joyce. Lawrence himself thought that Joyce's self-consciousness, which might have been entirely acceptable in a 17 year old and pardonable in a writer of 27 was 'obvious senile precocity' in a man of Joyce's years. Many other quite serious literary reviewers of the day, whose names have since become obscure, gave vent to sharp attacks on the author, and one could easily assemble a substantial list of epigrammatic views on the book: 'a dirty masterpiece', 'a morose delectation in dirt', 'the product of a frightened and enslaved mind', 'the screed of one possessed', 'rotten caviare', 'indecent as the alcoholic is intoxicated' and so on.

At a lower level of mass journalism the distaste for the work was probably best exemplified by the pseudonymous reviewer for *The Sporting Times*, who signed his lengthy and venomous attack with the name 'Aramis'. This was essentially a racing paper, known as 'The Pink 'Un' and immortalised by Sylvia Beach, who put its poster up on the walls of Shakespeare and Company, a poster which heralded the review under the title 'THE

SCANDAL OF "ULYSSES" ', and then listed racing win-
ners and their odds, to show where its heart and mind
really lay. 'Aramis' thought the book was the work of a
'perverted lunatic', that it was 'morbidly pornographic'
and 'the literature of the latrine', and that it was 'enough
to make a hottentot sick'. 'The Pink 'Un' had another go
at the book at the beginning of 1923 and told its sporting
readers that *Ulysses* could now be got for a mere ten
shillings. Curious racing enthusiasts, always on for a
gamble, sent Treasury notes to Sylvia Beach for their
copies.

After publication, a major concern was with the errors.
Some attention needs to be given to this, if we are to
understand and judge the claims on which later editorial
positions were based. There is also the question of the
extent to which any writer is affected, by criticism, in
his own judgment about whether he has got his own book
'right' and exactly at what point, if this can be
determined.

On the first of these, Joyce established his position
firmly enough. In the wake of the New York prosecution,
B. W. Huebsch, who was Joyce's American publisher, and
had published *A Portrait of the Artist as a Young Man*
and *Dubliners* in 1916, as well as *Exiles* and *Chamber
Music* two years later, got cold feet. He and Quinn had
been on the brink of negotiating an agreement at the time
of the trial, with the publisher debating the question of
whether or not to risk prosecution and a fine, with a
possible prison sentence, or to see the book going to
another publisher, Boni and Liveright, who were interested in taking on the rights to *Ulysses*. Huebsch said
alterations in the text would be necessary. Quinn, then
acting for Joyce in the negotiations, refused. Boni and
Liveright had also lost interest.

This was all at the stage immediately prior to Sylvia
Beach's tentative offer. Immediately after that, Joyce
told Harriet Shaw Weaver that the chief thing for him

was to hand the book over definitely and get it out of his sight. He was later to tell her that he wanted a complete rest to be able to forget the book. He used the metaphor of being able to round the 'last (and stormiest) cape'. The choice, with two episodes to go, was to abandon it unfinished or complete it. That was in April 1921. During only a relatively brief phase was there any serious question of Joyce being pressurised to change the book and it never got to the point of specific details being mentioned. Any committed reader of *Ulysses* would need no persuading of the impossibility of combing it for changes designed to satisfy censorship requirements, either in Britain or America. With the courageous and unswerving Harriet Shaw Weaver, the question was never raised.

With this area of alteration eliminated, once Sylvia Beach had committed Shakespeare and Company to the book, the problem of errors resulting from typesetting mistakes became paramount and remained so, not just until publication of the first edition, but through several editions after that. We have already seen how Joyce handled these and the at times quite light-hearted approach he adopted – as indeed did the elegant and witty Maurice Darantiere – to the successive rounds of mistakes which emerged with each printing of the book. It is fair to assume that behind this process, at least for a period of time, Joyce's concerns went beyond mere literals, and the changes which he proposed, for which either Sylvia Beach or Harriet Weaver paid, may have included alterations which were more structural. But the evidence of the book being completed, as a work, and still being in need of revision, as a text, is not hard to find. In the two letters written on 6 November 1921, mentioned earlier, he told Harriet Shaw Weaver of the irritation of all the printers' errors and he told Frank Budgen '*Ulysses* is finished'. He was then firmly locked, in his own mind, on an early 1922 publication date – by then he had been forced to substitute his birthday for the earlier projected publication in the late summer of 1921 – and for the writer this kind of pressure is a great concentrating force upon the mind.

Once Joyce started on *Finnegans Wake*, in February 1923, *Ulysses* began to fade – in the creative sense. He remained interested in the controversy which continued to surround it. He remained interested in the money which he derived from it. He remained interested in the gossip, the jokes, the exaggerations. He remained closely interested in the fortunes of the physical texts of the book and his polite outrage over Quinn's decision to sell the main manuscript is instructive in several ways. Joyce would have presumably taken a different line if it had achieved a really substantial price, half going to him; and at least some of his concern over the actual fiasco of the sale was about the damage to his reputation. But he does not express at this time or later the need to retain or have back the manuscript in order to satisfy a *writer's* need. He does not want it in order to complete a new, revised version of the book. He wants it because, morally, it is his property, and by Quinn's own decision to share the money, half of it was regarded by Joyce *legally* as his as well.

On the unlimited, cheap edition, priced at 60 francs, brought out by Sylvia Beach on 1 January 1924, the colours for the cover were reversed; instead of the lettering being white, surrounded by the printed, or lithographed blue, an easier solution was taken: blue lettering on white board. This was the edition seen in the window of a Paris bookseller's shop by the Prince of Wales, later briefly King Edward VIII, on a visit to France using the incognito of the Earl of Chester, which apparently fooled no one. He complained about the book being on display, or so gossip at the time claimed, and a variety of different stories about this episode soon circulated in the city. By mid-1924 the book had become remote. Joyce told Harriet

Shaw Weaver that he had to convince himself that he actually wrote it and he felt that he could no longer talk intelligently about it. Joyce's interest in the continuing critical analysis of the book was a mild one. He read and judged the various academic and scholarly autopsies, and joked about them. In the late summer of 1925, in the wake of several of these, he told Harriet Shaw Weaver that he was going to organise a piece of 'lower criticism' which would include textual analysis of the book, but that thereafter the book could look after itself. He was also more seriously interested and directly involved in the early translations. One in French, by Auguste Morel, was undertaken in 1925. A first part appeared in serial form in *La nouvelle revue française*. Morel, whom Joyce regarded as a bit *'sauvage'*, was not entirely satisfactory as translator, but critical reaction generally in France pleased Joyce; he regarded it as better than the German reception of the work.

On the structural side, Joyce was as diffident as one might expect any author to be. It is common today for the book to be described in terms of a host of external structures and definitions. The chapters are almost invariably identified and referred to by their classical titles, and there is a vast literature involving analysis, including of course comparison with Homer. The reader of *Ulysses* today, particularly the student and the academic teaching him, is expected to approach the book armed, or burdened, with such knowledge. Privately, from its beginnings, Joyce referred to the episodes in this way. But the extent to which he wanted there to be a public apparatus surrounding the book is difficult to judge. Would he have approved of us approaching his work by way of Homer's? More seriously, would he have wanted his readers to know in advance all the complexities of construction?

Even before the book appeared, there was a *séance* given on it at Adrienne Monnier's bookshop, in which

Valéry Larbaud, a leading French critic at the time, provided a fairly detailed analysis of the structure of the work which was subsequently published in *La nouvelle revue française* in April 1922 and in translation in *The Criterion* in October 1922. Larbaud was the translator of Coleridge, Landor and Samuel Butler. A wealthy man, unmarried, the last of a rich family, he was a well-informed lightweight rather than a serious academic critic; he was also poet and novelist, and dedicated to Modernism and its introduction. His criticism was the first significant piece of literary criticism of James Joyce. It analysed the episodic structure of *Ulysses*, pointed out Joyce's intricate use of symbol, his identification of each episode with a colour, an hour of the day, an organ of the human body, in effect creating an example of the art of mosaic. Larbaud then went on to explain how a work of such formidable labour could nevertheless live and breathe as a work of art. 'The manifest reason is that the author has never lost sight of the humanity of his characters, of their whole composition of virtues and faults, turpitude, and greatness; man, the creature of flesh, living out his day.'

Richard M. Kain and Marvin Magalaner, who are two of the founding fathers of post-war American James Joyce criticism, maintain that 'many errors of judgment and interpretation might have been avoided' if Joyce's early readers and reviewers had availed themselves of Larbaud's essay. It is a questionable view, the first heavy imposition of the implied *necessity* for reading Joyce criticism, rather than the idea, current in the books which appeared from the 1920s on, which were based on the belief that some people, if by no means all potential readers of Joyce, might *like* to be introduced to him but did not necessarily *have* to be introduced.

This was the view of the early works of criticism, which begin with Herbert Gorman's *James Joyce: The First Forty Years* (1924), which is the first biography of the writer.

Gorman had difficulties later with Joyce, who claimed a 'marriage' in 1904, 'supplemented by retroactive civil marriage according to English law in 1931' (the phrase is Paul Léon's, who in 1939 was acting as Joyce's secretary, writing to Gorman in that capacity), and insisted that Gorman emasculate the passage. According to Ellmann, 'Gorman left the matrimonial question bewilderingly unresolved'. In 1927 Paul Jordan Smith wrote *A Key to the 'Ulysses' of James Joyce*, which was published in Chicago and contained a map of Dublin showing the various places covered by the book. By then 'Bloomsday', 16 June, was already an established date in the calendar of Joyce enthusiasts, on which some of them sent him 'hortensias, white and blue, dyed'. Further introductory works appeared in 1932 (*James Joyce and the Plain Reader* by Charles Duff) and in 1933 (*James Joyce* by Louis Golding).

Of a different order was *James Joyce's 'Ulysses'*, by Stuart Gilbert, which was published in London by Faber and Faber in 1930. Gilbert was a Cambridge Classics scholar who joined the Indian Civil Service and lived for a time in Burma, where he first read *Ulysses*. He returned to Paris in time to become involved in the translation of *Ulysses* into French, working with Morel and Larbaud, and it was this collaboration which then led to the writing of his study of the work. If one considers Gilbert's own description of the collaboration, it becomes clear that a detailed analysis of the meaning of the book went on between the three men and the author such as to ensure that if *Ulysses* had errors they were not of the fundamental kind affecting either the meaning of the text, its sense, its direction, its whole narrative and psychological force.

Gilbert was ideally trained for the job of intermediary and adviser for the work of translation, particularly with his background in Classics. In his judgment a thorough understanding of the work was a first essential; 'any vagueness or uncertainty in this respect must lead to failure'. A close analysis, in his view, leading to all the implications being fully unravelled, was necessary 'before looking for approximations in the other language'. In this advisory role, long before he came to write his own book, he consulted with Joyce 'on every doubtful point, of ascertaining from him the exact associations he had in mind when using proper names, truncated phrases, or peculiar words, and never "passing" the French text unless I was sure we had the meaning of each word and passage quite clear in our minds'.

Gilbert was impressed at Joyce's patience with him. His career in the Far East had been a judicial one and he was used to the protracted, detailed inquiries 'East of Suez' so necessary to get at the truth. Gilbert, at the time, was rereading Homer's *Odyssey* in the original Greek, and picked up from Joyce hints and details about the origin of events in *Ulysses*, which he stored up for his own, later writing. But at that stage his priority was to ensure a full understanding of the book for the benefit of the translators and it is reasonable to assume that during this period all of them, but particularly Joyce himself, went through a process of checking on the text which would have brought to light, and caused to be changed, any fundamental errors of composition or omissions of matter. Gilbert also emphasised that his own study was read out to Joyce who gave it his full approbation and who liked the academic approach. It served as a counteracting force to the general perception, at the time, that *Ulysses* was a violently romantic work, and on this point Gilbert concludes: 'It was necessary to emphasise the "classical" and formal elements, the carefully planned layout of the book, and the minute attention given by its author to detail, each phrase, indeed each word, being assigned its place with *pointilliste* precision.' It would be a bold mind indeed that would assert, after the death of the author, that he had got a host of these words, phrases, names and other details wrong. Yet that is precisely what has happened.

Gilbert's points are made in the 1950 Preface to the edition published in 1952, by which time there was an abundance of critical writing on Joyce and on *Ulysses* in particular, and this may have had some influence on Gilbert's presentation of the collaboration between himself and the author during the second half of the 1920s. We do not have much correspondence between the writer and his critic. In other letters Joyce indicated his respect for Gilbert, his concern that Gilbert's essays, in French and English, should find a home in one or other of the various publications, in both languages, in which sections of his book appeared before it came out with Faber and Gwyer (as the firm was in the 1920s), and this gives Gilbert's interpretation of Joyce a standing which Joyce was perfectly ready to withhold from critics of whom he did not approve. There were many of these. Moreover, Joyce went on working with Gilbert, who gave him help and wrote about *Finnegans Wake* as it began to appear in segments during the 1930s.

Finnegans Wake exceeded *Ulysses* in everything except genius. It took longer to write, had an even more complicated publishing history, was conceived and executed under a greater range of symbolic and mythic guidelines, was dictated to more famous amanuenses, among them Samuel Beckett, was used as a weapon of revenge by Joyce, who mocked in it the people who had offended him, including Rebecca West; in short, it was the inscription on the walls of eternity of James Joyce's feelings, his prejudices and his obsessions. He put almost everything into it, including Nora, whose disposition to saunter into his life, characteristic for Joyce of the female temperament, is recorded there. He included the rest of his family and his favourite wine, Fendant de Sion, a Swiss white which was in fact the colour of urine, and was so described by Ottocaro Weiss, who was drinking with

Joyce when they discovered it, the pair of them holding their glasses up to the windows like test tubes. Yes, said Joyce, agreeing with the definition, but the urine of an Archduchess. On another occasion, drinking with Weiss, Joyce told him that breasts like the udders of she-goats were the kind he liked on women; and this is reflected in both *Ulysses*, where Bloom so describes to himself his wife's soft bubs, 'sloping within her nightdress', and in *Finnegans Wake*. No wonder Joyce soon became exclusively obsessed with this monumental repository into which he poured himself and about which he often felt defeated, as even those closest to him, among them Pound and Harriet Shaw Weaver, seemed to doubt, to lose their enthusiasm over or to become actively hostile towards its unfolding.

After the long period of gestation of Stuart Gilbert's elegant, detailed and extensive study, and notwithstanding the many books which were still to appear about Joyce and his writing during his own lifetime, there is a justifiable temptation to suggest that *Ulysses*, as far as textual changes were concerned, had reached a conclusion and that Joyce, along with many other readers, had simply to accept that errors by way of literals and misprints would go on for as long as the book survived. Differentiating between the two is itself hard enough. After all, several of the great howlers of the 1984 Critical and Synoptic Edition concern the alteration or omission of just one letter.

The importance among the early critics of Stuart Gilbert, in the context of this book, is his involvement in the translation which led to a very detailed analysis of the text. The main tide of critical attention was of a different order and need not detain us. There is, however, a certain finality in Joyce's remarks to T. S. Eliot in 1932. He was in correspondence with the poet on a number of issues, one of them the curious anomaly that *Ulysses* was being prescribed for certain Cambridge University examinations, despite the fact that students could not obtain the book and that, to bypass this, their professors were lending them their own copies of the book. There was then some question of episodes of *Ulysses* appearing in *Criterion*, the magazine which Eliot edited. Joyce rejected the idea in a letter of 22 February 1932. He gave several reasons, including the current idiotic state of British censorship. But his main reasons was that *Ulysses* has a beginning, a middle and an end, and should be so presented and experienced. And he thought that a private, limited edition, if highly enough priced, would avoid Home Office action – a hint to Eliot about what his publishing firm, Faber and Faber, might consider doing. One thing on which Joyce was emphatic: the text would have to be unabridged and unaltered.

There was a compulsion among writers who considered themselves literary figures to 'deal with' Joyce and it led to numerous absurdities. But it also led to some wonderful insights and tributes. Rebecca West was perhaps one of these, in her book, *The Strange Necessity*. Joyceans dislike West's view of *Ulysses*. They dislike her dismissal, in which is quite correct, of Joyce's poetry as sentimental rubbish. They dislike the style of her critical examination, very much the work of another creative writer, imaginatively casting her essay in the form of a day-long journey around Paris – a tribute of a kind to the day-long plot of the work she is studying. They dislike the more specific criticisms, which range from her description of Joyce pushing his pen about 'noisily and aimlessly as if it were a carpet sweeper' to her broad condemnation of Joyce as 'a great man who is entirely without taste', and a writer whose most fundamental error is gross sentimentality. Long before it became a burdensome platitude about Joyce and about *Ulysses*, Rebecca West investigated the situation in literature and life where people had become conditioned by a knowledge of the existence, if not the content and experience of *Ulysses*, in varying degrees. She writes about her subject as an outsider. She deals wonderfully with such concepts as the equal ranking in human experience of love and art, and her summary of Joyce is essentially that 'He is an artist, he has created a work of art, anything that helps me to understand that work of art . . . is welcome to me, because it helps me to establish myself in the universe.'

At a level quite different from the critical one, Joyce was lionised by the lighter figures of literary life, particularly on his visit to London in 1931, when at last he married Nora. Harold Nicolson, in his *Diaries and Letters 1930–39*, records such an occasion, sticky in the extreme, when the Joyces were guests of the Hartingtons (he was chairman of Putnam, the publishing firm). The first impression Joyce made on Nicolson was 'of a slightly bearded spinster'; then, 'of some thin little bird, peeking, crooked, reserved, violent and timid. Little claw hands. So blind that he stares away from one at a tangent, like a very thin owl.' Every time Joyce was asked whether he were interested in a particular subject, he replied, 'Not in the very least'. This had the effect of making all the guests and the host and hostess increasingly nervous. Nicolson, who had been given broadcasting work to do, in the form of a series of talks about modern literature, had been forbidden by Lord Reith to mention *Ulysses*, a fact which led to a row and the termination of Nicolson's BBC contract. This was the first item of information in which Joyce showed any interest at all. He promised to send Nicolson a copy of Dujardin's *Les Lauriers sont coupés*. Nicolson concludes: 'He is not a rude man: he manages to hide his dislike of the English in general and of the literary English in particular. But he is a difficult man to talk to. "Joyce", as Desmond [MacCarthy] remarked afterwards, "is not a very *convenient* guest at luncheon."' Later, in a letter to Vita Sackville-West, Nicolson spoke of Joyce as having 'the most lovely voice I know – liquid and soft with undercurrents of gurgle', and very courteous, 'as shy people are'. He describes Joyce's pronunciation of *Ulysses* as 'Oolissays' and suggests that in the mid-1930s, the Irishman was surrounded by worshippers but detached entirely from reality.

Even more absurd were the many critics who attacked Joyce for his obscenity, scurrilousness, obscurity. But the main tide of interest was dutiful, intense, scholarly and essentially dull. Upon this tide there travelled the small but growing vessel of a potential Joyce 'industry', and in all the different types of critical address to him and his work this perhaps represented the most threatening of all. It was this that would create a permanent readership around Joyce, which would puzzle over the problems and read about *them*, while at the same time reading less and less of the writer's work itself.

One other point Joyce made in a letter to Eliot at this time, on 13 February 1932, was that, at present, he was the owner of 'all the rights of *Ulysses*'. That he came to be abused in this somewhat limited benefit was an outrage to Joyce but inevitable. In the late 1920s, Samuel Roth, a New York publisher and religious crank, who believed he was called by God as a good man in his generation, proceeded to publish Joyce illegally and in spurious versions. His 'goodness in his generation' included the clandestine, though arguably not strictly illegal, dissemination of *Ulysses*, which he was busily bringing out at the time in a monthly magazine; he also went on to publish an incomplete version of the book, as well as a forgery of the Shakespeare and Company imprint on another spurious and unauthorised edition. Extraordinary as it may seem, this highly questionable version was used by Random House for the first, incorrect American edition of 1934.

The controversy over Roth and the pirating of *Ulysses* in the United States brought up the question of American copyright. At the time of the publication of the book in France, Quinn had emphatically advised both Joyce and

Sylvia Beach that serial publication in *The Little Review* had been sufficient to secure the copyright. Yet this seems not to have been the case at all and the issue of copyright remained a major problem for years to come. When the Roth action provoked an international protest in 1927, appropriately dated on Joyce's birthday, 2 February, it was stated that the appearance was 'under colour of legal protection in that the *Ulysses* which is published in France and which has been excluded from the mails in the United States is not protected by copyright in the United States'. Roth was described as taking advantage of the author's legal difficulties. The occasion demonstrated, in the remarkable series of signatories to the international protest, how effective Joyce was in summoning up support, much of it from people who were not particularly sympathetic to the book. Richard Aldington, Arnold Bennett, E. M. Forster, John Galsworthy, Wyndham Lewis, James Stephens, Rebecca West and Virginia Woolf are all numbered in the lists, as well as the champions.

The unbanning of the book in the United States came when Judge Woolsey, in a district court decision of December 1933, decided that *Ulysses* was not pornographic, but 'a serious experiment'. His judgment came as a result of the legal action by Random House to obtain a court reversal of the original banning. The man behind this was Bennett A. Cerf, a director of Random House, who was already the publisher, under the Modern Library imprint, of *Dubliners* and *A Portrait of the Artist as a Young Man*, which, according to Joyce, he had taken away from 'the helpless Huebsch'. He sent Joyce an offer for *Ulysses*. Joyce replied with a long account of his experiences as a writer and the difficulties he had faced over the publication of *all* his works. He was particularly incensed, at the time, about the unauthorised publication of his work in the United States and about the fact that, under United States law, he had been unable to obtain copyright. There is still, unbelievably, doubt about the copyright situation in the United States on *Ulysses*. (This is dealt with in the next chapter.) Under American law it was then a copyright requirement that any English book published elsewhere had to be republished in the United States within six months. This, of course, was not done. It was Cerf's intention to resolve the legal uncertainty over the book's banning, not the question of copyright, and then go ahead with publication, which would probably, though not certainly, assert a lasting and serious copyright anyway.

Judge Woolsey's views on *Ulysses* are eminently sensible. He distinguished between obscenity and whether the intent of this obscenity is pornographic, that is to say, written for the purpose of exploiting obscenity. In spite of its 'unusual frankness', Woolsey did not detect anywhere 'the leer of the sensualist' and held that it was not, therefore, pornographic. The judgment is itself a remarkable piece of literary criticism, written, as it is, from the standpoint of public interest and perceiving, as it does, a remarkable range of Joyce's qualities; Joyce's sincerity and honest effort, his 'astonishing success', his loyalty to a difficult technique and his courage in facing the clear implications of the intrusive mode of narrative are all contained in a summary which never loses contact with the broad, legal obligations which also have to be fulfilled. 'Brilliant and dull, intelligible and obscure by turns', the book was seen by the judge as a *tour de force*, the criticisms of it entirely countered by the book's rationale. Unlike the vast resources of criticism, the judge's view was that the law should be concerned with the feelings and responses of 'the normal person'. For such there were scenes in the book which represented a 'strong draught', but at worst they were emetic, thought Woolsey, rather than aphrodisiac in their character.

The first American edition from Random House appeared in January 1934. Random House counsel for the defence, Morris L. Ernst, wrote a Foreword, hailing a new deal in the law of letters and describing Judge Woolsey's judgment as 'a major event in the history of the struggle for free expression'. It was a rousing diatribe against the Bowdlers, the Mrs Grundies and the Comstocks. He went on to claim, with a prophetic degree of truth, that as a result of the *Ulysses* case, 'it should henceforth be impossible for the censors legally to sustain an attack against any book of artistic integrity, no matter how frank and forthright it may be.' The judgment coincided with another liberalising decision of the courts. In December 1933, Prohibition ended in the States. 'We may now imbibe freely of the contents of bottles and forthright books,' wrote Morris Ernst. He believed the repeal of the sex taboo in books would in time prove to be of the greater importance. 'Perhaps the intolerance which closed our distilleries was the intolerance which decreed that basic human functions had to be treated in books in a furtive, leering, roundabout manner. Happily, both of these have now been repudiated.' Only after the appearance of *Ulysses* was the district court judgment appealed, before the United States Circuit Court of Appeals. That court was not unanimous in its finding. On a two-to-one majority the decision of the district court, under Judge Woolsey, was upheld, but Judge Manton, one of the three, dissented, finding that the matter complained of had 'a tendency . . . to deprave and corrupt. Who can doubt the obscenity of this book after a reading of the pages referred to, which are too indecent to add as a footnote to this opinion? Its characterisation as obscene should be quite unanimous by all who read it.'

In October 1936 John Lane, who ran The Bodley Head in Britain, followed the American example, though without the necessity of a trial, and published *Ulysses*, in the first instance only with an edition limited to 1,000 copies. At the time Joyce was correcting the proofs for the book he was in Copenhagen; this was in August 1936. He met

Kai Friis-Moller, the Danish poet and critic, translator of T. S. Eliot into Danish, and told him that he had been fighting for this for 20 years. He rather proudly told another distinguished Danish writer, Tom Kristensen, that the war between himself and England was over, and that he was the conqueror. The first unlimited English edition appeared the following year. By the time these two editions appeared, *Ulysses* had sold not much over 2,000 copies per annum or, in total, 30,000, that is the same number of copies as T. E. Lawrence had sold of his book, *The Seven Pillars of Wisdom*, during the *three-month period* between March and midsummer 1927. Joyce had a hard old time of it, winning through.

FOUR

Which Version is Copyright?

'Jim, how beautiful you are!'
Nora Joyce, seeing James Joyce's face
through the vitrine in the coffin-lid

O N 13 January 1941, James Joyce, who had been operated on for a perforated duodenal ulcer, went into a final coma and died at 2.15 in the morning. Just over an hour before that, Joyce had woken and asked the nurse to send for his wife and his son Giorgio. They were summoned to the hospital, but did not arrive in time.

Permission was given, later that day, for the famous death mask to be made. Two versions were taken. Later still a Catholic priest approached Nora and Giorgio, offering a religious service. 'I couldn't do that to him,' was Nora's reply.

Two days later, on a cold snowy day, the body was brought to the Flüntern Cemetery, in Zurich, and buried. As the coffin was lowered into the grave, Joyce's face faintly visible through the tiny vitrine let into the lid, Nora, who had always loved his looks, called out to him: 'Jim, how beautiful you are!' The ceremony included speeches, one given by Heinrich Straumann, the new Professor of English at the University of Zurich. There was the singing of Monteverdi's farewell to earth and sky. There were no flowers. Joyce did not like them.

Among the wreaths was one with an Irish harp woven into the green, an emblem of the country with whose uncreated conscience he had wrestled all his life. There was no other Irish representation present, certainly none to lay claim to him in the way Irish people worldwide have done since. He was an awkward customer as far as Ireland was concerned and had been throughout most of his life. He was to remain so for some time to come. From the days before the First World War, when the prospective publisher of *Dubliners* had got cold feet and had burnt the entire first edition of the book, Joyce's writings had been increasingly embarrassing to Ireland. His fame and reputation were not of a character which could be easily accommodated within the narrow, censorious and bigoted atmosphere which had developed in Ireland during the first two decades of independence. With the exception of a few enlightened spirits, he was regarded with suspicion and distaste. It was certainly not politic, on the occasion of his death, for the state to become involved in the obsequies. Indeed, the only diplomatic official there was the British Minister in Berne, Lord Derwent, who made a speech which implicitly claimed the great man as a British writer. 'Of all the injustices Britain has heaped upon Ireland,' he said, 'Ireland will continue to enjoy the lasting revenge of producing masterpieces of English literature.' There was some justification for the ambiguities implicit in Lord Derwent's presence and the words he spoke. Joyce had been born British. Through the moderately good offices of George Moore, combined with the help given to Joyce by W. B. Yeats, he obtained a Civil List pension from the British Prime Minister, Asquith; moreover, all his working activity, his publishing aspirations, and his interest in an academic and popular reputation, as far as the British Isles were concerned, were focused on London, not Dublin. This never proved greatly to Joyce's advantage, however. It should be pointed out that, while the British banned

Ulysses, Ireland never did. But then Ireland had more subtle ways of registering its reservations. In truth, Joyce was neither English nor Irish, either practically or emotionally. He already belonged to the world.

Joyce's religion and religion as a force of censure within Ireland have a significance in the attitude of the family to Dublin and in Nora's own caustic view of a Catholic ceremony at the time of Joyce's death. Her own position was indeterminate; she actually went back to religious observance in her widowhood. But she was acutely aware of the fact that James Joyce had severed connections with the Church as far back as 1897, when it is thought, in a burst of piety at Easter, he participated in Mass for the last time. Before that, he had been quite religious. At Clongowes he excelled in religious instruction. He became an altar boy. He wrote a hymn to the Virgin Mary, which was much admired. He loved ritual and knew about it in some detail. The majesty of the Church excited him long after its power had ceased to impress him. But deep down the force guiding his spiritual development was probably his father's intense anti-clericalism. He thought of himself as a Jesuit, rather than a Catholic, and told Budgen so. Much later, when asked when he left the Church, he replied that it was for the Church to say.

Joyce's affairs at the time of his death were disrupted. He had left Paris just over a year before in such a hurry that papers, documents and other possessions remained in his flat, some of them impounded by the landlord, to whom he owed rent. His friend and long-time amanuensis, Paul Léon, gathered as much as he could together, and deposited with the Irish Minister in Paris, Count O'Kelly, a box of papers. The instruction was that, in the event of Léon's death (as a Jew, he was arrested, deported and eventually shot by the Gestapo), these were to be sent to Dublin and deposited in the National Library, with a 50-year embargo on them. The papers were sent over at the end of the Second World War, and opened and catalogued 50 years after Joyce's death, in the early spring of 1991. It was the Library's intention to sort, catalogue and exhibit the papers later in the year; first impressions were of no major discoveries. Nora was opposed to them going to Ireland at all. She resented the fact that Dublin had ignored her husband and she tried, unsuccessfully, to get the papers back. But that was later, and constituted only a minor problem among the many with which she and her family were faced.

Their main difficulties were financial and legal. They derived from a combination of the war, Giorgio's inability to provide for his mother, as well as his increasing dependence on alcohol, and the fact that they had moved to a neutral country and away from their friends. There was also the problem of Lucia, who was in Brittany, in a clinic where she remained throughout the war. The few people who had helped them in Zurich had done so for the sake mainly of Joyce himself. After his death, the widow met with a different attitude, exemplified in the sharp demand, made by Mrs Giedion-Welcker within one month of the event for the return of the substantial guarantee she had paid to allow the family into Switzerland. She also refused to hand over the two death masks, for which she had paid at the time they were taken. She had no hope of getting the money until the estate was settled and it is to this we now turn our attention.

Underlying many of the events of the next half-century, including control of the use of James Joyce material, the dictating of the publishing history of all his works and ultimately those decisions which were designed to achieve the creation of new copyright, including that of *Ulysses*, was the James Joyce Estate. The wheels for its creation were set in motion by Joyce's death, though the outline plans for the eventualities now being realised had been laid years before.

Joyce made his will in London in 1931, signing it on

5 August. He had then been married to Nora for just a month. The main purpose of the will was to secure inheritance for his children, just as the main purpose for the marriage was to secure their legitimacy. Under the will he made Nora the executrix *and* sole trustee, and he gave Harriet Shaw Weaver sole and absolute control over 'all literary matters relating to my writings published and unpublished'. His library and his pictures went to Giorgio; everything else to Nora. No material goods, though of course eventual income, went to Lucia. Eventually both Giorgio and Lucia, equally, were beneficiaries of the residuary estate, and their children, if there were to be any. Thus he left the income from the royalties on his works to Nora, during her lifetime, and thereafter to his children, Giorgio and Lucia, and to their descendants, of whom at the time there were none, though Giorgio's wife, Helen, was pregnant with Stephen James Joyce. He was born the following 15 February and remained the only issue of James Joyce's two children, and is today the sole surviving member of the family, though his father's second wife, who is also a beneficiary under the writer's son's will, is alive. James Joyce left all his worldly goods to Giorgio and nothing to Lucia. Stephen James (he regularly insists on the use of the two names) was to become head of the family and an increasingly important voice in James Joyce affairs after the death of his father, Giorgio, on 12 June 1976. Though the question of the legitimacy of his children was present in Joyce's decision to marry Nora and in the executing of his will, doubts were almost immediately cast on the success of this, and when it transpired that the family's residence in Paris might invalidate the terms of the will, Joyce required his lawyers to draw up a codicil which, in the event of the legitimacy being disallowed, would ensure their inheritance on the condition that they took his surname.

To some extent Joyce was acting according to con-

ditions which suited the changed social and moral cli-
mate. The light-hearted and relatively happy decade of
the twenties, the Jazz Age, when living in Paris seemed
to epitomise living at the centre of all that was exciting
and stimulating, gave way to something rather different
in the thirties. Sobriety, growing poverty, political polar-
isations in many countries and then the rise of Fascism
made some kind of thought for the future, even with
someone as careless of such thought as James Joyce, a
fuller necessity. It may seem odd, but the gaiety of the
twenties had existed side-by-side with a certain censori-
ousness about the wilder shores of literature. Whatever
gloom may have come in the 1930s, it included, ironically, a more liberal attitude towards drink – Prohibition
ended in 1933 after 14 years – and a certain degree of
liberalisation in respect of literature.

Joyce left all his manuscripts to Harriet Shaw Weaver,
as we have seen, and he also made her his literary executor. This deprived Nora of the ready cash which might
have been obtained from the sale of his papers. She was
soon in need. Poor as the family had been before Joyce's
death it became much poorer afterwards. The first problem was the will. Probate took time and while the
lawyers were dealing with this, all income from royalties
went to the Joyce Estate in London. The problems which
Joyce had intended to obviate, by making his will in London in the first place, returned. Legal questions over
recognition of his domicile meant that probate could not
proceed. Instead, the matter had to go to the High Court,
and this delayed its resolution and of course any money
for Nora.

Money was extremely difficult anyway. These were the
darkest days of the Second World War. Though Switzerland was neutral, it was surrounded on all sides by com-
batants, or, in the case of France, by that portion of
the country which, though with its own government
at Vichy, was effectively under German control. The

practicalities of getting messages to Switzerland were complicated enough; the transfer of money was considerably more difficult. Quite apart from its availability, the British Government had set up a 'Trading with the Enemy' section in the Board of Trade which was relevant, in respect of the money needed to finance Lucia, and which also covered neutral Switzerland. The department was not in favour of sending money abroad. In the case of Switzerland, that country's currency was in short supply in Britain and this imposed further restrictions.

There was no 'Joyce' money available, only the money from friends, including a group in America organised by Padraic Colum and his wife, and of course Harriet Shaw Weaver. Her association with James Joyce had tailed off substantially in the period following her guardianship of Lucia in 1935. Towards the end of Joyce's life there were brief exchanges, but the warm flow of correspondence had ceased long before that, and it was now Harriet Weaver's task to take on the family without Joyce and once again come to its aid. The first executor of the will appointed in Clause 1 was Nora; if she were not able to act, then the Public Trustee in London was appointed. Nora, from Zurich, was not able to prove the will. The Public Trustee declined. It seemed that Harriet Shaw Weaver would be obliged, more out of affection for Joyce than anything else, to become administrator as well as literary executor. 'Financial guardian' might be a better way of describing the role she assumed, since once again it was her own money which had to be used.

The question of Joyce's domicile, which had required a court judgment, was not settled until 1943 and probate on the Joyce Estate was not obtained until 1945. Some of the delay was due to Nora herself and to Giorgio. Nora was a poor correspondent, Giorgio ill-equipped for the complicated management of his own and his mother's affairs, despite the time he had on his hands. James Joyce's son had been badly prepared by his parents for regular self-sufficiency, even less prepared for the difficulties of the war and the immediate post-war period. He was unemployed and effectively unemployable. He drank increasingly and was on the way to becoming an alcoholic, drinking a brandy and water mixture at the Kronenhalle, in Zurich, which was simply known by the barmen there as 'Cognac Joyce!' A redeeming characteristic was his affection for his mother. Nora, according to Brenda Maddox, 'basked in his constant comfort and attention . . . Giorgio remained very precious to her, her only reliable companion, just as he had been as an infant in Rome. Her attachment to him only deepened as he grew to look more and more like James Joyce . . .'

But if their precarious and still essentially bohemian existence militated against the liberation of legitimate funds from England, the restrictions imposed by lawyers, by the Bank of England and by Harriet Shaw Weaver herself have also to be taken into account. Exchange controls were rigorous and there was little appreciation of the family's needs. It was not until 1947 that the Bank relented. Nora was recognised as a resident of Switzerland and it was agreed that any income due to her would be released. But Harriet Shaw Weaver, who remained effectively in control as self-appointed executor and administrator of Joyce's will, still imposed tight conditions, for Nora's sake and also to ensure that the money needed for Lucia was available. She restricted the flow of cash to small but fairly regular payments.

A year after the war, at the end of 1946, Giorgio's son, Stephen James, who was 14, left Zurich for America, where his education was to continue at the Phillips Andover Academy, in Massachusetts, and where he would be looked after by his mother's family. By 1948 the financial situation had improved for his grandmother, and from then until Nora's death, on 10 April 1951, she was adequately provided for.

The present structure of the James Joyce Estate developed from this period. Harriet Shaw Weaver effectively became both literary executor and administrator of the will. Essentially this was Nora's decision. For many years Harriet Shaw Weaver had been represented legally by Fred Monro, of the London firm of Monro, Pennefather (it had been known by other combinations of names earlier in the century, including Slack, Monro, Saw, and then Monro, Saw, but by the 1950s was named thus). Fred Monro, as a result of the association with Harriet Shaw Weaver, acted for James Joyce and Nora Barnacle at the time of their wedding, the making of the will and also in respect of action which Joyce sought to take at the time against the *Frankfurter Zeitung*. One of the witnesses of the will was Samuel Harrison, managing clerk to the firm, which was then called Monro, Saw and Company. Fred Monro was Joyce's solicitor when the question of publishing *Ulysses* in Britain arose, in the mid-1930s, and corresponded then with T. S. Eliot, who was a director of Faber. Responsibility for the Joyce family remained with Monro, Pennefather after the writer's death. When Nora died and Giorgio became head of the family, he reappointed Harriet Shaw Weaver as administrator and she retained the same lawyers. Fred was succeeded as the responsible partner by his son, Lionel, in 1951, and much later by his grandson, David Monro.

The development of other aspects of the Joyce Estate may also be summarised here. Harriet Shaw Weaver acted as literary executor with great dedication and care, considering carefully every kind of request for copyright and other permissions, and personally reading all relevant documents. Her policy was simple: to do what James Joyce would have done. She was the kind of person who replied to letters on the day of their receipt, whenever possible. The work escalated, however, and references to the activities of the Society of Authors, on behalf of authors' estates generally, attracted her attention and led to her requesting the Society to act on behalf of the James Joyce Estate, at least as an eventual replacement of herself as literary executor. This consultation appears to have been in 1950 and the person who then became responsible, from the Society of Authors' point of view, was Anne Munro-Kerr. During Harriet Shaw Weaver's lifetime the 'sole decision in all literary matters' affecting Joyce's writings, either published or unpublished, rested with her, while questions of policy would be decided by her in consultation with Lionel Monro. The firm of Monro, Pennefather remains as the Trustees' solicitor and now acts in cooperation with the Society. It would seem that Stephen James Joyce, in recent years, has used separate solicitors. In a letter to Peter du Sautoy of 25 June 1984, reporting on a lunch in the country outside Frankfurt, after the launch and presentation of the Synoptic and Critical Text to Stephen James Joyce, Ellmann wrote, 'Stephen told me that he was going "to assert himself with the Estate"'. If this in fact happened, then it may well be that the events of the past seven years or so owe more to Stephen James Joyce than he suggests or others suspect.

In summary, it would seem that the line of control, or power, within the Estate is operated by the family solicitors, or the Trustees' solicitors, or both, through the Society of Authors, and using either one or more Trustees. During most of the events covered by this book, Peter du Sautoy was the principal Trustee, acting with either Lionel or David Monro. In 1990 he was succeeded by Clive Hart, who is referred to as 'Sole Trustee'. It is not clear whether Harriet Shaw Weaver made over the literary Executorship to the Society, or not, and in what form if she did.

What happened to the manuscripts? What happened to *Ulysses*? Brenda Maddox records that, as early as 1940, Joseph Prescott, of the University of Connecticut's

English Department, placed an advertisement in a European newspaper seeking Joyce manuscripts. The search,
suspended during the war, started up again in the mid-
1940s. The race was on. Contenders emerged quickly
enough, among them John Slocum, an American State
Department official, later to publish *A Bibliography of
James Joyce* (1953). Nora herself owned one work only,
in manuscript, *Chamber Music*, which Joyce had given
her in 1909. It was a specially written version (the
book had been published two years before, and Joyce
inscribed it as a copy of his poems which had been
done by him in Dublin and completed on the 11th day
of November 1909), a 'fair copy' on parchment, bound
in cream-coloured leather, which Nora sought to sell
before the money situation eased, when she changed
her mind. Then, in 1948 and 1949, she went to Paris to
help sort out the papers and other Joyce possessions
which had been left in the flat in 1940. Following this
there was a sale of Joyce material at the Librairie La
Hune, where the family portraits were disposed of as
well as manuscript material. The rivalry between John
Slocum and the University of Buffalo was resolved when
Buffalo scooped the pool and acquired the main items
for $10,000, to Slocum's fury. He wanted it for his old
university, Harvard.

Many forces were in contention over James Joyce and
his manuscripts on that occasion. Nora and Giorgio were
mainly interested in money, Giorgio particularly so, and
interested in as much of it as he could get. Brenda Maddox makes the point that he was jealous of the amounts
needed to care for Lucia. Harriet Shaw Weaver was in a
more complicated position. She was concerned that the
family would be properly cared for, as a result of the sale,
which was organised, after all, for Nora's benefit. At
the same time, as literary executor, she wanted to
ensure that the physical disposal of manuscripts was
done in fulfilment of her duties as literary executor and

in the interest of Joyce's memory. Another interest was that of Joyce studies, though in a muted form. The Joyce industry was then embryonic. But, as we have seen, since 1940 active pursuit of Joyceana had become the domain of universities and of scholars acting on behalf of university libraries. At the same time the private collectors were also on the march, fully aware of the potential value of Joyceana, as they had been since the 1920s. On this occasion, partly because private buyers had limited funds, it was the universities which took the lead.

As part of the complicated *dramatis personae* of that episode, there were the friends, and the supposed friends, of the family. There were the real or imagined national interests, apparent in the fate of the manuscripts of *Finnegans Wake*. These, as Harriet Shaw Weaver saw it, would be best deposited in the National Library of Ireland and she had promised them to the Keeper of Manuscripts there. The Library had already received the sealed packages from the Joyce flat, rescued by Paul Léon. Nora, however, opposed this course of action quite strenuously. She had learnt with some distress of Paul Léon's action, felt that he should have consulted her, and had then tried unsuccessfully to untangle and reverse the transfer of those documents. She was also annoyed with Ireland for ignoring her husband. Unlike W. B. Yeats, whose body – one hopes – was brought back for burial in Sligo after the Second World War, there had been no question of Joyce being accorded the same honour. Rather, he was regarded still with suspicion and distaste. Upon this there pivoted the fate of Dublin as a repository for Joyce material and Dublin lost out. In deference to Nora's wishes, Harriet Shaw Weaver consigned the manuscripts of *Finnegans Wake* to the Library of the British Museum, now the British Library, and Ireland remains without major Joyce material of any kind. The other item of concern to her was a notebook for *Exiles*, Joyce's only play. Though this outlined many personal associations between real people and the characters in the play, Nora saw no problems here and agreed to publication. The contents of the notebook were subsequently published as 'Notes by the Author' as an appendix to the 1952 edition of *Exiles*, for which Padraic Colum wrote a sensitive introduction.* The notebook went to the University of Buffalo, along with the La Hune exhibition material.

As far as *Ulysses* was concerned, the greater part of the significant manuscript, typescript and corrected proof material, as well as the limited number of earlier drafts of work, had all been distributed and were either in university libraries or on their way to them. The proofs had passed to Mrs Johnson, owner of the Willard Gallery in New York, who bought them from Sylvia Beach. The complete Rosenbach collection of manuscript material would go to the Rosenbach Institute in Philadelphia in 1952, having been in Dr Rosenbach's private collection until his death that year. He and his brother had already set up the Rosenbach Museum in the city to be the final repository for the manuscript of *Ulysses*. On the publishing front no significant changes had occurred since the first, and then standard, British and American editions had appeared in the 1930s; the Bodley Head *Ulysses* appeared in a limited edition version in 1936, an unlimited version in 1937; the Random House edition, corrupt and, in copyright terms, muddled, appeared in 1934. There had been several reprints of the Bodley Head edition in 1941, 1947 and 1949, and of the Random House (or Modern Library) editions, in 1940, with a sub-edition which used corrected plates from the 1934 edition, and in 1961. But it was not until 1960, in the case of the former,

---

* It was Padraic Colum, incidentally, who encouraged the author of this present book to put the play on in Dublin in March 1958, in its first full run in the city. It was a two-week run in the Players' Theatre, in Trinity College, Dublin, with Terence Brady playing the part of Richard Rowan and Juliet Tatlow as Bertha Rowan.

and 1961 in the case of the latter, that *Ulysses* was reset, with all the opportunities and pitfalls associated with this.

It is difficult to imagine how anyone, in the late 1940s, could have conceived of the significance of what they were dealing with, as decisions were made about the disposition of Joyce material around the world. These manuscripts are the working capital on which the industry was to be based and then developed. They still represent a huge resource. Perhaps more importantly, they represent a source of power and influence. But it is not at all simple, in the sense of possession being in some way central to the exercise of power. Control of the material is only part of the argument. Control of its legal use is the overriding consideration. What Harriet Shaw Weaver held during her period as literary executor was control of two things. She had discretion over certain remaining manuscripts, one of them *Finnegans Wake*, which went to the British Museum, the other a notebook for Joyce's only play, *Exiles*, but, initially, she also had copyright control.

Joyce's published books throughout his lifetime were covered by copyright laws in Britain, the United States and elsewhere. For Britain and the other signatory countries to the Berne Convention there was a measure of uniformity in the pervasive influence of this international agreement. But the United States stood outside the Convention and this has complicated considerably the question of copyright in the country in which interest in James Joyce is now paramount.

That copyright lies in territory essentially alien for the literary scholar is clearly evident among Joyce experts, who in general show little understanding of or interest in it. It is a matter for lawyers and law experts. It is also a matter for publishers and for literary estates. On the whole they like to keep it that way. There has been, and still is, a great deal of obfuscation, beginning with the Joyce Estate itself, whose sole Trustee since 1990, Clive

Hart, declines to give details about the beneficiaries of the James Joyce will, or to indicate where the money goes.

Anthony Burgess, the novelist, and a man with a natural and understandable curiosity about the financial affairs of another writer, is bewildered about the Joyce money, and how it has been managed in the past. An equally protective view is taken by Stephen James Joyce, the writer's grandson, whose public statements frequently emphasise his commitment to the protection of family privacy. Anthony Burgess has reported publicly on a conversation with Stephen James Joyce about the money, to the effect that he understood the affairs of the James Joyce Estate to have been in a mess, but to have been recently improved. 'Things are better now,' he claims, on the basis of what the author's grandson has apparently told him. To his credit, Stephen James Joyce is emphatic about offering the works of his grandfather as an end in themselves and in opposing the massive apparatus of the Joyce industry as a huge handicap to the enjoyment of the books. He extends this also, though with less justification, to cover the intimate relations between his grandparents and other matters of a 'private' nature, including the more intimate letters. But the emphasis on privacy is also a defence against other intrusions. The detailed investigation of the various facets of Joyce's life are legitimately associated with Joyce scholarship. It is arguable that the same view should be allowed to affect the copyright position as well and all the financial issues which flow from it.

Copyright is no small matter to summarise. It affected Joyce from the beginning of the century and was of course relevant in the publication of all his work, but particularly the publication of *Ulysses*, which certainly fell foul of United States copyright law.

The creation of an author's right in what he had written was circumscribed in its relevance until the invention of printing. He controlled his thoughts, if he published them, as best he could. But once the technique of printing had created the possibility of widespread reproduction of such works, the effectiveness of this control changed. No longer could the idea of the protection of the work remain bound up in the ownership of the object by which thought or creative writing was set down, that is, the manuscript. The ideas were important, in classical times, as was the way they were put, the two constituting 'style', in the broadest interpretation of that word. But not until we have the exactly repeatable reproduction of the work does a problem arise. This is the separation of the ownership of a right in what is contained in the written message, our copyright, and the ownership of a manuscript, which now becomes the first version of the message and not its sole or rare means of distribution.

Thus the printing and publication of a work creates the need for copyright. It was not satisfied immediately. Nothing happened hastily. It only came about three centuries later, firstly, in the Copyright Act of 1709, which gave to the author a 14-year right of sole publication, renewable for a similar period. It was necessary, under this law, to register with the Stationers' Hall in order to gain benefit. This situation was echoed, 200 years later, in the American legislation which affected Joyce, where registration was also a factor. This was one of the differences between American copyright law and the law in Britain.

A quantity of case law under the 1709 Act and under subsequent amending legislation, together with certain amending Acts, materialised during the period up to the Copyright Act of 1842, which repealed the preceding legislation and then became the basis for existing law. This Act changed the period covered by copyright, giving 42 years copyright cover to a work, from its date of publication, or for the natural life of the author together with seven years after his death, or, if the book were to be published after the author's death, for 42 years from that publication date. One of the odd aspects of this legislation was that the rights were to be 'the property of the owner of the author's manuscript', which would as often be the author's publisher as his descendants.

This Act also provided for the lodging of copies of author's works in the Copyright Libraries (British Museum, Bodleian, Cambridge, Edinburgh, Dublin University). It was still an essential part of the law that a work had to be registered at the Stationers' Hall, so there was a register of copyright works and no action for infringement of copyright could be taken without this record having been made. The 1842 Act defined in its preamble an objective which was the encouragement of 'literary matter of lasting benefit to the world'. Case law extended and altered the definition of this. It led to the extension of copyright to cover journalism, the listing of stocks and shares in newspapers and periodicals, the catalogues for the major department stores and trading enterprises, so that the broad definition of something open to copyright became a matter in which the labour of the brain and the expenditure of money had been dispensed. Private letters were not deemed to be published, either by being written or being sent. Copyright in these remained the property of the author. Conventional publication only created a copyright period. One other point, which might arguably have been of some relevance to James Joyce's work, was that copyright protection under this Act prevailed only for 'innocent publications'. Books of an immoral tendency were not 'capable of being made the subject of copyright'.

Following this Act of 1842 was the Copyright Act of 1911, which came into force on 1 July 1912. Between the two occurred the Berne Convention on copyright, agreed at a conference in the Swiss capital in 1885, ratified by Britain by an enabling Act in 1886 and ratified by the other signatories in 1887. The Convention defined the entitlements to copyright and established common ground based on the simple idea that work which was copyright in one signatory country was copyright in the other signatory countries, though the duration of such copyright could not exceed the duration in the country of origin. Authors from outside the union of signatories were given equal rights by a revised Convention, signed in Berlin in 1908. The definitions of works were wide-ranging. The revised Convention also defined the present period, the life of the author and 50 years after the author's death, extended to 1 January of the year following the completion of the 50-year period.

The United States remained outside the Berne Convention until 1989. Moreover, in the Act which Congress passed in March 1909, the United States established its own copyright laws which were inferior to the British Copyright Act of 1911 and of the provisions of the Berne Convention. Whereas both of these measures had removed the need for formal copyright registration, the American legislation required that a work published abroad had to be deposited at Washington within 60 days of such publication, had then to be republished within the territory of the United States within a period of four months following the deposit of the original edition of the work. The work had also to be registered in order to confirm the copyright, such registration involving the deposit of copies of the *American* edition. The point of the American printing for permanent copyright purposes was tied up with the strength of the American print unions, who sought to protect themselves. It does not require a great effort of imagination to see how good the author's timing or that of his publishers in the United States had to be, in order to satisfy the strict timetable under the terms of the Act. The protection, under American law, was for 28 years, a period which could be extended for a further 28 years, but only if application for the extension was made one year prior to the expiry of the first term.

The British 1911 Copyright Act established the 50-year period after the death of the author. It came into effect after *Chamber Music* (1907) and only two years before the publication of *Dubliners*. Its writ ran throughout the British Colonies and Dependencies, and was largely copied by the Dominions, Canada being the weakest in terms of similarities of legislative rights, a condition which resulted from being a neighbour of the United States, but one which penalised its own authors rather than those who came from countries which were signatories to the Berne Convention.

The legal conditions on copyright which applied to James Joyce throughout his lifetime were essentially those outlined above. To a great extent, they still contain the major provisions governing his works. At times he adopted a quaint view of the potential complications, mainly out of a desire to see his works in print. One of these occurred with *A Portrait*, which provoked hesitations among a number of the printers who were approached by Harriet Shaw Weaver. Ezra Pound then became responsible for a hare-brained scheme for by-passing this censorship by organising the printing of *A Portrait* with 'largish' blank spaces where the offending passages in the book had been. Into these spaces would be pasted manifolded versions of these passages. The actual copyright in the work would be obtained for the *printed* portions only, and presumably for the spaces, since these would have become integral, as far as copyright was concerned. Pound offered to paste the pieces of paper into each copy of the book himself! Joyce agreed with this scheme. Harriet Shaw Weaver plodded on meanwhile with the task of finding a printer prepared to do the book, unexpurgated. Nothing, fortunately, came of the 1915 cut-and-paste job. The copyright problems it would have created would undoubtedly have been horrendous.

Quite obviously, the copyrighting of *Ulysses* in the United States presented difficulties. The original edition of 1922 could not be deposited at Washington; and certainly, within four months, no subsequent American edition could be brought out, since the book was banned. Joyce was concerned about this and particularly so when Samuel Roth pirated *Ulysses*, first printing the early episodes in a slightly expurgated form in 1927. Joyce first tried to get John Quinn's surviving partner to take legal action on his behalf, then, through Ezra Pound, to get the poet's father, who was a lawyer, to take the case. He finally ended up with an American lawyer in Paris instructing a New York lawyer. As Joyce said, in a long letter to Harriet Shaw Weaver, there was never a case against Roth for breach of copyright. The case which was talked about aimed at stopping Roth by challenging the use of Joyce's name. It was a common law issue, of property, of misrepresentation and of fraud.

But the issue of copyright, both then and now, presents us with much greater complexities. To begin with, British and American copyright need to be seen as entirely separate legally. The British copyright laws have not changed substantially, the American law has. Under British law the basic situation is still covered by the Act of 1911. On the author's death, all published works are covered by copyright. Substantial revision, with new material added, may allow for renewal of copyright in the revised and changed work, but does not alter the ending of copyright in the original versions of the works as published. There is, therefore, an onus of scholarly justification involved in works seeking new copyright, and this is obvious in the cases of *Dubliners* and *A Portrait of the Artist as a Young Man*. It is central to *Ulysses*, but leaves all the other versions of the book which appeared before the author's death in January 1941 free to enter the public domain on 1 January 1992.

The American situation is different. From 1962

Congress had intended reforming American copyright legislation and several preliminary Acts had been passed, culminating in the 1976 Copyright Act which came into force in 1978. Because of the long delays in legislating, what is called 'grandfathering' had taken place in the provisions and special extended copyrights were allowed, permitting the 75-year copyright period to be applied retrospectively. The original Act gave 28 years protection, renewable for a further 28 years. Thus, if the 1922 *Ulysses* had been properly published in the United States, its original copyright protection would have been for 56 years, to 1978. Because of 'grandfathering', the Act passed in 1978 extended that copyright cover, so that 47 years were added as the renewal period. Added to the original 28 years this gives to works published after 1906 a 75-year copyright under the new 1976 Act, so long as their new copyright was renewed.

As far as *Ulysses*, as published in 1922, is concerned, all of this is hypothetical. Indeed, the whole framework for dealing with the copyright questions surrounding the book in the United States is bound by conjecture. The factual situation seems to be as follows. When *Ulysses* was first published in 1934, a copyright claim was made for the edition, citing four dates: 1918, 1919, 1920 and 1934. Added to the first three dates was the name of Margaret Caroline Anderson, the principal editor of *The Little Review* and the owner of its copyright. Assuming that she filed copies for copyright, the situation would appear to be that the copyright claim in 1934 included separate claims for the portions of *Ulysses* which appeared between 1918 and 1920 in the versions prepared for *The Little Review*, constituting 13 complete episodes of the 18 which make up the book, together with part of the 14th episode, up to the point where *The Little Review* was prosecuted for obscenity and publication of *Ulysses* brought to a halt. The 1934 copyright claim was therefore made for the unpublished balance of 'Oxen of the Sun', together with the final four episodes. But the copyright that was claimed had little to do with the version which was published. This was taken from Samuel Roth's pirated version of the book, which was at least partially corrupt; and it was later corrected. We have therefore the actual American copyright on *Ulysses* based on an early version of the book for half its total content and on a corrupt version for the rest, but claimed in respect of a relatively satisfactory version.

A point of considerable interest arises here. The differences between the parts of *Ulysses* which were actually copyrighted and the version of *Ulysses* as printed in 1934 are more substantial than the differences between the accepted, pre-Gabler version of the book and his revised version. If there is justification for the Estate in claiming copyright on the Gabler version for *another* lengthy copyright period, then there is, by the same token, no justification for claiming that any earlier version of *Ulysses*, except the Roth and *Little Review* versions, enjoy any copyright in the United States at all. *Ulysses*, as subsequently revised and now out in a reprint based on the 1961 edition, and offered by Random House as an alternative to *Ulysses: The Corrected Text*, is not copyright in the United States and never has been.

What is under copyright, in defective or superseded versions, enjoys its copyright protection for periods which are of varying lengths within the one volume. The portions covered by the copyright claims dated 1918–1920 run out, under the 75-year-rule, in 1993, 1994 and 1995 respectively, while the 1934 corrupt portion of *Ulysses* runs out of copyright in 2009. All of *Ulysses* as used by Random House for this copyright claim, quite distinct from the actual text as published in 1934, corrupt or not, was superseded by Joyce's revisions and by the careful editorial work carried out for other editions by Stuart Gilbert. If, on the other hand, an argument is sustained for *Ulysses* being under copyright in some way or other in America, then we see here a divergence between the copyright coverage of *Ulysses* in Britain and the Commonwealth, and indeed many other countries, and the much less stable position existing in the United States.

Finally, the Americans, having adopted an essentially isolationist view of copyright towards the rest of the world throughout most of the 20th century – a type of literary Monroe Doctrine – have now conformed in another way as well. On 31 October 1988, Ronald Reagan signed the Berne Convention Implementation Act which made United States law compliant with the 1971 Paris text of the Convention. Though the action of the President has little or no impact on the subject matter of this book, its intent is a welcome if belated acknowledgement of the unfortunate impact of America's international attitude to copyright throughout much of the rest of our century.

FIVE

The Coming of the Scholars

'How did you bury Joyce?
In a broadcast Symposium.
That's how we buried Joyce
To a tuneful encomium.'

Patrick Kavanagh

SEAN O FAOLAIN, the Irish short story writer and literary critic, opens his essay on William Faulkner in *The Vanishing Hero* with an anecdote about James Joyce scholarship. 'Not long ago I said to an intelligent critic of Joyce: "Tell the truth! Do you not sometimes get utterly exasperated by him?" The critic smiled a slow smile and then replied with disarming honesty: "As an avant-garde critic I can never afford to be exasperated."'

O Faolain confesses that it was several days before he realised how insulting this attitude was to the author concerned. He felt that there was an insincere type of author, too smart to exasperate authors or critics, but that the true writer must inevitably do this often. O Faolain did not comment on the extent to which this reflected on the 'intelligent critic', yet his reported encounter indicates a significant shift in the attitudes towards Joyce scholarship on the part of such critics collectively, as well as a shift in the character of their critical objectivity.

Another shift also occurred quite soon after the Second

World War. The point which demonstrates it was made by another Irish literary critic, Denis Johnston. Writing in the Dublin literary magazine *Envoy* in April 1951, he painted a light-hearted picture of obsessive American college students of Joyce, unable to read him for amusement because of the burden of having to write about him in order to qualify academically. Johnston describes Joyce as 'our bad boy from Belvedere' and reminds us that Gogarty, whose rage against the thesis-mongers is part of the argument, was perhaps justified in feeling mild resentment at the way such supposed scholars pursued him 'as the character in a book of an early hanger-on whom he never liked'. The sin is against the writer; the conscientious scholarly workers have broken the Geneva convention that is observed in all professions 'from barristers to bootleggers. Outsiders must not foul the pitch.' And Niall Montgomery, in the same publication, refers 'to subtle overseas doctors in whom, under martial aid, are vested the exegetic rights'. (In this, 'martial aid' is a pun — Montgomery was full of them — on the post-war Marshall Aid package which encouraged many demobilised GIs to study in Europe.) When he quotes them, of course, they turn out to be less subtle than at first supposed. Montgomery, who had an eye for a monocle, saw the absurdity in Herbert Gorman's solemn discovery that Joyce's father always wore his 'in one eye'; and he quotes extensively the heavy definition of terms like 'desire' and 'joy' which are preambles to weighty judgments on Joyce in critical documents which Montgomery apostrophises as clauses in the Joyce Factory Act! Professor Levin of Harvard defines reading as 'some process of critical chemistry' and Montgomery, who defines Levin as 'the best of the psychoanalysts who have written on Joyce', describes this as fancy.

Here are three Irish writers taking ironic notice of a new phenomenon, that of Joyce himself being surrounded and appropriated. Patrick Kavanagh has a poem in that same issue of *Envoy* called 'Who Killed James Joyce?' The commentator killed James Joyce. He did it with a Harvard thesis. Joyce was buried in a broadcast symposium. 'Who carried the coffin out?' asks Kavanagh.

> Six Dublin codgers
> Led into Langham Place
> By W. R. Rodgers.*

A man from Yale is given the credit for polishing off *Finnegans Wake*, not quite getting his PhD, but a BLitt and Masters, and a scholarship to Trinity College. And after that everyone made the pilgrimage 'in the Blooms-day swelter' from the Martello Tower to the cabby's shelter.

There remained, side by side with the new academic high seriousness about Joyce, as well as the possessive-ness, the older style of critical assessment. Indeed, Sean O Faolain himself in *The Vanishing Hero*, a remarkably good book about fiction in the 1920s, published in 1956 but based on a 1953 series of lectures at Princeton University, also includes an essay on Joyce entitled 'Virginia Woolf and James Joyce, or Narcissa and Lucifer'. It is a model of the writer's – as opposed to the academic's – assessment of James Joyce's work. But it is not frequently cited, nor is O Faolain for his other writings on and edit-ings of Joyce, because he does not easily fit in. He is one example of a vast continuing literary tradition, of the *belle-lettres* approach to Joyce, as opposed to the aca-demic, but increasingly an awkward element. Apart from the works of exhaustive bibliographical summary, these essays are not widely recorded and belong generally to a genre which is collateral to academic analysis of Joyce.

* Rodgers was a poet from Northern Ireland who worked for the BBC. The headquarters of the BBC were then in Langham Place, at the top of Regent Street.

O Faolain, Johnston, Montgomery and Kavanagh are all Irish writers who deliberately took issue with the process by which James Joyce was being engulfed by the academics. But it was good-hearted badinage for the most part, and totally insufficient to combat the wealth, seriousness and sense of purpose of the academic system which was turning itself into an industry. Nor did they entirely wish it, at least, not to the point of alienating the university faculties dealing with Joyce studies and those who directed them, since most of these writers from time to time did teaching courses in literature and sometimes even in Joyce studies, and were therefore dependent on the support of the scholars they in part deplored. They saw the threat for what it was, made fun of it and got on with the central problem of writing their books. The machine rolled on.

Up to the Second World War there was a predominance, in scholarly as opposed to scurrilous criticism of Joyce and his writings, of men and women who were writers, friends, supporters and disciples. They did not anticipate making their living out of writing about Joyce, studying and teaching him. They would have starved if they had. They wanted to contribute to knowledge, perception and understanding about Joyce and his books, but only as part of their own use of words and very often as a small part. After Joyce's death and then with the end of the Second World War, and also with the distribution of much of his manuscript material completed, there came the rise of the academic institution with a vested interest in this material, and therefore in the related scholarship. This in turn led to a new and quite different kind of scholar studying Joyce. This was the professional, who had a long-term interest in the study of the man and his writings, largely to the exclusion of all other study; and by long-term is meant, in most cases, lifelong.

Richard Ellmann is one of the key figures and the author of the definitive biography of James Joyce.

Anthony Burgess, a man fond of superlatives, described it as 'the greatest literary biography of the century'. It is a powerful work indeed, though not without its flaws, perhaps one of the more serious being the writer's tendency to rely on *Ulysses* and other works by Joyce as unqualified source-material for biographical fact. Sometimes this is thrown out with irresponsibly damaging effect. As Ulick O'Connor has pointed out, in his book, *Biographers and the Art of Biography*, Ellmann casually suggests that Joyce called Gogarty 'the counterjumper's son'. The 'source' for this, as offered by the biographer, is *Ulysses*. It is not Joyce referring to Gogarty; it is Simon Dedalus referring to Buck Mulligan. Nevertheless, Ellmann's life is an outstanding achievement, the nature of his mind and scholarship put to remarkable use in dealing with a complex genius who left many problems, which his biographer transcends superbly. The very qualities which Ellmann brought to the job of recreating James Joyce the man, and which include an ability to absorb vast amounts of material, changing and adapting his view of the meaning of that material, reveal Joyce to us very fully indeed. Though it is often overlooked, they also reveal a good deal about the biographer himself; something of Ellmann's character, as he sifts, separates and then reconstitutes the character of Joyce, comes through in his sustained openness to every point of view. Later, in the context of the events in this book, we shall see how badly this open and flexible approach served him when it came to judging the strict and quite different rules of editing.

Another commentator on Ellmann is Dr Patrick Henchy, former director of the National Library, who travelled with Ellmann in the west of Ireland during early researches for the book, and often had a difficult time restraining the American scholar from indiscretions and misjudgments about what he could ask, in a Barnacle household, and what was definitely not to be referred to.

On one occasion, when Ellmann was embarking upon a catechism which would lead inevitably to questions about the effect in Galway of Joyce and Nora not getting married until their children were in their teens, he successfully headed him off and saved a fruitful encounter from absolute disaster.

Ellmann conceived of the idea of his life of Joyce in 1947, when George Yeats, widow of the poet, showed him an unpublished 'preface' in which Yeats described his first meeting with Joyce. He did preliminary work over the following five years and then settled steadily to the biography which was published in 1959. From then until his death he published many further works of importance in the Joyce canon, and many less important ones as well, only in the 1980s turning to another subject altogether, Oscar Wilde. Ellmann died in 1987. His life of this other Irish writer was published posthumously. During that period, from 1950 until his death, Ellmann assumed a dominance in Joyce scholarship, not always benign, as we shall see. Though Ellmann was not a textual scholar, his imprimatur is on the revised, new copyright texts of two Joyce works, *Dubliners* and *A Portrait of the Artist as a Young Man*, both of which were revised in the 1960s, with new copyright being claimed. When it came to the revision of *Ulysses* he played a much more extensive role. This was entirely consistent with the position he had established for himself in Joyce scholarship generally.

He was part of a rapidly growing army of academics whose work during that same period, 1950 to 1980, broadly followed the pattern which Ellmann could be said to have established. These academics became swiftly enough both competitive and generative. Inter-university rivalries, which had manifested themselves in the pursuit of James Joyce's manuscripts, had a similar purpose in pursuing students and scholars, and in establishing reputations for the teaching of Joyce. This could be done in part with the possession of Joyce collections, in part by the publication of Joyce books and articles, and in part by the setting up of Joyce centres with Joyce periodicals. The scholarly vehicle gathered momentum and the more it developed the heavier it became. As to the personalities involved, they enjoy a kind of hierarchy. When Richard Kain died, on 11 April 1990, Hugh Kenner became the senior Joyce scholar, worldwide. When I put it to him during a discussion in the summer of 1990 that he was now the academic who had been continually working on Joyce material for longer than any other, he was mildly pleased with the idea, accepting it as some form of accolade. Stalwarts, like Richard Ellmann, have passed on, and the mantle was now being transferred to a new generation which revered the older men.

Joyce scholars constitute an international order of academic freemasonry. There are rites to be performed, in order to gain entry, consisting of a thesis, a work of scholarship, a level of publication. Then there are levels of seniority and hence power. There are meetings and international conferences. It is an entirely new development, post-Second World War, where a single author can produce a lifetime of study and teaching for a not insubstantial number of academics, and can proliferate the armies of toilers in the field, the students and their myriad fruits, in the form of a vast panoply of written and published words.

The most powerful organisation in the James Joyce world is the James Joyce Foundation, established on 16 June 1967. This Foundation is responsible for the two-yearly International James Joyce Symposiums, the last one being held in 1990 in Monte Carlo on the theme 'Images of Joyce', the next to be held in 1992 in Dublin. Its first symposium was in the year of its foundation, but it missed a year in order to hold a symposium in the centenary year of James Joyce's birth, 1982. The current president is Karen Lawrence who succeeded Morris Beja at the end of the 1990 meeting in Monte Carlo. No formal electoral procedure is followed; there are no nominations, it simply emerges at the behest of the men who run the Foundation's affairs, among the most senior of whom are Bernard Benstock, of Miami University, and Tom Staley, Director of the Humanities Research Center at the University of Texas at Austin. It produces a newsletter, but calls it a 'Newastlatter'.

Another considerable organisation is the Zurich James Joyce Foundation, the creation of Fritz Senn, who began a rich collection of Joyceana many years ago, and has contributed uniquely to scholarship and interest in the writer. There are also Joyce centres in other countries, notably Ireland, where the Sandycove Martello Tower, the setting for the opening of *Ulysses*, is a James Joyce Museum, and where also, in North Great George's Street, there is a Joyce study centre. Though the Princess Grace Irish Library, in Monaco, has wider interests than Joyce, it has an expanding collection and has organised Joyce events other than the 12th International Symposium. It is associated, for the purposes of scholarly publishing, with Colin Smythe, the English publisher who is on the board of the library, and he has become a regular publisher of Joyce books.

Many other scholarly presses publish Joyce books and there are several journals. The most important of these is the *James Joyce Quarterly*, published by the University of Tulsa, in Oklahoma, and edited by Robert Spoo. There is a *Joyce Studies Annual*, edited by Christine van Boheemen, *European Joyce Studies*, edited by Fritz Senn, *The James Joyce Broadsheet*, edited in Leeds, and *The James Joyce Literary Supplement*, published by the University of Miami and edited by Bernard Benstock.

Joyce, the exasperator of everyone during his own lifetime, a writer who has provoked innumerable divisions within criticism and scholarship since his death, has left

an even more lasting memorial in the enforced transfer
of attention to his work from the writer to the critic. This
is the scholarly shift, more than any other, responsible
for the development of the industry. It is no more than
he predicted, no more than he sought. He claimed to have
put in all the enigmas and puzzles in the work for the
very purpose of ensuring his own immortality by keeping
the academics busy. He thought their work would go on
for centuries.

What he almost certainly did not anticipate is the shift
in the character of the critical attention and analysis
away from the broadly-based considerations of style,
character, plot, narrative skill, humour, irony and satire,
which had generally been the collective headings under
which his writer-critics assessed him, into a rather different academic approach, which increasingly considered
myth, symbol, allusion, pun, word-play and textual
analysis. Perhaps even more important than this, he did
not anticipate a quite distinct though associated shift
from the broad mixture of favourable and unfavour-
able judgments, which had been his general experience
during his lifetime, to an increasingly adulatory critical
starting-point adopted by the predominantly academic
people who had made an often irreversible, lifetime commitment to Joyce studies. Such people, and of course one
is adumbrating a general principle, start out from a position which largely removes from their critical canon the
possibility of finding *against* Joyce the writer in any serious or fundamental way. Since Pound spoke, James Joyce
has been a genius; by dint of pressing the case, this view
is widely accepted in the academic and non-academic
worlds. For the 400 or so serious Joyce scholars, there can
be no real argument about this. As a position it separates
them from writers such as O Faolain. This has not, however, removed the conflict, the argument and the bitter-
ness; but it has largely confined it to Joyce scholarship.
The non-Joyce critic needs to be a major figure indeed in

order to impinge on the industry with any serious critical contribution.

Relatively early in this period, certainly by the beginning of the 1960s, the issue of texts was being addressed by scholars, and within that decade two major Joyce works were re-edited, with new copyright *in the new versions* being claimed by the James Joyce Estate. Richard Ellmann was involved in both of these events. As a prelude to the more controversial issue of *Ulysses: The Corrected Text*, which was to follow as a textual and copyright project during the 1970s and 1980s, it is worth considering what happened to the much less controversial works of Joyce's earlier life, which are dealt with here in the order in which they were re-edited for copyright purposes, though this was the reverse of the order in which Joyce wrote them.

By the time *Ulysses* appeared in 1922, Joyce already had two 20th-century 'classics' to his name, *Dubliners*, his collection of short stories, and the novel, *A Portrait of the Artist as a Young Man*. In the case of *A Portrait of the Artist as a Young Man* the changes in the edition which now claims a new copyright are minimal. So much is this so that the note in the current 1985 Jonathan Cape edition does not specify them. The principles adopted for this, the newly copyrighted 1964 edition, are set down and are significant. In this case the Dublin holograph, or 'final, fair-copy manuscript' in Joyce's hand, together with other changes listed by Joyce during his lifetime and not all incorporated in the many, many editions of the book, were offered as proposed corrections, were then pronounced on by Richard Ellmann and then incorporated in the published version. The edition is called 'definitive'. 'Lists of corrections and changes noted by Joyce, some of which were never made in any of the published versions', were also part of the apparatus of the editor, Chester G. Anderson. The work of making these lists and of setting out 'an extensive list of possible corrections' constituted his doctoral thesis at Columbia University in 1962. Ellmann was 'asked to act as arbiter, and made the final selection'. It is interesting that, in 1981, in a letter which Ellmann wrote to Peter du Sautoy on 7 December, dealing mainly with *Ulysses*, he said, '. . . I know that *A Portrait of the Artist* was badly edited by accident, and needs a bit of touching up, but that would seem to me a minor matter. . . .'

Whether or not this justifies new copyright is open to question. Its position as such can arguably only be checked if the edition is challenged by an alternative edition employing some, or indeed all, of the changes which are incorporated. There is no automatic assumption of the right simply as a result of claiming copyright in the normal way, by putting either the word 'Copyright', or the letter 'c', usually inside a circle, followed by the date and the name of the claimant. In the case of all of these titles the claim is made on behalf of 'the Estate of James Joyce'. But the legal reality behind this claim is that it requires to be established or proved, rather than simply lying there, as an established fact. In other words, there is no copyright register, internationally recognised, to which people can appeal, or within which those asserting the right can inscribe it, thus warning off any challenges by others.

The new 1967 copyright in *Dubliners* is argued at greater length in the version currently on the market. It is claimed by the James Joyce Estate on the 1988 reprint of the Jonathan Cape hardback edition of 1967, which was 'The Corrected Text, with Explanatory Note by Robert Scholes'. The same claim is made on the Penguin paperback. It is similarly claimed for the American editions. It is based on relatively few changes. These include verbal alterations and alterations in the punctuation, which are worth looking at, at least in outline.

Joyce favoured dashes instead of inverted commas for direct speech. In his lifetime he got them only in *Ulysses* and *Finnegans Wake*. But he *wanted* them in the earlier works. Unfashionable at the time in Britain, though the norm in France, his original London publisher, Grant Richards, rejected Joyce's stylistic oddity and used inverted commas. He was in a strong position. It was Joyce's first published work in England. Publishers' rules and typesetting styles were more rigidly held then. They prevailed in subsequent editions. In the 1967 edition dashes have at last been introduced. In addition, 37 textual changes of a minor kind have been made, based on a surviving copy of the book from the aborted, Dublin Maunsel edition, with Joyce's corrections in it. This copy, which is at Yale and dates from 1912, two years before the Grant Richards edition, has changes which seem, on the face of it, odd. Two examples will demonstrate the nature of what has been done and also the kind of questions which are provoked in textual editing of this kind.

In the final story of *Dubliners*, 'The Dead', Miss Ivors, a woman of Republican persuasion and a guest at the Misses Morkan's annual dance, challenges Gabriel Conroy with being the author of a column in the *Daily Express*, which, in the 1914 edition, she refers to in these terms:

> – Well, I am ashamed of you, said Miss Ivors frankly. To say you'd write for a paper like that. I didn't think you were a West Briton.

In the 1967 edition 'paper' becomes 'rag'. A moot point: which of the two is preferable? Using the slang term – only justified in the political sense, the *Express* being a newspaper which represented the 'Establishment' and which would have been anti-Parnell – slightly weakens Miss Ivors. The use of 'paper' is appropriately neutral. The overall context of the encounter between her and Gabriel, which is an extended one, suggests that she would have preferred the neutral rather than the deroga-

tory term. She is careful, as a character, not to disdain him and her carefulness thus outlined, if it mattered, was certainly the way Joyce left it, during his lifetime. More compelling, perhaps, is the fact that Joyce not only accepted 'paper' for 1914, but never sought to change it subsequently. The book went through many printings and editions in his lifetime, and none of these changes were attempted. So what is the justification for the change, made so many years after Joyce's death? Are we really able to know what he finally wanted, when he seems not to have known, or sought it, himself?

One other example will clarify further the basis for which copyright is sought in this particular work. In an earlier story, called 'Clay', Maria, the central character, is twice described as wearing a 'raincloak', this word being a replacement for 'waterproof', which is used in the 1914 edition and all subsequent editions of the book. The reintroduction of 'raincloak' is archaic, notwithstanding the fact of Joyce *perhaps* having *once* preferred it.

In the 1967 revised edition of *Dubliners* there are four categories of change. The first of these is the replacement of inverted commas with a dash, in compliance both with Joyce's later style and with his expressed wishes at the time of the 1914 publication. The second is the restoration of the 1914 first-edition punctuation, though the details of what this entailed are not given. The third is the introduction of an unspecified and undetailed number of changes, from a list of 28 written out by Joyce for Grant Richards, some of which were done, others not. All now have been incorporated. Finally, there are the 37 other changes, two examples of which have been given. If this constitutes a basis for new copyright in *Dubliners*, then it does so on the strength only of the last of the four. Two of the other three could have no legal status and the third is minor. This means that any publisher, seeking next January to bring out a public domain version of

Dubliners, could introduce the dashes or not, as he saw fit, and then print the 1914 version, or a later version, of the book in its entirety, just as Joyce saw and lived with it throughout his life, with no serious attempt to revise or change the text. This would conform with current copyright law and would be the correct procedure to follow, once James Joyce's works come out of copyright on 1 January 1992.

These views are based in part on an analysis of the law and the comparison of cases. As recently as March 1991, in a copyright case in America before the Supreme Court, Judge Sandra Day O'Connor repeated one of the principles governing the creation of copyright, that it should be based on creativity rather than on hard work. 'Copyright rewards originality, not effort,' she said, 'and in no event may copyright extend to the facts themselves.' The case itself concerned the compilation of database material such as telephone listings and its use by other than the compilers. But by extension, the idea that the introduction of a dash to replace inverted commas throughout a work could have any copyright relevance has less validity as a result of the judgment. The use of the dash in Joyce's work, to replace inverted commas, is the equivalent of a fact and the change fulfils a single idea long known to all Joyce scholars.

What happened with Joyce's first two books was then extended in the next decade to the biggest prize of all, *Ulysses*. If we accept the editorial changes, then *Dubliners* and *A Portrait of the Artist as a Young Man* in the versions of 1967 and 1964 respectively have qualified, as it were, for renewal. But we have to accept the superiority of the texts. If we do, then this means that the Estate will continue to enjoy royalty income for 50 years from 1967 and 1964 respectively for these two works in their latest versions. But it also means that a publisher can go back to an earlier, or an alternative version of either title and publish from next 1 January, not paying any royalties and not requiring permission. What he needs, of course, is an alternative and equally persuasive authority, if he is to do other than simply reprint one of the versions which appeared during Joyce's lifetime.

SIX

Ulysses for Everyone?

'I would like to know how we stand in this matter and whether the extent of the changes will justify a new copyright. I hope you will all assist me in resolving the dilemma that the estate is likely to face.'
Peter du Sautoy to Philip Gaskell,
5 May 1983

*U*LYSSES: *A Critical and Synoptic Edition*, edited by Professor Hans Walter Gabler, a Munich-based Joyce scholar, was published on Bloomsday 1984. Two years later, on the same day in June, there appeared *Ulysses: The Corrected Text*. The first version was a three-volume scholars' edition; the second a commercial edition, in hardback and paperback, published over British and American imprints. The first of these two editions claimed a new copyright for 'The Trustees of the Estate of James Joyce' in the 'reading text' of Ulysses. It was this reading text which was then used for the 1986 edition. Copyright was also claimed by the Estate in 'draft texts' and 'revision material'. Hans Walter Gabler's copyright was confined to 'Presentation of Genetic Synopsis, Notes and Afterword'.

In the summer of 1988, a young American Joycean, John Kidd, published a substantial attack on the edition in *The New York Review of Books*. It was not the first attack, nor was he the only serious critic of the edition, but he brought to wide, non-scholarly attention what he considered its defects and raised the controversy to a level not generally associated with academic disagreements. The reaction at first was to belittle John Kidd's scholarship, and specifically his textual capacities, and to berate him for taking the matter into the public arena and away from what was represented as the calmer, less emotional, less 'journalistic' atmosphere of scholarly journals and conferences. This ignored the fact that Kidd had first presented his criticisms to the Society for Textual Scholarship in New York on 26 April 1985, in Gabler's presence. Indeed, Gabler, forearmed with a copy of Kidd's paper, replied to it in withering terms, dismissing Kidd, expressing the wish that he had been asked to respond to a worthier challenge and concluding with the assertion that nothing had emerged from Kidd's criticisms to undermine his work. It was as a result of this failure to respond in like manner to what was a scholarly assessment of defects in Gabler's work that John Kidd chose a different and much broader public platform for the controversy.

Then, in December 1988, Professor Charles Rossman, of the University of Texas at Austin, published a report in *The New York Review of Books* of an investigation into the Ellmann papers at the University of Tulsa, in Oklahoma, which revealed misgivings among the editorial team about the edition, as well as copyright motives in organising the project, and monitoring its direction and extent. These two events, the Kidd article, entitled 'The Scandal of "Ulysses" ' and the Rossman article six months later, together with many letters which appeared in the *Times Literary Supplement* in London and in the *New York Review of Books*, focused worldwide attention on the controversy. A committee, called the Tanselle Committee, was set up to investigate the criticism, but never met and was subsequently disbanded. The American publishers brought back into print the 1961 edition of *Ulysses*, removed from the covers of certain printed versions of the

Gabler edition any reference to it being 'The Corrected Text' and awaited developments. In the late summer of 1990 one of the principal publishers, Viking-Penguin, set up an editorial team under Seamus Deane, of the National University of Ireland, to re-edit all of Joyce's works, including *Ulysses*, though it was not clear how far this re-editing would use or dispense with 'The Corrected Text'. An Irish publisher also embarked on a new, post-copyright edition of *Ulysses*, using John Kidd as editor. It was widely accepted that *Ulysses: The Corrected Text* had not succeeded in establishing itself as the best possible version of the book and that more work needed to be done.

In 1977 Hans Walter Gabler put to the James Joyce Estate the idea that he should prepare a new critical edition of *Ulysses*. Gabler was then Professor of English at Munich University, a position he still holds. He had an established expertise in editing and was academically well-equipped for the task of dealing with a major editorial project of the kind represented by *Ulysses*, which, despite the complexities of *Finnegans Wake*, far exceeds that later work in the editorial problems which had been created by the earlier book's publishing and printing history. Gabler is solidly academic, a severe and quite fluent campaigner on behalf of his own theories and practices. He is in the field of editing at times prone to a somewhat stiff use of English, which was to provoke reservations by his colleague in the project, Richard Ellmann, over his command of the idiomatic English used in Dublin in the early years of this century, and perhaps of the use of English generally. Gabler had earlier offered to re-edit *A Portrait*, but the Estate had turned down this proposal. The Trustees of the James Joyce Estate agreed to *Ulysses*, however, and the work commenced. It was backed by a grant from the Deutsche Forschungsgemeinschaft, a cultural agency of the German Government, and this, according to the chief editor, was 'unprecedented' and 'alone made the seven years' work on the edition possible'.

The direct editorial team of assistants for the project consisted of two principals whose names appear on the title pages of both *Ulysses: A Critical and Synoptic Edition*, of 1984, and *Ulysses: The Corrected Text*, the commercial edition which appeared in 1986. These are Wolfhard Steppe and Claus Melchior. Both were in the English Department of Munich University. Claus Melchior was initially student assistant on the project, and Gabler credits him with 'skill and knowledgeable independence of judgement'. He pays tribute to Steppe's 'experience and mature understanding of editing'. Both men, who are younger than Gabler, are very supportive of him and constitute a 'team' in a visually obvious way. They move together at conferences; and they debate together at sessions. The two men did the computer-aided groundwork of editing, under the chief editor's instruction. The three men worked together on the penultimate and then the final version, the 'textual states', of the edition over a three-year period of discussion during which each of them read 'chapter after chapter of computer printouts of the given edited versions'. Melchior was also responsible for tabulating the dates and the relationships of the proofs of the 1922 edition.

This basic team for the project, of editor-in-chief and two full-time assistants, was vastly augmented by a number of other helpers, including the principal Trustee of the James Joyce Estate, Peter du Sautoy, who was at the time of the inception of the project a director of Faber and Faber. He is credited with an involvement in the undertaking 'far above the call of duty' and is said by Gabler to have led the project 'further along the road' on which du Sautoy, acting with Marshall Best, a senior editor with Viking, the publishers, had originally set it. Peter du Sautoy is not a scholar in the accepted sense of the word, but has a background in editing and publishing, mainly with the distinguished firm of which he became a director. He was in his early 70s during the time of the publication of Gabler's two editions of *Ulysses*. He was educated at Uppingham School, where he was a Foundation Scholar, and took a first-class degree at Oxford in English before joining the library staff at the British Museum. He was in the Royal Air Force during the Second World War, joining Faber and Faber in 1946, and becoming a director in December of that year. He was subsequently vice-chairman and then chairman of the company up to 1976. He was active in publishing associations, both in Britain and abroad, throughout his career, travelling quite widely to discuss publishing issues at a variety of international conferences.

Reserved in his attitude towards the complexities which soon emerged over the scholarly editing of *Ulysses*, he was dependent on his advisers to explain, in some detail, the ramifications of Gabler's theory and practice. He also relied on them for copyright advice, which seems odd, given his own background in the one profession where exact knowledge of the subject is essential. The Trustees, soon represented by Peter du Sautoy on his own, did, however, recognise that a copyright issue was involved from the start. Indeed, the claim that the 'initiative' for the new edition was Gabler's, rather than the Estate's, is somewhat naive, since, apart from asking for permission to edit *Ulysses*, Gabler could not proceed any further at all until the Estate had decided and agreed. In effect, the edition was jointly initiated.

The Estate appointed a three-man committee of academic advisers: Richard Ellmann, Clive Hart and Philip Gaskell; and two assistants to this committee were also appointed, A. Walton Litz and Michael Groden, under much pressure from Gabler. Ellmann was regarded as the leading Joyce scholar of the day and his imprimatur, as we have seen, was a *sine qua non* of many Joyce enterprises. He had been Goldsmith Professor of English literature at Oxford since 1970. His early academic career, including his doctorate, had been at Yale, though he also had a degree from Dublin University. His publications were mainly, though not exclusively, on Irish subjects; Yeats first, then Joyce and finally Oscar Wilde, whose life was published after Ellmann's death in 1987. In his style he was a generalist; in the sheer volume and reputation of his output, particularly on Joyce, his position was much more than that; but he was not, as previously stated, a textual scholar.

Philip Gaskell was educated at the Dragon School, in Oxford, at Oundle and then at King's College, Cambridge, where he held various positions, including Dean and Tutor, after war service in the Royal Artillery. His principal expertise was in bibliographical matters, on which he published widely. In 1967 he became librarian at Trinity College, Cambridge, and occupied this position at the time of the commencement of the project. He is undoubtedly a distinguished textual scholar, though not an expert in James Joyce's works. He keeps a lower profile than his colleagues in the *Ulysses* project and has arguably been bruised by the later bitternesses, unusual in so public a fashion in the other spheres of editorial and bibliographical work in which he has been involved. Philip Gaskell shares with Peter du Sautoy an enthusiasm for music, though with du Sautoy this finds expression in his support for, and involvement in, the Aldeburgh Festival, while Gaskell, who at one time played in Humphrey Lyttelton's Jazz Band, likes his music less formal.

Clive Hart, who subsequently became a Trustee of the James Joyce Estate and is now the Estate's Sole Trustee, is a Joyce scholar who published as early as 1963 *A Concordance to 'Finnegans Wake'*, followed by several other books. He has a forceful style of delivery and debate, and a habit of arguing from first principles, quite often turning on their heads the kind of basic assumptions with which ordinary people address specialised problems. When Robin Bates, for example, was interviewing Clive Hart in the autumn of 1989, he suggested that it was *at least interesting* that there were major disagreements among the scholars involved and that it was astonishing that Ellmann expressed enthusiasm publicly, while privately he had doubts. Hart's immediate denial that these attitudes were anything of the kind created the kind of stimulus of conflict which is characteristic of him.

Gabler credits the latter two members of the committee with closer work on the edition than is given to Ellmann, who is thanked for his 'perceptive comments'; they, on the other hand, are said to have involved themselves in Gabler's own conception of the problems in the text and also to have 'regulated' his editorial decisions. Their 'regulations' later evolved into published disagreements when they brought out, in 1989, *Ulysses: A Review of Three Texts*.

The two assistants to the academic advisory committee, Litz and Groden, are referred to by Gabler as 'godfathers' to the project. Both are distinguished Joyce scholars, Litz a significant name in the field of James Joyce criticism since 1961 when he published *The Art of James Joyce: Method and Design in 'Ulysses' and 'Finnegans Wake'* and Michael Groden since his *'Ulysses' in Progress* of 1977, an enlightened and well-written book. They pledged their faith in the project from the beginning, and out of enthusiasm for Joyce and friendship for Gabler they helped throughout the work, both on fundamental issues and in 'unstinting immersion in minute points of detail'. Six other named helpers are listed on the title page of the three-volume edition. Groden in particular maintained a steady campaign on Gabler's behalf, the latest salvo of which was released in late 1990.

More general support was also given by two other major figures in Joyce scholarship, Hugh Kenner and Fritz Senn. Hugh Kenner, doyen of Joyce scholarship, has already been mentioned; Fritz Senn, who is director of the Zurich James Joyce Foundation, is a perceptive critic and lifelong Joyce enthusiast. Many others, including student assistants, were more directly engaged in the project.

Gabler credits the computer and its staff with a major role (while at least some of his critics assert that it was a far from benign element in the project). Either way, it was a significant participant. Wilhelm Ott, of the computer centre at the University of Tübingen, pioneered the programme, TUSTEP, which was regarded by the editor as ideal for editing work and was used throughout. Kuno Schalkle was its chief programmer. It 'took over the mechanical operations', and allowed Gabler and his team to concentrate on 'the decisions that render valid the editorial result'.

These participants, together with many others who are mentioned by Gabler in his 'Acknowledgements' at the end of the three-volume edition, were not all in place from the beginning. By the time the book was published, however, they presented a powerful phalanx of critical opinion and judgment in support of the edition. This became a significant element in the story, as did the fact that many of them, having had a hand in the edifice, then became its reviewers and supporters, explaining and praising what had been done, and finding few if any mistakes. This suggests a logical sequence in line with the view ostensibly taken by the James Joyce Estate, that the critical edition would appear, be debated by scholars and, if found satisfactory, provide the basis for a commercial edition which would replace the earlier version of the book and become the standard *Ulysses* for the future.

There was a hidden agenda, however. There usually is. By 1979, two years after the commencement of the project, when the annual James Joyce Symposium was held in Zurich, work on the edition was sufficiently advanced to provide the main public focus of discussion. Indeed, in anticipation of that conference, Hans Walter Gabler published privately, not for sale, but for the use of the scholars attending that meeting, *Ulysses II.5: Prototype of a Critical Edition in Progress*. This was a version of the eighth, 'Lestrygonians', episode from *Ulysses*, which has Leopold Bloom in the centre of the city, among other things walking under the 'roguish finger' of Thomas Moore's statue, where Westmoreland Street joins College Green: 'They did right to put him up over a urinal: meeting of the waters.'

Debate at this conference was essentially calm, though the direction taken by the editor was later to provoke criticisms from the advisers. Yet there is a strange time-gap in this surfacing. Widespread public attention upon what was being done to *Ulysses* was then focused on the project by one of its supporters, when Hugh Kenner published 'The Computerised *Ulysses*' in *Harper's*. This was in April 1980. In Charles Rossman's bibliography of the Gabler–Kidd controversy, published in a special edition of *Studies in the Novel* (summer 1990), this essay is described as 'The single most influential essay in establishing the initial reputation of Gabler's work, this expression of gratitude and praise brought the edition – then still four years from publication – to the attention of the public and scholars alike.' Kenner, in detecting a radiance emanating from the work, was reflecting his own enthusiasm for the idea of a computerised 'solution' to the *Ulysses* and James Joyce editing problems, enthusiasm which went back a long way, and was entirely consistent with his own style and approach as a scholar. He had whetted the appetites of Joyce scholars for a new approach, quite different, even revolutionary.

Behind the scenes there was a rather different perception of the revolutionary nature of what was going on, less to do with modern technology than with old-fashioned conflicts of personality. Though it seems to have taken quite some time to come to a head, in the summer of 1981 there was considerable correspondence – as indeed one would have expected, since those responsible for the project were four years into it – between the editor-in-chief, his literary advisers and the principal Trustee. There were meetings. There is also clear evidence, in the few letters that have become available, of confrontation. In a letter of 2 October 1981, from Richard Ellmann to Peter du Sautoy, Ellmann referred to 'rather considerable intimations of thunder in the correspondence before the meeting' and then with some relief claims that 'the meeting had no Wedgy Benns', and that future disagreements would not be any worse than they had been on that day.

The meeting in question had been held in Philip Gaskell's rooms, in Trinity College, Cambridge, on 21 September of that year, and seems to have brought to a head an argument about Hans Walter Gabler's methods and his progress to date. Despite the fact that Gabler had placed on record details of his working methods, two years earlier, in the published 'Lestrygonians' and with it an example of its practical impact, the reservations felt about it by at least some of the advisers were not made until two years later. Though the thought is unworthy, it would seem, from the tone and direction of the correspondence during 1981, up to the 21 September meeting in Cambridge and after it, that the advisers had not given sufficiently serious attention to what was happening. They did now, but from the classically weak position of non-participants making judgments about a vast amount of work already achieved by the editorial team. Clive Hart, Philip Gaskell and Richard Ellmann – the scholars in the case – all started from different positions, editorially, while Peter du Sautoy was in a different category altogether: not a scholar, and therefore dependent upon his advisers in that area, but very much a man concerned for the interests of the James Joyce Estate, which meant, among other things, copyright.

Gabler, in all these developments, had the strength of being one against many. This came out particularly in his letter of 15 September 1981. He had already heard from Peter du Sautoy, offering him £100 towards his expenses from the Joyce Estate. Gabler responded by announcing that he would bring his assistant, Wolfhard Steppe, and also that he would have in his possession estimates for the computer typesetting costs. These had been prepared for Gavin Borden, of Garland Publishing, and represented 'the final piece of information required (I believe) towards the contract'. If he had it, he announced, he would take it to Roma Woodnutt. Roma Woodnutt was the person at the Society of Authors responsible for the affairs of the James Joyce Estate. Earlier in the same letter Gabler had announced that it was 'absolutely essential' for them to come to total agreement on procedures and on the expectations for the advisers. He added: 'I am very anxious to put before you all some specific suggestions for *Finnegans Wake* funding and editorial organisation which, in my present view, should involve basing the *Finnegans Wake* edition in the UK.' While these comments do not exactly represent Hans Walter Gabler dictating to his advisers or to the Trustee, Peter du Sautoy, they do show him involved in contractual arrangements, plans for printing, negotiations with the person who emerged later as responsible for copyright, and dealing firmly with the need for 'procedures and expectations'. Into the bargain he was raising wider editorial ambitions, affecting the most complex of all James Joyce's books.

At this point another matter of great importance arises: the contribution to the editing of *Ulysses* by Jack Dalton, a brilliant scholar of the University of South Carolina, of whom Clive Hart wrote to du Sautoy (29 September 1981), 'for all his faults there was a touch of the editorial genius in old Dalton'. 'Old Dalton', who may be regarded as the first person to attempt a comprehensive editing of *Ulysses*, had nearly completed revisions of the 1961 Random House *Ulysses* when he died. His revised copy turned up in Random House and was itself copied, the photostat going to Gabler in Munich. Perhaps more important were the several thousand notecards on *Ulysses* which were in his papers at the time of his death and which Jack MacNicholas, also of the University of South Carolina, reckoned 'would represent a correct text'. They represented 95% of the required work and it appears that the only thing which stopped Dalton completing his edition was Random House's refusal to guarantee that *all* his corrections would be incorporated. MacNicholas persuaded Dalton's heirs to make the cards available and they were sent to Gabler on condition that 'Jack should be given some sort of credit'. Gabler's ideas of credit, in his 1984 Acknowledgements, were limited. His intention, over Dalton, expressed in a long letter, dated 6 December 1981 to the advisers, was to cite him selectively, that is 'where his suggestion agrees with our decision or where we have taken a decision because he saw a problem'. All coincidences would be passed over without comment and, because Dalton's work was unpublished, disagreements would be ignored. Given the magnitude of Dalton's work and its stage of development with Random House, this approach was less than generous in scholarly terms. It was, however, much more than would in time be extended to John Kidd.

The issue of copyright does not feature in the correspondence of 1981, except by implication. Hans Walter Gabler maintains that he was never involved with the issue of copyright, yet what he was doing was seen by the Trustee, Peter du Sautoy, in the context of copyright.* In a letter dated 5 May 1983, from du Sautoy to Philip Gaskell, but copied to Ellmann, Hart and Gabler, the writer referred back to assurances given him in September 1981,

---

* Interview between the author and Gabler, June 1990.

by Clive Hart, that 'there is a significant element of fresh creativity in the new edition . . .' 'Sufficient change' for an extension of copyright was an important argument, as far as the James Joyce Estate was concerned, and this situation did not change. The attitude of the Estate to the project, in this respect, was known to all five correspondents at this time. It was not an argument of great substance. In a memorandum to the advisers, dated 4 December 1981, Peter du Sautoy maintained, 'I don't attach all that importance to the extension of the copyright period as I think the larger sales will still go to the older uncorrected texts which will be out of copyright and cheaper; students will be told to read the corrected texts but will that be enough?' Ellmann, however, corrected him: 'It would seem intolerable that different version of *Ulysses* should be circulating together once the Gabler text has been fixed and issued.' What Peter du Sautoy did not know was the precise legal position over copyright, when set against the direction which the project was taking, with its emphasis on the extent of changes, in numerical terms. But he was reassured by Clive Hart's statement that, 'in the overwhelming majority of cases', there was editorial agreement.

The 1981 correspondence among the three advisers, the editor-in-chief of the project and the Trustee of the James Joyce Estate was principally concerned with editorial progress. It records a distinct advance over the earlier and experimental 'Lestrygonians' ('very impressive indeed' is Gaskell's judgment on his reading of the 'Cyclops' episode and the episodes from 'Eumaeus' to the end of the book, the last three). But there were reservations, on Gaskell's part, about the extent of the notes. He was concerned, not that there are too many, but that there are too few. 'Only six Textual Notes for the whole of "Cyclops"?' he asked, in his letter of 7 May to du Sautoy. He went on to take issue with Hans Gabler's apparent decision-making on readings, unsupported by textual argument of any kind. On two specific issues, which he cited, he was at odds with the editor and their differences were to go unrecorded. For a scholarly edition, which it was intended should be the subject of extensive scholarly debate after publication, this is slightly alarming.

What is more disturbing is the letter Gaskell wrote to Clive Hart, on 21 August 1981, in which he suggested a meeting with Hans Walter Gabler in advance of a general session on the edition in London. This became the 21 September meeting, attended by Gabler, Hart, Gaskell and Ellmann, but possibly not by Peter du Sautoy. At this stage, Gaskell, Clive Hart and Gabler were concerned with editorial details, and Peter du Sautoy in keeping a watching brief on issues which his own letters reveal he was generally unclear about. In the memorandum cited above he wrote: 'I ask myself, with regard to this whole enterprise, *cui bono*? Not, I think, the general reader of Joyce, or the general publisher: mainly Joyce scholars and of course Hans himself, though he is of course entitled to devote his very considerable skills to a project of this kind.' Richard Ellmann 'would be very welcome if he wanted to come', but it is anticipated, in the event wrongly, that he would stay out of the discussion at this stage. However, though the purpose of the meeting in Cambridge is for detailed textual discussion, in advance of the general session in London, Gaskell went on to say that he and Hart had to thrash out several important points about *general editorial principles*. Thus, four years after the commencement of the project, and with drafts of the new edition which include the final three episodes being read by the advisers, there was the question of general editorial principles being raised for discussion. Gaskell also suggested a *preliminary* preliminary meeting, between just himself and Hart, to prepare and compare their positions before meeting with Gabler, for the meeting which was to take place in Cambridge before the 'general' meeting, later, in London. These rumblings (in part, since we do not have the complete correspondence) were the 'intimations of thunder' referred to earlier; and indeed there were disagreements between the two advisers and Gabler at the September meeting. In actual fact, they were barely rumblings, let alone thunder and in the event the storm passed over. Gabler was 'tractable', 'willing to make concessions', 'far from being inflexible'. Into the bargain he was still supremely confident. In another long letter, late in 1981, he wrote to Peter du Sautoy about the Garland contract that he looked upon the *Ulysses* project as 'the beginning of a long-term publishing connection which should see out the eventual publication, in stages, of a complete critical edition of the works of James Joyce . . .' For this there was needed the 'sincere involvement, sustained attention and unreserved dedication' of the editor, and he felt that his work on *Ulysses* had indicated clearly that he had this in mind.

The only other point of interest to emerge from those parts of the 1981 correspondence which the writer has seen is the shared view of Gaskell and Hart that there should be no publication of a sample of the edition in advance of its completion. Effectively, this meant that deliberations about its progress and about the still apparently unresolved question of general editorial principles remained confined to the advisers, the editor-in-chief and the Trustee, apart from deliberations at conferences, which were by definition controlled occasions. The hidden agenda was to remain hidden.

It seems that the thrashing out of the differences over general editorial principles either did not take place or did not reach any kind of conclusiveness. It also seems that Gabler took a fairly tough line on the simple issue of who would have the last word. As editor-in-chief for the project he assumed that he would. This view was challenged by Peter du Sautoy. Instead, assurances were sought by Hart and Gaskell, and given by du Sautoy, that the advisers would have the last word. As Trustee he wondered whether, 'at this stage', his most productive contribution might be to state the position of the Estate, which was that the final text of *Ulysses* would have to have the blessing of the advisory committee: 'I would like to establish the last word with you three.'

Clive Hart's response to this was very positive. He welcomed the assurances that the Trustees (acting on behalf of the Estate) would have the last word and went on to say that 'Hans's attitude' would need to be modified. At the same time he expressed himself concerned about undermining his confidence in his position. All of this suggests that instead of the disagreements over general editorial principles being thrashed out, the simple question of 'authority' had been invoked. If we do not know what we are talking about, at least let us be sure who will have the final say!

Gabler worked away during 1982 without there being any further recorded debate, either on specific points or on any issue of principle. For Joyceans it was a busy year indeed, being the centenary of the author's birth, celebrated worldwide in a variety of different ways, the most impressive being the slightly dramatised, but essentially faithful reading of the whole of *Ulysses* by Radio Telefis Eireann in Dublin. This beautiful and powerful rendering of the book has become one of the most attractive ways of absorbing it, and is given in authentic Dublin style by a large cast of actors and actresses.

The fundamental question over the editing remained, however, and at the end of the celebratory centenary year a more serious storm loomed for all the participants. Within the body of correspondence for 1983, which runs from January to November, a key letter is the one sent by Peter du Sautoy to Philip Gaskell on 5 May, in which he expressed himself unhappy that principles of editing are still being discussed and that they have become more, rather than less, fundamental. His view was that principle should be set aside in favour of consideration of each disputed reading, with a view to resolving the difficulties in this piecemeal way. He then referred to the interests of the James Joyce Estate. There were, according to his letter, 'two points that are important'. The first was the presence in the edition of significant fresh creativity. He had already received assurance on this from Clive Hart in the September 1981 letter. What he also found assuring in that letter were claims that the advisers and the editor-in-chief would be in agreement on the overwhelming majority of cases. Peter du Sautoy had been reassured by this at the time. Now he asked, 'Have I got to relinquish that sense of assurance?'

The second point, which seems to be the first point put in a different way, was simply that there should be sufficient textual change to justify new copyright and that this change should rely on material which could be traced back to Joyce. He then highlighted a claim made by Hans Walter Gabler, in an article for *Text*, that there were between 2,000 and 8,000 transmissional errors in *Ulysses* to be put right. This article is Gabler's most important statement on editing *Ulysses*. Though written in 1981, it was not in fact published until 1984. It is entitled 'The Synchrony and Diachrony of Texts: Practice and Theory of the Critical Edition of James Joyce's *Ulysses*'. Peter du Sautoy asked Gaskell: 'I would like to know how we stand in this matter and whether the extent of the changes will justify a new copyright. I hope you will all assist me in resolving the dilemma that the estate is likely to face.'

So here we have the principal Trustee, within a year of the actual publication of the new copyright edition of *Ulysses*, calling for the abandonment of the unresolved debates on general editorial principle, the resolution of differences on a reading-by-reading basis and help with the basic problems peculiar to the Estate. These concern matters of law. Yet there is no evidence of lawyers having advised on the editorial intricacies which had emerged over a period of three years and which had clearly not been resolved. The man who at least should know the answers, as far as copyright is concerned, was asking a textual scholar and his academic associates, neither of whom appeared to be well informed on copyright law, to help him. A distinct shift had taken place between 1981 and 1983 on the importance of copyright.

Peter du Sautoy, in that 5 May letter of 1983, was endeavouring to resolve two quite distinct problems: the editorial confusion and the copyright issue. Gaskell's advice on copyright was brief and unequivocal. Whatever might emerge in other areas, the number and the importance of the changes to the text would amply justify a new copyright, in his view. This was opinion, no more. Yet it seemed to suffice. The question of help or finality over copyright did not emerge again in the correspondence. It is a matter of supposition, but Gaskell's finality on the point of substantial and serious change could well have sealed the fate of the advisers. For a new storm was mounting and this was one which would not pass over as easily as the 1981 'intimations of thunder'. In his article on method, published in *Text*, Gabler adopted in the title a curious order: 'Practice and Theory', rather than the other way round. At least it seems, in the general content of the correspondence dealt with in this chapter, that the advisers were certainly much clearer on practice, and the detailed approach of the editor-in-chief on individual episodes in the book, than they were on Gabler's theory of editing. It is to this that we must now turn: the fundamental issue of differences between what had now become two sides, with the Trustee, Peter du Sautoy, acting as referee.

Before doing so, however, we must complete details of this 'hidden agenda' of division and uncertainty as it developed during 1983, the year in which Philip Gaskell and Clive Hart resigned from the project, A. Walton Litz

and Michael Groden were brought into it, Richard Ellmann sided with Hans Walter Gabler, Peter du Sautoy
accepted all the changes, and said goodbye to his earlier
advisers, and then everyone came together again. Well,
it was *almost* the same as before. It happened in the
following way.

Conflict between Hans Walter Gabler and the rest of
the project team was expected as early as February, at the
end of which month an adviser's meeting was planned.
In anticipation of it Peter du Sautoy wrote to Richard
Ellmann on 7 February regretting that Ellmann would
not be able to attend. 'I shall try to be there, as if there
is a real conflict between Hans and the others the Estate,
under the contract, have to decide the issue, that in effect
means me. I shall have to do some work to be sure I
understand at least something of what is at issue. Have
you any advice yourself?'

Ellmann grasped that they had reached a point of crisis
and said so to Clive Hart, in a letter, though he seems
not to have replied directly to du Sautoy with the much-
needed advice. It was in the letter to Clive Hart that
Ellmann first expressed his doubts about Gabler's insufficient 'native command of English'. The crisis did not
break immediately, but in a letter of 18 April Clive Hart
told Philip Gaskell that unless things 'get somewhere in
June . . . our ways may have to part'. In May there was
clear difference over procedure between Hans Walter
Gabler and Philip Gaskell, with Gabler pointing out that
Gaskell would have difficulties advising over a concept
which did not conform to his (Gaskell's) view of how to
edit. This prompted Gaskell to write to du Sautoy on 7
May to say that Gabler was using Rosenbach material
'outside the line of descent' and he would not accept this;
'Clive and I are in fundamental disagreement with Hans's
episodes.'

The crisis came to a head at the beginning of June. A
meeting was held on Saturday 4 June in Cambridge. At a

late stage in that meeting the Trustee and the advisers, with it seems Gavin Borden of Garland Publishing, withdrew to consider their position. They were faced with Gabler's refusal to conform to their conditions, which questioned the principles on which he was editing the text of *Ulysses*. The advisers, or at least two of them, either intimated or said clearly they had no option but to resign. Ellmann, both then and in a letter after the meeting, tried to persuade Hans Walter Gabler to modify his position on the editing 'so as to make it seem less dependent upon fixed principles'. Gabler still did not bend; the advisory board effectively resigned, though the Estate decided to go ahead with the edition 'regardless'. Ellmann felt that Gabler's view was that to concede was to deny all that he had done. He also felt that Gabler was being 'doctrinaire' and 'rigid'. Without concessions by Gabler, Ellmann viewed the enterprise as 'clouded from the start'. He sent copies of his letter to Gabler to all those involved, including Gavin Borden, to whom he wrote: 'it is always conceivable that he might change his mind'.

Gaskell wrote on the Monday to Peter du Sautoy confirming his withdrawal from the *Ulysses* project. What Gabler was doing, in Gaskell's view, would have an important but undesirable effect on the final text of *Ulysses* and he felt he had to withdraw entirely. He added: 'I do not want my name to be used, or my advice to be acknowledged in any way, either in or with reference to Hans's edition of *Ulysses*.'

Peter du Sautoy wrote to Richard Ellmann to say that he agreed with *every word* in his letter to Gabler, yet he left no time for any response. Two days *before* expressing this agreement, he had written to Gaskell accepting his withdrawal and asking him to return to Gabler all the documents circulated for the purpose of advising. To this extraordinarily rapid disposal of Gaskell's services he added a significant piece of information. This was that

Gabler had asked the Estate if it objected to him seeking the 'unofficial advice of other Joyce scholars, particularly Litz, Groden and perhaps Kenner, "on questions of editorial decision during these coming last few months on the project". I cannot see that we have any right to object, even if we wanted to, which I don't think we do.' Whatever may have been the meaning of the word 'unofficial' (since Litz and Groden became official 'assistants' to the academic advisory committee, and appeared on the title page of the 1984 *Ulysses* as such) the suggested change is remarkable for its speed and for the fact that it gave immediate indication of support for Gabler, strengthening his hand substantially.

Gabler himself acted with characteristic determination, with a letter dated 16 June 1983. Instead of responding to Ellmann's letter by offering a modified or less rigid stance, he listed many faults in the way Gaskell and Hart had worked, and then told Ellmann that he had Peter du Sautoy's knowledge and approval to ask Litz and Groden to advise. 'Would you, I wonder, at all care similarly to be approached with questions . . . ? . . . I would like to think that I may read your letter as an offer of continued exchange, albeit divested of the official nature which your former appointment by the Joyce Estate lent to it.' Gabler's dismissal of Gaskell and Hart in this letter is fairly withering. None of their objections was 'new . . . or showed up a neglect of fact or circumstance in my approach to the textual analysis & editing'. Most other scholars, it seemed, supported Gabler; 'the advisers' were 'the last to become even aware that there was something of uncommon interest in some parts of the transmission'; they made clear they did not 'like the editorial solutions'; 'they closed themselves to my considered adaptation of textual theory . . . in our increasingly fruitless altercation in Cambridge I was never confronted with new views or perspectives to which a flexible reaction would have been called for . . .

Going by numbers alone, the Estate's ex-advisers are even now in a minority . . .'

Quickly enough Gabler was working with Litz and Groden. Richard Ellmann went away. From the end of August until December he was in Atlanta, Georgia, at Emory University. Before leaving he wrote to Gabler and to du Sautoy. His letter to Peter du Sautoy appears to respond to a suggested draft letter from du Sautoy to Gabler which followed a Trustees' meeting on 8 August. This meeting gave formal confirmation to the publication of *Ulysses: A Critical and Synoptic Edition* on Bloomsday 1984. There was an 'important' proviso: that the Trustees would 'pass for press' prefatory acknowledgements, particularly references to the Trustees and the academic advisory committee. No decision was offered on a trade edition. The letter alerted Gabler to the fact that the advisers were responsible to the Estate, but could only perform if they consulted with the editor. The Trustees, du Sautoy suggested, would consider whether a public statement would be made.

Just how unstable things had become is indicated by the final part of du Sautoy's draft letter.

'He said there that the Trustees had agreed to the publication of the Critical Edition, notwithstanding the advisers not accepting it in full. He welcomed the cooperation between Gabler, Ellmann and Litz in achieving agreement, and hoped that something as close as possible to general agreement could be reached. 'The Trustees don't expect more than that.' The edition could then be presented 'to the world' as a solution to the problems of *Ulysses*, as complete 'as is humanly possible at this stage'.

Peter du Sautoy, in the draft letter, did not see the need to reappoint. He judged that, through what Ellmann had done, the advisers had been kept 'still in action'. From the Trustees' point of view they could be called on for further advice. He then expressed confidence in Gabler, on behalf of the Trustees, and said that they had been influenced by the critical apparatus, which gave an opportunity for scholars to make up their own minds. The point had not been reached, he said, where formal approval was forthcoming for Gabler's 'final reading text'. 'We hope that one day that point can be reached.'

Ellmann thought du Sautoy's position 'a master stroke' and said so in a letter of 25 August which gave some suggested outline of how the Trustees might present things at the time of publication. Ellmann raised the possibility of 'mentioning' Jack Dalton, the single most comprehensive worker on the editing problems before Gabler, then said, 'Perhaps he shouldn't be mentioned'. Ellmann concluded by giving *his* view of how the James Joyce Estate might have wished to present things: 'The Estate, eager to have an edition corresponding more closely with Joyce's intentions as these were apparent in manuscripts and typescripts, encouraged him and appointed three advisers to watch over the edition. These, although they were not always in perfect accord with Gabler, found his work generally admirable. Variants are registered in an appendix so that an interested reader can see what has been done. The new edition is in no sense a different book, but Joyce's devoted readers will find a multitude of small corrections which will facilitate reading and eliminate doubts about whether something is a printer's slip or a Joycean eccentricity.'

This could hardly be said to conform with the events of the previous few months, which went a long way beyond the advisers being 'not always in perfect accord'. More seriously, it was not the course followed, as we shall see, when publication actually took place.

In a final letter to Gabler before his departure, Ellmann raised the question of 'Love, yes. Word known to all men,' and said he felt Joyce would have been too subtle to use it in the 'Scylla' episode and he advised: 'put it among the prominent variants in the back'.

Clive Hart remained unconvinced. Gaskell remained distant. Peter du Sautoy expressed his gratitude to Ellmann for working with Litz and trying to break the deadlock. He thought it more important to get Gabler to accept Ellmann's and Litz's suggestions than it was to get Gaskell and Hart back in agreement. At this stage they represented a problem: 'We shall have to decide later how to deal with the question of giving acknowledgements, if any are to be given, to the various advisers; at the moment there is to be nothing said, as I understand it.'

Gabler remained intransigent and told Ellmann in mid-August that if any question of reinstating the advisers arose it would be a matter between Ellmann and the James Joyce Estate. The advice of course was for the editor's benefit: '*not* to have received the quality of advice I expected over the past year has been my real frustration'. But if they were to be reinstated Gabler was quite clear about the terms: 'the advice should be given on the basis of the edition's own explicit conception and stated editorial policy'. Secondly, 'as the editor finally responsible, I am free (as Walt Litz also put it) to accept or reject advice received'.

For four months nothing happened to heal the breach. Peter du Sautoy drafted a letter to Gabler which he sent to Ellmann but not to Gaskell or Hart. Additionally he sent it to David Monro (also Monro's father, Lionel), Roma Woodnutt of the Society of Authors, Walton Litz, Gavin Borden and John Bodley.

On 26 October Gabler told Ellmann he had heard nothing from Gaskell and Hart, 'so it seems they have finally opted out altogether'. Gabler was not distressed. He went to Princeton and worked there with Litz and Groden. In December differences were resolved and Gabler was relieved for the Estate, but he saw 'no further occasion to call on Clive's and Pip's active assistance'. Nor is there any correspondence, at least at Tulsa, to suggest that the two advisers came back into the picture. Six months later, when the first copy of the book was presented to Stephen James Joyce in Frankfurt by Hans Walter Gabler, he said, according to a letter which Ellmann sent to du Sautoy on 25 June 1984, that the advisers had helped, but that they were only 'the tip of the proverbial iceberg'. Gabler was firmly in charge. He had advisers now who were prepared to work 'to compensate for the loss of time and disproportionate expense of energy caused by the events from January to June' and he was content. In a sense he had won all the important battles.

SEVEN

A New, Original *Ulysses*

'It is new in that it presents the work as it has not
before had a public existence. It is original in that
it is based with the greatest possible consistency on
the author's manuscripts. In this, the edition aims
to be radically conservative . . .'

Hans Walter Gabler's Afterword

I N EDITING *Ulysses*, Hans Walter Gabler sought to
write new rules for the editing process. He did so in
the context of the computer age. He chose for his
subject the most complicated and intractable editing
problem of the 20th century, possibly of any century. We
have seen how Joyce himself treated his own book as a
flexible text, right up to the final month before its publication. Like Marcel Proust, he added vast quantities of
material to the novel after typesetting had begun. He
became his own copy-editor, as well as proofreader. As
Hugh Kenner has said, James Joyce generated text and
meant his readers to be aware of his writing as text in a
way that is at least unusual among writers. It has been
demonstrated by more than one critic that his eye for
error was occasionally blind, but always inventive: he
could, on occasion, accept, absorb and then build further
material upon a mistake by a typist or an error in typesetting. In the end this meant that, in a totally bizarre way,
those around him who were involved at all in the book

could well add to its content and alter, if ever so slightly, its direction and purpose. This process stopped almost immediately on publication, and within a few years Joyce had adopted an essentially conventional writer's view of the text of *Ulysses*; the heat went out of it, it belonged to the past. *Ulysses* was there, with a few hundred typographical errors the correction of which, on past experience, would lead to the introduction of more errors, so it was best left alone.

In conventional editing terms Joyce would seem to be a classic case for the conservative approach of taking, as copytext, either the best published version of the book, or the last version of the book approved by the author before his death. This would at least have the benefit of setting against the most ill-disciplined and prodigal of writers a system of rigour and conventional control. The precedents and practice are there. The rules have been laid down by textual scholars of great repute; and the confrontation of opposites would be a logical way of minimising the damage of Joyce having abandoned the task himself, leaving – some would say deliberately – a vast array of problems for scholars of every kind, including textualists. But in keeping with the curious irony of Joyce's own approach to his greatest work, he attracted, as the *only editor* of *Ulysses* since its first publication to complete his task, a scholar whose methods were to be as fluid as the author's were in the composition of the book. One of the more fluid methods, and possibly the most controversial adopted by Gabler, was his 'continuous manuscript text'. Though this is considered in greater detail in a later chapter, some idea of it is necessary at this point. Hans Gabler's view was that the computer basis for editing allowed the reconstruction, within the user-friendly electronic machine, of all the material used in the writing of *Ulysses*, from notes and drafts, through manuscripts and typescripts, to printed and revised editions. This then conformed to the idea that James Joyce wrote 'continuous copy' which could be treated as 'essentially transitional stages in a dynamic process of artistic creation'. Combined with Gabler's unique combination of critical and textual expertise, mentioned below, this allowed for the unlimited mixing of sources to arrive at a 'perfect' text. At one point in the Afterword, Gabler refers to a 'comprehensive text in the author's hand'; he then goes on to include material not in the author's hand, but in typescript and in print, including the *Little Review* extracts, which were edited and changed without Joyce proofing them. On this mass of computer material Hans Gabler and his team were to work. Imagine the console of a vast, 1930s cinema organ, or the lighting control panels in a modern theatre. Electronically, an almost unlimited range of effects can be drawn forth, and the power and discretion of the controller are vast. So are his responsibilities. This was Gabler's position. He explains it rather differently.

Hans Walter Gabler's approach is set forth in both his own Foreword to the 1984 edition and in the Afterword. In fact there are two Afterwords. The one to the three-volume 1984 edition runs to more than 20,000 words. This is reduced in the 1986 edition to less than 3,000 words, for reasons which have considerable significance. The Foreword is a modest introduction. It asserts the need for a critical edition and suggests that the existing editions, from the first edition on, are 'replete' with error and require 'pervasive' correction. He claims further that the corruption of the text goes beyond Joyce's complaints about 'printers' errors'. He then writes that 'recovery' of what Joyce wrote and revised is possible, because of the many versions which have survived; and it is the survival of these versions that 'defines the possibilities' of the critical edition. The by now famous claims are then made: that the critical edition reports 5,000 'departures' from the author's text in the first edition and nearly the same number of 'departures' in the 1961 Random House edition. Thus, he claims, there is an average of seven departures per page from any printed text of *Ulysses*. The range of these is not particularly broad – from words and phrases down to commas and full-stops – but the impact, given that it is Joyce who wrote it, is rated highly. Gabler offers his edition as a 'new original text of *Ulysses*' and he defines his terms: 'new' because never before presented to the public in the form in which now he presents it, 'original' in that it is based on the author's manuscripts 'with the greatest possible consistency'. He describes this as being 'radically conservative'. The new version offered by Gabler 'claims to replace' all other printed versions, but adds that such a claim can only be as good as the scholarship on which it is based. Seven years' work is therefore put to the test.

The 1984 Afterword is a substantive statement of theory and practice, a prodigious essay in its own right on the nature of the writing of *Ulysses*, indeed of its protracted conception, back to 1906, when Joyce, who was in Rome, considered writing an additional story for *Dubliners* and calling it 'Ulysses'. Gabler discusses Joyce's manner and habits of writing, the relationship of documents to each other and 'the descent of the text' from these documents to the eventual printing. We begin with the notebooks. Despite Gabler's contention that Joyce based his composition on 'compendious note-taking', only three certain notebooks have survived, with the possible recent discovery of a fourth. For a book which Joyce himself likened to the equivalent of five normal-length novels, this is not an excessive number of notebooks. Of course Joyce depended on his notes, and Gabler is right to stress this and to give them a place in the 'descent of the text', but as material for the editing process – distinguishing it from an analysis of the creative process – they are marginal. There were also 'Notesheets', four times the size of a quarto page and presumably the result of Joyce's periodic struggles with blindness. From

the notes came the drafts which, unsurprisingly, are seen
by Gabler as descending from a pre-existing text. In other
words, Joyce did various drafts and we cannot be sure
whether what we have constitutes a major or minor part
of the whole compositional material. As between episodes in *Ulysses*, there is considerable variation. For some
episodes, notably 'Proteus' and episodes 11 to 16, pre-fair
copy drafts have survived, in two cases complete, the rest
fragmentary. In the preparation of his material Joyce is
characterised by Gabler as both author and scribe; as
author composing and revising unceasingly, but as scribe
'prone to inattention and oversight'. This stricture on
Joyce's capacities introduces a theme in the essay,
repeated within a page, where we find emendations being
suggested which would restore the 'text of Joyce, the
author, that was impinged on by Joyce, the scribe'. He
wrote out fair copies, sometimes catching himself in an
unintentional departure from a particular textual draft.
He is said to have missed phrases and reinserted them
later. He is also said – unnecessarily, perhaps – constantly
to have attempted the achievement of two distinct goals:
development by expansion and stylistic improvement,
and retention of narrative detail.

This problem is invoked in the context of 'Eumaeus',
which survives in a copy-book draft and in a loose leaf
fair copy in the Rosenbach Manuscript, in Philadelphia,
which was originally John Quinn's manuscript version of
the book, bought piecemeal, as we have seen, from Joyce
as composition proceeded. Gabler identified omissions
from the Rosenbach which are in the copy-book version,
and suggested we are faced here with 'Joyce the scribe'
inadvertently omitting what Joyce the writer intended
to put into the book, notwithstanding the fact that the
manuscript came later and that Joyce was emphatic
about not adding to it in order to conform with some
other version. He did not say it was definitive – the word
would have been a form of blasphemy to Joyce – he

just left the problem. Gabler proposes that the problem constitutes a category and he calls it 'invariant contexts', something for which an editor must have a formal system so that the group of variants can be dealt with as a logical whole. It sounds tidy, but it ended up being controversial.

It will already be readily apparent that the compositional and the bibliographical have been amalgamated. We are considering Joyce the author and Joyce the scribe, and making judgments on which he was, when and to what extent. The argument in favour of this is a powerful one and Gabler sets it out in authoritative terms. At its very heart is the more essential departure it represents from the idea – generally central to all literary editing – of a basic text of any kind. Though his skills are textual and his objectives textual, the creative and compositional nature of Joyce the man, and the effect of this on the writing, is invoked at an early stage in Gabler's account of his theory and practice, and becomes a fundamental additional consideration in the editing process. Viewed generously, it would seem to be a sensible response to the practical ways in which Joyce arrived at *Ulysses* as published in February 1922; but only if the process goes right. If it goes wrong, then the disentangling of judgments and opinions about what Joyce intended, and more crucially when he intended it and if he changed that intention, from the quite different discipline of diagnosing textual developments, clearly was capable of creating a nightmare, or Doomsday situation. We have phrases such as 'seems to make enough sense . . . to be authorially intended'. Bernard Benstock, in his paper to the Monaco Conference in 1985 entitled '*Ulysses*: How Many Texts Are There In It?' identifies both Gabler's suitability to tackle this precise problem and the potential pitfalls involved as well, when he writes: 'Although no one appointed or elected Hans Gabler, his voluntary undertaking seemed in most ways a perfect compromise, since he has credentials both as a textual editor and a

Joyce scholar. Yet as we attempt to read his explanations for choices made in this new edition, a discrepancy between the two halves of his expertise seems to present itself. When, as an editor, he paints himself out onto a gangplank, as a critic he quickly turns around and walks on water.' What Gabler describes as 'an overriding decision' is to consider Rosenbach omission from the copy-book version, where they occur in invariant contexts, as the scribal errors of Joyce or his amanuenses.

A further word about the Rosenbach Manuscript. This complete version of the book, written in longhand by Joyce, was the typists' source for only ten of the book's 18 episodes. The other eight were typed from a different ('collateral') draft. The major argument between the editor and two of his advisers, Clive Hart and Philip Gaskell, outlined as part of the 'hidden agenda' in the last chapter and repeatedly referred to from now on, derived from a fundamental difference of opinion over use of those portions of the Rosenbach Manuscript which, because of this, were 'outside the line of descent'. There is general agreement among scholars that the episodes which derive, in the proper line of descent from the Rosenbach Manuscript, are 1–4, 10, 12, 15–18. Those typed from a 'collateral' manuscript are 5–9, 11, 13–14. As Gabler says, the Rosenbach is technically a manuscript of *Ulysses*. But it consists of fair copies and of episodes in draft form, and there are variations in it, and between it and other drafts, which need to be observed. Nevertheless, it represents a decisive stage in composition. Again, as Gabler points out, the drafts lead up to it, the typescripts derive from it. Its tidiness derives, however, from need and from cupidity. It is a book collector's item, of immeasurable value now, in monetary terms, and of very real interest in textual and compositional terms. But it is an item overtaken by time, in the writer's terms, and it should serve to remind us of the two fundamental options mentioned earlier: best published, or last published text approved by the author. Writing, if it reaches its right, true end in a published work, is about finality, not speculation. The Rosenbach is only a milestone item on the road to this goal of published book.

Typescripts present Gabler with his next challenge. They are there in the linear descent of the text of *Ulysses*, either actually or by implication. We know the details from an earlier examination of Joyce's work in creating the book. Initially using his friend, Claud W. Sykes, with whom he fell out, Joyce established a typing system which involved a top copy with two carbon copies. He mixed the three sets of identical pages in an entirely unsystematic way, distributing two for serial publication and keeping a third, generally unrevised, which he then prepared for Darantiere. Much of this third copy has survived. Further alterations, if made to one or other of the lost copies, can be inferred from the printed versions, in serial form, for which they were used. This is of greater importance in the case of early chapters, since the typescripts did not survive. There is a further complication: serially published sections of *Ulysses* were expurgated and the impact of this on the purity of the text also has to be taken into account.

Many of the textual changes which relate to this background of different versions and sources are essentially uncontentious. Some, raised and examined at length, produce in the end no change. Let us go to school on this. (For those who have spent time looking out of the window, some prudent skipping through the next few pages may be helpful; they are dense with the editorial heart of the matter.) If the reader, for example, now takes up his 'old' copy of *Ulysses* and turns to the opening of the first chapter, or episode, he will find at line 38 a paragraph beginning, 'He pointed his finger . . .' Its second sentence reads: 'Stephen Dedalus stepped up, followed him wearily halfway and sat down on the edge of the gunrest, watching him still . . .' That word, 'wearily',

is examined at some length in Gabler's Afterword. It is
pointed out that the word was dropped by the typist altogether, as indicated by the agreement of *The Little Review*
and *The Egoist* texts (in the case of *The Egoist*, which did
not publish the first 'Telemachus' episode, we have to rely
on galley proofs, dated, in Harriet Shaw Weaver's hand, 1
March 1918). 'Wearily' was then restored by Joyce in his
typescript for Quinn, but in the wrong place, after the
word 'down' in the sentence, so that Stephen, instead of
following wearily, sat down wearily.

When Joyce came to the Sylvia Beach edition and
looked into the typescript which had lain uncorrected in
his various apartments, with no mention at all of Stephen
being weary – and why should he, a young lad, in the
early morning, unless it was weariness with the world? –
his correcting was different and he produced the result,
as quoted in full, which we have been reading for the last
70 years. Gabler does not change it. Nor is it in any way
controversial, except in so far as it indicates the deliberate entry, by the editor, into an enormously complicated set of constraints, or options. He concludes with
the statement: 'Yet each individual instance must be
critically weighed.' In this case that weighing process has
to take into account the mind of the writer of this epic
of fiction over a period of no less than four years. We have
to take into account Joyce's creative disposition when he
looked at the typescript after it had come back from the
typist, when he did the fair copy for Quinn and when
he corrected the final draft after coming to agreement
with Sylvia Beach, some time in 1921, and sent it to
Darantiere.

The diligence and thoroughness of the searches through
variant readings are breathtaking, the judgments re-
sonant. What is absent from the Afterword, however, is
any sense that the logic of the pursuit through variant
texts for the correct final version was established in
advance according to any clear principles. In some

respects, of course, it could not have been; only by the discovery of the example can the point be teased out, leading to some kind of principle. Quite genuinely, therefore, we approach the problem paradigmatically, through example.

There is a kind of principle involved, from the start. It derives from the sequential nature of Joyce's composition, monitored by his desire to put episodes in print as he went along. This creates the linear descent, from manuscript to typescript, episode by episode, with the chronological detail provided by actual publication in *The Egoist* and *The Little Review*. But at the same time it creates the collateral pattern, through the existence, side by side, of versions which begin their life as identical presentations of Joyce's *Ulysses*, but then become altered side by side with a published and therefore fixed version. It is not exactly a critical but a human judgment that is invoked by this collateral development, since what Joyce meant to do in 1918 and what he meant to do in 1921, together with the existence of different versions from which to diagnose his intent, brings us into the realm of the writer's ultimate purpose. *Ulysses* as a book was a very uncertain prospect in 1918 – there was neither contract nor publisher – and it got worse rather than better in 1920 and 1921, up to the time of his agreeing terms with Sylvia Beach. At that point, as Gabler makes abundantly clear in his Afterword, nobody, not even Joyce, fully realised how far from completion the book was. He suggests that the contract itself may have been the decisive catalyst to get Joyce moving on the extensive revision of the first 16 episodes and on the writing of the last two, 'Ithaca' and 'Penelope', which, when completed, would represent almost one-sixth of the book.

For all that, the 1922 first edition, with all its faults, real or imagined, has always represented the most significant milestone in Joyce's life as a writer. Textually, the version of the book which appeared then has exercised a powerful claim to being taken as the basic copytext for any editor; and there is certainly an argument, in the light of the supposed and actual unreliability of the editions which followed, in favour of Joyce or the Joyce Estate carrying out a basic editing of *Ulysses* to see what kind of approach needed to be taken. Joyce, as we have seen, did not undertake the task. If the Joyce Estate ever considered it we do not know of its decision, though presumably the Estate had agreed with the Random House re-editing by Jack Dalton, which was the subject of an actual contract and advance, in 1967; the work was never finished, partly because of differences between publisher and editor.

In Hans Walter Gabler's Afterword one might have expected a full account of his own consideration of this. Yet the argument against taking the 1922 first edition of *Ulysses* as copytext is not stated at all; and the setting aside of the edition is done in terms which are not acceptable as an argument. After giving over 12,500 words – more than half of the Afterword – to arguments about composition and the development of the text in manuscript and typescript drafts and fair copies, we come to a section headed 'THE EDITION', which begins with the assertion that the February 1922 *Ulysses* came closest to what Joyce aimed for as the public text, but then says immediately that it does not offer *Ulysses* 'as he wrote it'. There is no analysis of this statement whatsoever. No consideration is given, even, to the supposition which we must have, that Joyce himself considered what he published in 1922 as what he wrote. The preceding 12,500 words, which have analysed the composition and textual preparation leading up to the printing and publication in France are treated as the analysis and argument *against* the 1922 edition, and instead of offering even a summary of the arguments, for and against, Gabler goes directly into a quite different argument that this 'situation' (of the first printed text not being the work as Joyce wrote it) raises a number of problems of some complexity, 'theoretical, critical and editorial'.

There then follow three sentences of dense and prolix prose which appear not to correspond with the preceding rejection of the text, in terms of whether it represents what Joyce wrote or not, nor to lead on to the next crucial assertion about the failure of the 1922 first edition to 'validate' *Ulysses* as a work. The sentences are worth quoting in full: 'The definition required of the status that the work and its text attain on publication and of the degree of textual authority conferred upon the typescripts and proofs by the authorial control over the pre-publication transmission are essentially theoretical. From the ways in which the control over the pre-publication transmission was exercised in conjunction with a constant compositional alteration of the text arises the critical need to distinguish corrections from authorial revisions and expansions. Together, the theoretical and critical considerations lead to the specific editorial concerns of choosing a copytext for the edition, of declaring the rules and procedures for editorial decision towards the establishment of a valid critical text and of devising forms of apparatus presentation which make those decisions transparent and are commensurate with the nature of the text and textual materials recorded.' Hold on, one is tempted to say, one of those materials to which Joyce himself attached enormous importance is the 1922 first edition. Do we not need to hear the prosecution's case before the prisoner is sent down for eternity? But this does not appear to be a need. Gabler sweeps on: 'This edition's whole rationale is based on the assumption that the legal act of first publication did not validate the actual text thereby made public to the extent of lending authority to its high incidence of corruption. Instead, the act of publication is conceived of as an ideal act, to which the edition correlates an ideal text freed of the errors with which *Ulysses* was first published.

Thus, it is taken to be the main business of the critical edition to uncover and to undo the first edition's textual corruption.' This final point would also be the case, of course, if the first edition of 1922 had been adopted as copytext. But the earlier idea, of the first edition not validating the text, however corrupt, is strange indeed. It is of course arguable. But because of its strangeness, and because it is the fundamental issue on which the Gabler edition is founded, it does actually need to be argued – and it is not. No further attention is given to the 1922 first edition of *Ulysses*. We take up again the arguments about documents of composition, and documents of transmission. 'By common consent,' Gabler writes, at the end of this section, 'an editor chooses as the copytext for a critical edition a document text of highest overall authority. This eliminates the first edition of 1922 as copytext for a critical edition of *Ulysses*.' If this rule were applied to Shakespeare, a good deal of scholarship would be stopped in its tracks. And what of the Ancients? How would Gabler deal with Plato?

What he has done, as the main argument in the Afterword, is to use the complicated structure of surviving manuscript and typescript material to suggest the corruptions which the 1984 edition itself is there to 'prove'. The argument *for* the textual approach adopted in the critical edition, of a continuous manuscript text, is fully stated; the argument *against* the more obvious use of the 1922 edition as copytext is not. Gabler claims, *probably* correctly, that 'the text of highest overall authority on which to base a critical edition of *Ulysses* resides in Joyce's autograph notations'. But not alone is this an arguable claim in itself; being able to extract that text of 'highest overall authority' is quite another day's work – in fact, a labour of seven years by a team of many workers. Whether they achieved it or not has created and sustained the scandal of *Ulysses* for a further seven years, and this seems likely to go on.

EIGHT

Floundering On

'I think what I have to say is going to blow the whole
Joyce establishment wide open.'
John Kidd in the Washington Post, April 1985

HUGH KENNER was delighted with the three-volume edition of *Ulysses* when it came out on Bloomsday in 1984. He reviewed it for *The Times Literary Supplement* in an article entitled 'Leopold's Bloom Restored'. In his review he deplores only one editorial decision in the whole work, the insertion of a comma after the word 'man', in a brief, cryptic statement by Davy Byrne: '– I wouldn't do anything at all in that line, Davy Byrne said. It ruined many a man the same horses.' It would appear that Kenner picked this point up from the essay in *Envoy* of 1951 by Niall Montgomery, referred to in an earlier chapter. Montgomery, who drops a treasury of allusions and subtleties in the same work, and who marvels at 'the precision of the dropped comma', should have alerted Kenner that a mistake against which warnings existed of 30-year vintage might indicate that a more detailed and careful examination of other sections of the book was required. Kenner's review, which runs to almost 3,500 words – a major essay for the *TLS* – is as comprehensive an assessment of Gabler's work as any to appear in a serious but essentially widely read literary publication. In scholarly terms, this was a rave review.

Gabler had fulfilled all Hugh Kenner's expectations, and had justified the support and encouragement which Kenner had given to the project, including the early supportive article in *Harper's* of April 1980, 'The Computerised *Ulysses*', which had really been the first to alert public and scholars to the wonders that were to come.

Kenner presents the critical text in dramatic terms. He paints a picture of the 26 French compositors of the first edition, with no command of English and the composing room foreman with just enough to cause trouble, beavering away over Joyce's words. He presents other sharp images of Joyce's army of amateur typists and of Joyce himself, wrestling with the composition of two episodes at the same time, with the correction of proofs to which he was adding another third to the book in fresh composition, while at the same time suffering from the agonising eye infection, iritis, which his doctor said should preclude reading and writing altogether.

But Kenner soon begins to grapple with the rectification of error, rather than its production, and gives us a succession of sensible changes carried out by Gabler in the edition. He gives an example of the sentence lost through the compositor using a visual checkpoint in the text, the capital letter, W, but then picking up the wrong capital W on a page and, from typescript to hand-set letters, dropping from the transfer the words between the two capital Ws. By going back to typescript, Gabler recovers words not only lost throughout all editions of *Ulysses*, but actually corrupted in later editions as well as by a 1936 Bodley Head proofreader, totally bewildered by the earlier mistake and simply trying to correct it by his own punctuation. This example, straightforward enough, is not peculiar to the special system adopted by Gabler. The recovery could as easily have been achieved by a more conventional editor, working from the 1922 edition as his copytext and checking against manuscript versions. But Kenner attributes it to Gabler's method.

Slightly more marginal is the case which derives from Bloom's interior monologue as he goes down Grafton Street and sees the cascades of finery in shop windows. These provoke a memory of Meyerbeer and a passing internal quotation of the Italian words, *lacaus esant*. The French compositor corrected what he thought was bad French, to '*la cause sainte*'. When this got back to Joyce in proof, *he* then corrected it back into more proper Italian, '*la causa è santa*'. It has remained this ever since. Is this Joyce as Joyce intended? Or is this Joyce correcting Joyce and making a botch of it? Either way, the end result is not, in Kenner's view, nor in Gabler's, 'the fine phonetic rendition' that went through Bloom's mind. We are asked to accept that Joyce himself slipped in his recall – precision fading between 1918 and 1922 – and that the version *now* offered is the closest to what Joyce really intended. One wonders.

More complicated are the changes made by Joyce's typists, who in some cases introduced hundreds of commas, as well as reparagraphing his writing, while another typist, mentioned in Gabler's Afterword as an example, dropped exclamation marks from the first 'Telemachus' episode. Kenner refers to 47 of these 'Mulliganesque vulgarities' being dropped, since they are used deliberately for a character who is seen by Joyce as essentially hollow, no master of the interior monologue (and gets given none by Joyce, though even Blazes Boylan gets three interior monologue words!). The author's latter-day disdain for the model for Mulligan, Oliver St John Gogarty, was heartily reciprocated by the poet and memoirist, who declared that Joyce, who had been an early hanger-on of his, was a phoney and *Ulysses* a joke, a declaration that was tantamount to Gogarty deliberately and loudly belching at Mass.

'Everywhere, in this new version, the book is firmed up,' Kenner claims, and gives a succession of more briefly presented examples. He also deals at some length with what has become one of the most controversial changes by Gabler, the insertion of the passage naming the 'word known to all men', of which more anon. At the beginning of his review Kenner tells his readers that the alterations number 5,000, or roughly seven per page, and that they range from the recovery of a comma to the restoration of 'whole lost sentences'. At the end, as we have already seen, he finds fault with just one comma inserted: *ergo*, a prodigious and almost totally admirable achievement.

Other reviewers, dealing more briefly with the project, began the process of exaggeration and distortion which was to prevail over the next few years as the controversy developed. The 5,000 'alterations', or changes in the text, became 5,000 'gaffes' in Paul Gray's review in *Time* magazine; unheard of for this popular news magazine, which usually devotes a couple of pages in most issues to books and avoids heavy literary subjects, to take on a three-volume critical and synoptic text of a classic. But such is the appeal of Joyce, and such were the claims made for the clean-up job which had been done, that it proved irresistible. The reviewer called the book 'a palimpsest of confusion' and referred to Joyce as hectoring his printers to get the job done in time for his 40th birthday. The book that was then placed in Joyce's hands 'was not exactly the one he thought he had written'.

This travesty of reality makes stimulating reading. The tone was maintained, but the rest of the review is much more moderate in its message: vast majority of corrections, punctuation and spelling; word changes and additions, only a fraction of the overall work of correction; less to this huge edition than meets the eye? It is at least a possibility. Most important of all is what he said in conclusion: 'This new *Ulysses* will give scholars plenty to talk and quarrel about for years to come.' He reminded everyone that this was exactly what Joyce wanted and what he predicted would happen. In common with Hugh

Kenner, Paul Gray gives extended time to that 'word known to all men'.

The word known to all men is love. In the 'Circe' episode, when Stephen is drunk and hallucinating in the brothel with Leopold Bloom, he has a vision of his dead mother and asks her to tell him the word known to all men, if she knows it now. She refuses. In the new version there is no change to this part of the text, but much earlier, in the 'Scylla and Charybdis' episode, the same phrase, 'Word known to all men', is murmured by Stephen Dedalus in an exchange with Best and is preceded by 'Love, yes'. This sets in place the understanding, so that Stephen's request to his mother is for confirmation rather than for information. The full quotation is as follows:

> – Will he not see reborn in her, with the memory of his own youth added, another image?
>
> Do you know what you are talking about? Love, yes. Word known to all men. *Amor vero aliquid alicui bonum vult unde et ea quae concupiscimus . . .*

In *Time* magazine, the context of this new portion of prose, set against a tinted background, was given at the foot of the page of the review, with the added lines set on an untinted background, the whole piece in a panel introduced with words claiming that the new sequence 'was accidentally omitted from the first edition of Joyce's novel and never restored in print until now'. This, of course, is a very long way from the truth; what the claim needed, in bold type, were the words 'Maybe, and maybe not'. Much more hangs upon the new material than either its accidental dropping or its inspired restoration. We shall come to it again, in still greater detail, later on. For the moment, however, it can be claimed as one of the more substantial and important changes in the book, quite fundamental if one adds to the textual change the significance of the answer – love – to the question about any word known to all men. At least one senior and distinguished Joyce scholar, Hugh Kenner, believed and maybe still does that the word known to all men is death, not love.

Unlike the reviewer of *Ulysses* in *Time* magazine, who, though he may have read the work, displays no serious scholarly knowledge of it and is disposed to take on trust the claims made about it, *The Economist* in Britain, which also, unusually for a weekly publication not overly enthusiastic about detailed literary subjects, responded to the publicity and the generous distribution of review copies of the $200 three-volume work by giving it almost a page for review. Moreover, it managed to hand it to a writer who knew a good deal about Joyce and his writings. Brenda Maddox was then working on her life of Nora Joyce. Only the week before she had attended the Frankfurt Ninth International Symposium of the James Joyce Foundation. There, one of the participants had made the unexceptional claim, for a diligent and numerate scholar of Joyce's work, that *Ulysses* contained the word 'love' 29 times. 'Not any more' was the correction offered by Hans Walter Gabler, the publication of whose three-volume new edition actually occurred during the conference. So great had been the publicity, however, that Brenda Maddox – wisely as it turned out – predicted that the American publishers, Garland, would regret the fact that they had only printed 2,000 copies.

She went on to claim that the retrieval of the five lines containing the explanation of the word known to all men was 'the major retrieval of the new edition' and that 'the new lines offer grounds for reinterpreting the meaning of the book'. Of course they do. It would be a major alteration indeed if the haunting subtlety of Stephen not knowing the word known to all men and searching for it, not as a word but as a reality in his life, were to be known and expressed by him long before he confronts his mother.

That confrontation would then be a challenge to her, to speak to him of love, something which she had been unable fully to offer him in her own lifetime. The change would change Stephen's character. From being the embryonic writer, the cool observer, analysing other people's feelings and having none of his own, he would draw closer to the really great creations in *Ulysses*, Leopold and Molly Bloom, both of whom live out their lives in repeated speculation about the very varied possibilities offered by that word known to all men.

So we are persuaded, in this new edition, to accept the fundamental change. And it is, of course, worth a multitude of commas and exclamation marks, respellings and freshly discovered individual words. The word known to all men was debated at the Frankfurt symposium and Brenda Maddox referred to it in her review, reporting on an attack made by Richard Ellmann against Hugh Kenner for getting it wrong in thinking the word was 'death'. The burden of Ellmann's statement, as reported by Brenda Maddox, is that *Ulysses* is 'an affirmation of love in a world of hate and violence and that critics who suggest that it is a cold, misanthropic work are wrong'. The strains of 'All You Need is Love' are close to our ears as we listen to the critics telling us what the book deals with. Somewhat cripsly, Brenda Maddox concluded her details of the conference by telling readers of the *Economist*, 'Scholars now have two years to enter their comments on the revised text before the standard trade edition is published.' Perhaps without fully knowing the background details, she had touched here on a fundamental issue of a quite different kind.

In a short letter from Richard Ellmann to Peter du Sautoy, dated 9 July 1984, very shortly after the publication of the majority of reviews of the three-volume edition, reference was made to Gavin Borden, the publisher at Garland, having 'two-year rights' and possibly being prepared to give them up. Perhaps more significantly he referred to there being an 'acceleration', presumably in the publishing schedule for the trade edition. Ellmann wrote: 'So far as the edition is concerned, I doubt that in two years there will be any major assault on it, so I should not myself have any objection [to going ahead with publication of the commercial, or trade edition]. Clive and Pip have presumably reconciled themselves to the new text except for minor quibbles. Does Gabler feel comfortable with the acceleration? Nihil obstat, from my place on the Holy Seat.'

If one considers the scale of the project with which the James Joyce Estate and the various publishers in Britain and the United States were faced in bringing out an entirely new, re-set version of *Ulysses*, in both hardback and paperback, and doing so at the end of a two-year rights period for the special scholarly edition, then the concept of scholars actually *having* two years in which to debate is ludicrous. The planning, production, publicity and printing, even of a modest 80,000-word novel, takes upwards of a year. Here we are addressing a book five times that in length, the main essence of which is the clean purity of its text, and the heavy attention to detailed changes in words, punctuation and meaning, not to mention design, binding, variations for 'student text' versions, followed by the great vehicle of publicity and promotion. The scholars, did they but know it, had a brief six months in which to try to get across their criticisms, if they had any; and the view of the team of advisers was that these would be few and essentially marginal.

It was not to be. What was thought to be marginal quickly became central; and Richard Ellmann himself, from that assured feeling of trust in the edition expressed in the 1984 letter, was soon at odds with his earlier self. In company with other Joyceans, Richard Ellmann reviewed *Ulysses: A Critical and Synoptic Edition* (1984) in *The New York Review of Books* and his edited review later became the Preface to *Ulysses: The Corrected Text*. This telescopes the period between the two editions, where Ellmann was concerned, turning his judgment of 1984 into his imprimatur of 1986. His position, if we consider it as stated in the letter of July 1984, was already clear: *Nihil obstat*. The authority of his position, made, he said, from the 'Holy Seat', was indeed somewhere near to the authority of God among other Joyceans. Effectively, Ellmann, limited though his understanding of textual scholarship was, was still the greatest living authority on James Joyce and he had given his blessing to the 1984 edition, opening the way for its publication on the commercial market.

The critical line he took, in reviewing the book, was not unlike that of Hugh Kenner. The difference is that Ellmann's review is permanently with us, while Kenner's, along with all the others, has to be dug out of the original place of publication, and carries the inevitable dust and datedness of time. Ellmann's deals with the original nature of the book, its subleties, its difficulties and its flaws. He briefly analyses Gabler's 'fairly complex' approach to the job of editing the book and comes to the conclusion that he sought 'an ideal text, such as Joyce would have constructed in ideal conditions'. He characterises this as a work heavily reliant on existing manuscript sources and, when these are lost, as an edition which 'attempts to deduce from other versions what the lost documents would have contained'. Ellmann presents Gabler as 'conservative' and the majority of changes as non-controversial. He gives a number of examples, concluding with the now famous example about the word known to all men. John Kidd later claimed that Ellmann was fully supportive of inserting the words, to the point where his review, giving details of the insertion, becomes the Preface to *Ulysses: The Corrected Text*. Ellmann is actually ambiguous, referring to Gabler having settled the matter by recovering the passage, but then goes on to say that 'Whether Joyce omitted it deliberately

or not is still a matter of conjecture and debate.' Though
this was originally said when the matter of conjecture
and debate really was intended as such, we now read it
after the pre-empting of that debate. This is not good
enough and shows quite serious dereliction on Ellmann's
part. There is about it a laconic, apple-in-the-brantub
speculation which leaves readers having to make editorial decisions which the book was there to make for
them. The truth, as the correspondence shows, is that
Ellmann was much more emphatic in opposing the
decision Gabler made over the 'love' passage than he
appears to be in his Preface. Yet his Preface is the most
permanent and most widely-read version of his views on
this crucial point and on his judgment of the job generally.

Whatever Ellmann's view then, he was prone to second
and third thoughts. The discovery itself, anyway, was
not Gabler's, if indeed it can be called a 'discovery'. The
passage, drawn from the Rosenbach Manuscript, had
been published in 1975 when the facsimile had come out
and was known as a possible alternative, the issue, of
course, being whether or not it should be put in. Ellmann
and Gabler debated the issue in an exchange of letters
immediately after the Monaco Conference. Gabler
appeared to take the position of accepting Ellmann's
objection, on *editorial* grounds, but promoting his own
view that the passage should stay in on *critical* grounds.
The critical grounds he put forward included views about
whether or not Stephen is in doubt, as early as the 'Proteus' episode, of what the word is and how this will affect
'character consistency' when the issue of the word known
to all men comes up in the 'Circe' episode. Gabler, in
his letter to Ellmann, discussed the co-existence of the
different treatments of the word – spoken, unspoken,
uttered or articulated silently – and concluded: 'In short:
I do not propose to remove the "Scylla" passage.'

What is more serious, because of more general – and

arguably more mistaken – implication for the work as a whole, was Gabler's assertion, in this letter, that as a principle he did not intend to change things in his 'established text' when the new arguments brought forward issues that had already been carefully weighed. Yet the only person who could make any judgment on whether or not the careful weighing was sufficient was the person who had done the careful weighing! He supported this position by arguing that critical editions can never aspire to being definitive; *ergo*, he would live with his own ultimate critical position, right or wrong, because definition of 'right' or of 'wrong' is ultimately open to debate, and is, at least to some extent, subjective. He felt, according to his letter, that the reader ultimately had to go along with the edition's principles, and if he could not do this, then he must do an edition according to principles with which he could agree!

Whatever Ellmann made of all this, he finally came down against the inclusion of the passage dealing with the word known to all men. He did so, in part, before the appearance of the 1986 commercial *Ulysses*. In the June 1985 Monaco Conference he began the process of demolishing his own arguments in a paper called 'A Crux in the New Edition'. In this he refers to Gabler telling him, well before the appearance of the three-volume edition, of his 'recovery' of the now famous passage about the word known to all men. 'He thought I would be pleased,' Ellmann says, since Ellmann himself had been quite precise in an earlier book, *Ulysses on the Liffey*, in stating that love was the word, indeed that love was central to the entire work. But Ellmann was far from pleased. Despite the gratifying confirmation, he in fact had grave doubts and he put them to Gabler, 'But to no avail'.

All of this was put on record at the 1985 Conference, in a full and detailed paper devoted to the single issue of whether or not the passage should be included. He suggests that it is reasonable to surmise that Joyce saw

the passage, particularly the garbled version of St Thomas
Aquinas, as 'tortured and self-defeating', and that Joyce's
example was simply 'to give up love'. He went on to
confirm this and to develop his arguments even further,
in an article for *The Georgia Review*, in the summer
of 1986, where he distinguished clearly between two
approaches: the usefulness of having on record that Joyce
meant love, as the word known to all men, and the argument about including the discovery in the text of *Ulysses*.
'It should not be included in the final text,' is his considered judgment. Unfortunately, along with the other
critics, he made the point too late. Or, to put it another
way, the James Joyce Estate allowed the public version
out too early.

With the exception of the letter referred to, no other
correspondence has yet come to light from 1984 and,
though the tone of the letter is far from enthusiastic,
either about the future fate of the edition, in terms of
attacks upon it, or about the wholeheartedness of the
support for it of the other two advisers, there is a note of
inevitability. Having gone through the traumas of 1983,
with the advisers all withdrawing, then coming back to
the project again, and with Hans Walter Gabler revealing
an iron-hard determination in sticking to his point of
view on the edition and eventually winning the day, Ellmann, in the correspondence that has been made public,
was not in the mood for an aggressive reopening of the
private wars among the inner editorial team. This is clear
from the detailed analysis of the correspondence made by
Professor Charles Rossman and in part published by him
in *The New York Review of Books* in December 1988.
Nevertheless, Richard Ellmann is revealed in his correspondence during 1985 as a man unhappy with the whole
direction of the edition, one who had in a sense only just
woken up to the enormity of what had been done to
Ulysses. In a letter of 22 August 1985, he wrote: 'That we
are publishing an edition not as Joyce intended it to reach

readers but as he wrote it, no doubt with many implicit ideas about changing it before publication, is really dismaying. I feel that Hans has been most tendentious about this theory. If we wanted it as he wrote it, we would have a facsimile of the manuscripts – the use of print argues different criteria.' In the same letter he claimed that a real debate with Hans Walter Gabler 'doesn't seem possible' and that 'his refusal to reconsider now what he considered earlier is certainly a discouragement'. Richard Ellmann had really dithered his way through a continuous confrontation, never really coming to any sticking point. The merit of Clive Hart and Philip Gaskell is that they, at least, did come to the sticking point, however briefly, over the matter of principle raised by the disparities within the Rosenbach Manuscript. They did their best to arrest a process which they felt would lead everyone into trouble – as it did. But Ellmann, to put it bluntly, floundered on.

Bad feeling had been generated, Ellmann claimed, and this would cause Gabler to reject any suggestions coming from John Kidd, as he had already done in a famous encounter of April 1985 (see below). It was much worse than that. The events of 1985 are a sorry record of uncertainty, doubt and disagreement. The pivot for it all was the Monaco Conference. This consisted of a series of papers and discussions about the 1984 *Ulysses*. Nineteen essays were subsequently published in a book edited by George Sandulescu and Clive Hart called *Assessing the 1984 'Ulysses'*. The conference was in no small measure a response to the first wave of John Kidd criticisms of the edition. However, Kidd did not attend and in his report to Peter du Sautoy after it was over Clive Hart said that his (Kidd's) specific criticisms 'were at no stage taken up in detail'. But there was widespread criticism from other points of view.

The letter, which was a lengthy one, detailed two types of criticism. Firstly, there was the criticism of editorial

judgments, a piecemeal delivery from all sides of disagreements about specific textual changes. These did not,
according to Clive Hart, invalidate the edition; nor were
they unacceptable, in principle, to Hans Walter Gabler,
who expected this kind of reaction and was ready to
absorb the points and make individual judgments about
them. This is the very heart of the scholarly debate, as
far as committed Joyceans are concerned. This is the territory they know intimately, each of them having
specialist knowledge of different aspects and areas of the
text, and often decided views about words, phrases and
treatment to back up the basic knowledge. It was not to
get sufficient airing. Secondly, there was the criticism of
editorial principle. This was much more serious, in Hart's
view, and reinforced his own and Philip Gaskell's serious
doubts about the basis of the edition. 'Considerable
vigour' was exercised in one of the papers attacking the
concept and Clive Hart thought this appropriate. More
seriously he said that the objections along these lines
were sympathetic to the position which Richard Ellmann
had adopted all along, that Gabler should have been more
conservative in his proposals for editorial changes. The
worry at the conference was that the 1984 edition, and
the Gabler approach generally, while it captured fairly
accurately what Joyce wrote at various stages, did not
take account of the kind of artist Joyce was. This argument was to become a major point of alarm with Peter
du Sautoy that summer, but is not teased out in this
first report from the Monaco Conference. What is clearly
underlined, however, is that the fundamental criticisms
of the principles for the edition were 'so deeply rooted'
that 'to meet them would require a complete rethinking
of the edition, which is of course out of the question'.

Clive Hart then reported the general view on Gabler's
edition that it was too mechanical and over-reliant on
the concept of the continuous manuscript, even when
that continuous manuscript did not exist and had to be

invented. He placed himself in support of this criticism and went on to confirm general agreement at the conference (in which he himself shared) that the editor had paid inadequate attention to 'authorial quirkiness and fallibility'. But he resigned himself and the others involved in the edition to having to live with this. His suggested solution was a rather weak compromise: that revisions should be made, that Hans Walter Gabler should hear from as many people as possible on detailed proposals for further change and that no one should try to hold up the progress of the edition towards its trade version. What he considered them now to be involved in was an edition based on Gabler's much-challenged editorial principles 'however questionable they may be' and that, with some cleaning up, to which, according to Hart, Gabler agreed, they should go ahead with the best possible text under these circumstances.

There was here a serious abnegation of duty and function. For the scholarly debate to have any meaning at all, in the circumstances of Gabler's stubbornness as had been made palpably clear to Ellmann and the rest of them, there was the need for the advisers to monitor and judge the scholarly criticisms. Yet here was the most active of the three advisers leaving that process to Gabler to organise and preside over.

Peter du Sautoy was dismayed at the outcome of the Monaco Conference and the degree to which it represented a set of wholly new views on the edition. He had not been aware of the implications of what Gabler had been doing. He had no real understanding of editorial theory. He felt that he had become entangled in textual developments of which he was ignorant. He knew nothing of 'the new bibliography'. He did not understand the theory of the copytext. His views on the editing of writers' works were essentially simple ones, based on a concept of the scholar 'completing' what the author had left imperfect and he saw this process as a somewhat romantic one. He confessed to having been originally reassured that Gabler was only working with what came from Joyce and was not inventing material. Only latterly, under the growing thunderclouds of disagreement and criticism during 1985, did he come to the conclusion that a different kind of 'invention' – 'personal' editorial decision-making – was at the heart of the project. He expressed himself disconcerted that what Joyce intended as the published text of *Ulysses* had been replaced by the *written* text of the work. Peter du Sautoy even wondered if the Gabler *text* ought to be published at all on its own. It had emerged, as far as he could judge the matter, that the real contribution by Gabler had been the editorial work, not its end product. But he was constrained, even more than Clive Hart, at least at that time, by the copyright considerations.

Among those who gave papers at Monaco that summer was Rosa Bosinelli, an experienced Joyce scholar and associate professor of English at the University of Bologna. She commended Gabler for showing up the 5,000 'imperfections' and seeming to have put 'all the cards on the table'. What seemed and what was were far apart.

The essays present an interesting cross-section of critical opinion. Before coming to them, however, some consideration should be given to the situation which had developed publicly. As early as the beginning of April, 1985, a public broadside against the three-volume edition of *Ulysses* had been delivered in the form of a newspaper article by David Remnick, in *The Washington Post*. Entitled 'The War over *Ulysses*', or, with edition changes, 'Jolting the Joyceans', and bearing a Charlottesville, Virginia, dateline – the university in which John Kidd was then a fellow at the Center for Advanced Studies – it quoted a laconic Kidd, 'in his spare, one-bedroom apartment near the medical school', saying that 4,000 of Gabler's changes were unnecessary. Immodestly, but accurately, John Kidd went on: 'I think what I have to say is going to blow the whole Joyce establishment wide open.' The project, he argued, had been rushed and had got out of hand.

John Kidd asserted through this interview a sudden and significant role in Joyce scholarship for himself which was to grow steadily. He swiftly became the main critic of the work done by Gabler, indeed the only critic so far to emerge who was prepared to do the fundamental and essentially difficult work of taking apart the changes made, in all their complex detail, analysing them and then making judgments about their validity. In order to embark on this it must have been at least necessary to make certain judgments about Hans Walter Gabler himself. In doing this Kidd revealed devastating perception. Unlike those who had worked with Gabler over a number of years, and were duty-bound to judge his capacities and performance – a judgment on which all of them fell down – Kidd had no such obligation. Yet he made the judgment anyway and it was in the extreme form of finding against the edition fundamentally, in theory and practice, and laying this at the door of the editor himself, whom he believed to have made 'a hash' of *Ulysses*. Kidd also seems to have judged sufficiently of Gabler's stubbornness and determination to realise that a major onslaught was necessary, with no holds barred, if the Joyce fraternity was to be brought to its senses. Even then he would face problems.

John Kidd had handicaps of his own. Relatively young, untried in the field of extensive, scholarly editing, brash, aggressive, at times alarmingly outspoken, his proven Joyce expertise in the relatively arcane field of numerology, he had few allies and few friends. But he had a burning conviction about the wrong that had been done to Joyce and he effectively committed his immediate future career to setting things right. His role is a classic one. Parsifal-like, he emerges from the forest to redeem a damaged situation. His method is confrontational. His motive is the argument itself. In lectures or debates he can be light-hearted, humorous, witty, almost indulging in vaudeville; but then a challenger will emerge to confront him and a change immediately takes place: John Kidd becomes a hard-faced fighter, clear and devastating in his presentation of argument, which he does with admirable simplicity and clarity for so complicated a subject.

The article, based on a lengthy interview with Kidd, but also on discussions with other figures in Joyce and general editorial scholarship, contained the essentials of the row which was then inevitable. Kidd claimed then what he was to go on claiming for years, as the controversy developed; his list of criticisms began with the broad ones, that Gabler ignored traditional bibliographical standards, overlooked archival sources and made changes which were not necessary. Kidd accused Gabler of wilful ignorance, of making changes based on no evidence or argument and of ultimately producing an edition of *Ulysses* with *more mistakes* than the 1922 first edition.

John Kidd's scholarly supporters were assembled in the article and some are quoted, among them Decherd Turner, then Director of the Humanities Research Center at the University of Texas, and Jerome McGann, a scholar whose judgments and criticisms of the Gabler edition, and of Kidd's own criticisms, have been much admired. The writer of *The Washington Post* article also contacted Gabler in Munich, and reported from there the editor's dismay and astonishment, but not surprise, at the Kidd attack. 'What I'm watching with some sadness is that John Kidd is fascinated with the popular appeal of the edition and has tried to catch some of the limelight for himself.' Kidd claimed in the article that he 'likes and admires' Gabler, that they had worked amicably together and enjoyed a friendly, professional relationship. Gabler was reported as referring to the help he had given to the younger scholar, but concluded by saying that it's all about the old motto, 'No good deed goes unpunished'. *The Washington Post* article preceded a programme of events in the United States, involving both Gabler and Kidd, and reference was made to these. The article, in addition, detailed most of the main areas of John Kidd's criticism and delivered his view that *Ulysses*, if it went ahead and ended up in the bookstores, would 'be a mess'.

The story behind *The Washington Post* story, given much later by Kidd and offered to ameliorate the unfair charges that he went after media coverage of his own position, and took the scholarly war out into the open plains of newspaper drama, is simple enough. John Kidd resisted David Remnick, refused him an interview, but did make the remark about blowing the Joyce establishment wide open. Remnick then pursued his story elsewhere, coming back to Kidd with the classic argument of the journalist that he had so much other material it would look silly if Kidd did not also participate: 'I gave in to Mr Remnick.' Not for the first time had that paper come up with doggedness as an answer. The story was a prelude to the meeting in New York of the Society for Textual Scholarship on 26 April 1985. John Kidd delivered there his paper, 'Errors of Execution in the 1984 *Ulysses*'. Dense in style, but essentially clear in its arguments, Kidd's paper dealt first with the basic issue of copytext and described Gabler's approach as 'revolutionary in its redefinition of the term'. Kidd then went on to demonstrate a wide range of departures from the approach, including the changing of the word 'filtre' back to 'filter', Joyce having made the change in the other direction, with Gabler giving as his justification that the revision was 'an apparent contamination by French'. He also pointed out that the collation of editions and impressions was defective, that no proper investigation of the substantial variation between the 1932 and 1933 Hamburg versions of the book was carried out and that vital documents, including correspondence between Joyce and two early helpers, Claud Sykes and Stuart Gilbert, were overlooked. Nor is the synoptic – overall view – claim justified, since many variants are relegated to the third volume and are not present where they should be, opposite the reading text.

John Kidd also addressed the problem of the dashes, pointing out that, while reviewers had been misled into thinking that there had been a restoration of Joyce's intent, in the placing of the dashes flush left with the margin, this is not what Joyce wanted. He wanted an indent for the dash, which generally is the French approach. Ironically, in the light of revelations yet to come, Kidd took up the point of difference between Jack Dalton, another Joycean textual scholar, and Gabler, and between Gabler and yet another Joycean scholar, Clive Driver. He quoted Gabler's explanation, from the Afterword, that 'where we disagree, we disagree silently', and went on to express mild surprise that, where two teams undertook the same transcription, involving thousands of hours, and arrived at different end results, the explanation of the differences was denied to the scholarly users who were meant to make judgments on the success or failure of the result and on which of the two approaches was the more successful, in individual cases.

Kidd gave a summary at the end of what he had found; and it represented an outline, in brief, of the storms yet to come. It is worth quoting in full:

The errors of execution in the 1984 *Ulysses*, as I see them, begin with the decision not to examine Joyce's unpublished correspondence and the archives of his associates. Failure to collate three editions and at least twelve impressions during Joyce's life left the printing history incomplete. Nor were we offered an essay on the transmission of the work in print or an estimate of Joyce's role in corrections. Among the considerable facts which *are* gathered in the apparatus of the 1984 *Ulysses*, I have noted errors in transcription, the absence of Joyce's instructions to the printers, and hundreds of variants not recorded in the historical collation. The synoptic left-hand pages do not represent the document *per se*, because emendations are inserted and authorial readings tucked away in the notes. These are the problems with the analytical bibliography and presentation of data in the 1984 *Ulysses*.

Hans Walter Gabler, who was present for John Kidd's contribution, rose in the audience with a 'reply' which he said he had been asked to deliver, though he also said in the first sentence of that reply that no defence against John Kidd's criticism was necessary. Kidd, who knew nothing of this prepared, on-the-spot response, was unsurprisingly rather shocked. He was even more upset at the direct, personal nature of the attack, which contains machinegun-like repetition of Kidd's name. Kidd was accused by Gabler of polemic, of not grasping the principles of the edition – 'neither . . . was even remotely fathomed' – and of having delivered into the debate 'a shambles of undigested editorial lore in an argument that, for lack of stringency and incisiveness, collapses into triviality'.

Gabler's arguments for much of the paper were about his own editorial theory and practice, and are not altogether easy to follow. When he addressed the involvement of John Kidd his tone became patronising and sarcastic. The title of Kidd's paper, 'Errors of Execution', 'reveals unfortunately how, desperate to get a perspective . . . he ran off to the textbooks yet did not realise . . . he might have made further headway . . . had he more patiently read . . . his carelessness of reading . . . it is acutely troublesome to discover that Kidd doesn't even appreciate truly bibliographical reasoning . . . actually badly bungles the issues . . .' Gabler concluded by wishing that he had a worthier challenge to answer and that '*nothing*' had emerged to change the critical text.

By all accounts it was an astonishing performance and represented a marked change in the character of the debate, and promised to prejudice adversely any future encounters by Joyceans on the issues raised by the controversy, and not just between the two principal protagonists in what were to become the Joyce Wars. It should have had the additional function of alerting the advisers to the need to impose upon Gabler a consideration of Kidd's criticisms as well as those of other Joyce scholars. Yet clearly this did not happen and several months later the aspiration was still being privately expressed, in correspondence between the advisers and the Trustee, that Gabler would, of his own free will, give serious critical attention to the points being made. It is quite remarkable, with the growing evidence of Gabler's refusal to accept criticism, taken in the context of Kidd's wealth of example and the seriousness with which his arguments were taken, by, among others, Clive Hart, that no structure was imposed on the editor to address the points raised that was better than a vague expectation. This reflects badly on all those involved in the advisory committee, and on Peter du Sautoy.

One other person of some significance in the debate as it developed from the spring of 1985 and who was present in the audience, was the editor of *The Times Literary Supplement*, Jeremy Treglown. He listened to John Kidd's paper and then to Gabler's blistering response to it. He was the first person to raise any questions, asking Gabler if there was really 'nothing' that needed to be changed. Were there not missing manuscripts and documents, uncited by Gabler? Had not certain evidence been omitted from the synoptic part of the edition, misleading Treglown's own reviewer of the book, no less a person than Hugh Kenner? The answers did not satisfy the *TLS* editor. He reported on this conference of the Society for

Textual Scholarship in the issue of the *TLS* for 10 May 1985, giving a general account of the various contributions, reporting Kidd's criticisms and Gabler's rejection of them as 'all unfounded or misconceived'. Then he went on: 'The main text of his [Gabler's] edition, without apparatus, was intended to go into paperback and would inevitably become the new standard version, assured of huge sales. Permission had to be given, though, by the Trustees of the Joyce Estate, who are represented by the Society of Authors. Until Kidd's detailed findings are published, it is hard to judge how much difference they would actually make. If textual scholarship is fully to serve all readers, rather than just a group of academics, the Society should delay any decision. It may take a while; but scholars can already read Gabler's edition in its hardback form in the library; and the rest of us have got by all these years with the Penguin anyway.' Even as Jeremy Treglown was delivering this wise advice, the go-ahead for the printing of the new edition was being given, and its direction was already in the hands of John Ryder of The Bodley Head. In July, two months later, he was at work with the typesetting.

Another editor who sided with Kidd, on the basis of the evidence presented up to the autumn of 1985, was Robert G. Lowerey, responsible for *The Irish Literary Supplement*. He published in the autumn issue 'Gaelic in the New *Ulysses*', by John Kidd, which Lowerey thought should have been headed: 'GABLER GARBLED GAELIC'. The article demonstrated a number of errors in the presentation of Irish, in the edition, the most obvious example being the omission of the *fada* (accent) from the word '*sláinte*' by Gabler, throughout the edition and without comment. The word is correctly spelled, with the accent, not only in the 1922 edition but in the previous serial publication of episodes, both in *The Little Review* and *The Egoist*. Moreover, as Kidd shows, while '*slainte*' was being thus spelled by Gabler, without the

accent, he was busily correcting Egan's faulty French, in two words, *'sétier'* and *'bréton'*, which, though incorrect, had passed muster when presented to the French printer, Darantiere, and remained intact until, in the 1932 Hamburg edition noted otherwise for its purification in the hands of Stuart Gilbert, who did considerable editing work on it, an efficient German compositor decided that Egan must have brushed up his French in the interim and so it was put right. What did Joyce intend? We shall never know. Certainly, in these instances, the Gabler edition does not help.

The Irish Literary Supplement piece was far more substantial than its title might suggest and ranged over many languages other than Gaelic. Joyce was a truly brilliant linguist. He learned languages easily, and used them with wit and mischief in *Ulysses* and later in *Finnegans Wake*. Kidd demonstrates an impressive critical brilliance in dealing with the many linguistic problems which arise in the book, some of them created by Joyce's wish to use language in the defective forms which suit his characters, among them Bloom, who has poor Spanish and even poorer Irish. Gabler mends the former, but ignores the latter. It must be said, however, that Kidd did not start out in his Gaelic criticisms as a Gaelic scholar. In fact he was a novice in the Irish language; and he was less than fair in acknowledging the full help he received from various people – a fault on which he strongly criticised Gabler.

In his editorial comment, headed 'Piracy in the Joycean Ranks', Robert Lowerey suggested that the 1984 *Ulysses*, if it had the errors attributed to it by Kidd, might become 'the Spruce Goose of academia'. He also mentioned, in an aside, that a representative of Garland Publishers, who attended the conference at which Kidd gave his first paper, did the handing out of Gabler's bitterly worded response. Lowerey anticipated a continuing debate: 'We expect there to be responses and counter-responses in future issues, so stay tuned.' Little did he know that the printing was already in hand and the point of debate had been pre-empted.

There was to have been a conference at the University of Virginia in 1986 to consider the 1984 *Ulysses*. This was cancelled, specifically in response to Gabler's reply to Kidd. Kidd himself claimed, in an article entitled 'The Context of the First Salvo in the Joyce Wars', published in the 1990 summer edition of *Studies in the Novel*, that 'Mr Gabler had, in the mind of more than one dean, turned a disagreement about editing into a personal feud.' The cancellation meant that the debate on the 1984 edition of *Ulysses* would now transfer to the Monaco Conference. Undoubtedly, then, by the time that conference took place and although he did not attend, John Kidd was seen as the major troublemaker, despite the fact that many others were critical.

One of the contributors was Donald Phillip Verene, of Emory University in Atlanta, Georgia, an expert in the work of Vico, who saw a long and complicated exchange between scholars, for whom both the 1984 and the 1922 texts were essential. 'The problem is the latest will be thought to be truer than the original.' Fritz Senn, another contributor, admitting that he was 'wholly untrained in textual scholarship', revealed, in his lengthy and sensitively written paper, a deep knowledge of the text, which makes his judgments, placing many readings in doubt, all the more valuable. But he confessed that the apparatus of symbols on the left-hand pages defeated him: 'I cannot bring those symbols to serviceable meaning.' His defeat, he felt, was widely shared, and there existed a gap between textualists and the rest which would not be easily bridged. Charles Peake, using as one of his examples the decision to replace the word 'goner' (very Dublin) with 'doner' (not very anything), indicated the heavy interrelationship between textual, or bibliographical, judgments and critical ones, inherent in the method and very much a complicating feature. This was criticism which went to the heart of the theory and one of several essays which implied the need for lengthy consideration of the 1984 *Ulysses*. On this issue, the Ellmann papers in Tulsa yield an interesting group of five index cards, two of which suggest strongly the Wiltshire, un-Joycean origin for the word, and one of these has the catchy quotation, no doubt from a Wiltshire son of the soil, referring to a pig in his charge: 'Thuck ould sow be a dunner; her'll be dead afore night'. Charles Peake might have paused over it, wondering whether he was right in his assertion that 'the balance of probability . . . lies with Gabler'.

One contributor, Suzette Henke ('Reconstructing *Ulysses* in a Deconstructive Mode') claimed, contrary to Gabler's claims, that 'we now have a "definitive" version of the text of *Ulysses*'. Richard Kain, who opened with a delightful paper on the atmosphere in Dublin in 1904, did not address the text at all. Clive Hart came down, with fairly strong emphasis, *against* the edition, particularly against that part of it – the right-hand page – destined to become the commercial edition. This page, he felt, 'turns synopsis into conflation, generating, in many places, an impossible work of art'. There had been too little attention to the overall effect of inserting a new and different word, often 'more inspired', to replace weaker substitutes (by Joyce)' which had greater propriety in the context. Hart concluded by expressing a clear preference for Joyce's, pre-Gabler *Ulysses*. Given the private correspondence, and what was *not* being done, or even contemplated, this is truly astonishing.

Clive Hart conceded, in a letter to Peter du Sautoy dated 15 August 1985, that Kidd's researches were clearly based on far deeper analysis of the primary textual material than could possibly have been undertaken by the advisers. (He did not, at this stage, recognise that Kidd might have done more research of this primary kind than even Gabler had done.) What he did suggest was that Kidd was working on the critical apparatus against the edition more or less full-time and that it was quite clear, from the 'hard-core evidence', that Kidd's allegations against the edition were 'so damaging as to need at least some consideration'. It is difficult to know who was most at fault. Hart had identified for Peter du Sautoy the seriousness of Kidd's criticisms, but did not press for formal responses or the setting up of any systematic way of involving Kidd and absorbing his help. But then Hart had lost out in the earlier confrontation, was now inescapably and formally involved in the published 1984 version, and was possibly reluctant to engage in what could well turn out to be further fruitless confrontation.

Peter du Sautoy, alerted by Hart to the problems, adopted a weak way out, expressing distress that he had not treated more seriously the warning signals from the advisers and perceived the way things were developing. This also persuaded him to the view that Gabler needed to be warned of the substance in Kidd's criticism, *but he doubted if he would take any notice.* What he did say very firmly was that the experiences over *Ulysses* had put him off any consideration at all of proposals for the re-editing of the other works, particularly *Finnegans Wake.*

This is perhaps an appropriate time to address in more detail the other themes in the correspondence of 1985, dealing with the trade edition and the timing of its publication. This was handled with extraordinary ineptitude.

The commercial arrangements on which the two editions were based clearly consisted of several different contracts over which Peter du Sautoy appears to have presided. These not only involved the principal publishers, The Bodley Head in Britain and Random House in the United States, but also Garland Publishers, for the three-volume scholarly edition, and Hans Walter Gabler for his part in both editions. Then there were the sub-

sidiary paperback rights, presumably in all three contractual areas, since even Garland produced the three-volume
work both in hardback and in paperback.

The contracts with the three principal publishers, Garland, Bodley Head and Random House, were signed in
March 1982. This together with the two-year licence
period for Garland implies that the whole process of
bringing out the two editions in sequence was planned at
the one time. Peter du Sautoy told Ellmann, in a letter
of 13 August 1985, at the height of concern about criticisms of Gabler's work, that the James Joyce Estate
reserved the right to say whether or not a trade edition
was desirable and therefore whether the Estate would
go ahead *at all*. This option had been considered by the
Trustees in July 1985. It was agreed then that the trade
edition would go ahead, but that the two-year period
between the first, critical edition and the commercial one
would be adhered to. Peter du Sautoy, in the same letter
to Richard Ellmann, actually said that this meeting of
the Trustees, and its decision in favour of minimum and
essentially cosmetic delay for the two-year period, had
been made in the light of John Kidd's criticisms, and the
reports from both Ellmann and Hart after the Monaco
Conference – in other words, the opposite of what had
been outlined, as the critical and publishing procedure
was undertaken by the Trustees. Instead of pausing, and
allowing as much time as possible to put right the errors
and misjudgments, which were clearly more substantial
and more distressing than anyone had anticipated, as
little time as possible was being allowed. Peter du Sautoy
told Ellmann that the Trustees were bound under the
contracts to give a decision by 16 June 1986, but were not
precluded from making that decision earlier. In June 1985
they made the decision. The copyright motive for making
that decision is clearly stated in the same letter. It is an
important consideration.

In the summer of 1985 the main question, concerning

possible postponement, had been resolved, against all the arguments and primarily, it seems, because the contracts had constructed in advance a situation from which it was extremely difficult to extract *Ulysses*, should the editing prove to have been inadequate. Clive Hart, so long as changes were made, was reluctantly of the view that the trade edition should go ahead. Philip Gaskell also went along with this. Neither was happy about it. Both had fundamental reservations. Both anticipated, perhaps naively, that Gabler would try to hear from as many of his critics as possible and incorporate the suggested changes which would emerge from this. But they realised that this reliance on Gabler, even if it proved fruitful, would essentially deal only with superficial criticisms. It could not address the more fundamental disagreement about the overall textual approach; and in any case, by their decision of June 1985 to go ahead anyway, the Trustees had pre-empted this completely.

Even on the straightforward, critical changes to the text, Gabler's compliance was not in any way assured. It simply depended on his goodwill and his acceptance that there were many things still to be put right. There was no structure allowing for further consideration. Perhaps, in the light of events between the summer of 1983 and the post-publication criticisms, it might have been better to have set in place such structural terms for vetting the criticisms. But this was not done and it turned the atmosphere in the summer of 1985 into one in which the whole sequence of events is referred to by more than one of the principal figures as a *fait accompli*. Richard Ellmann's position was summed up in the remark made by Hart to du Sautoy that Ellmann would have preferred it if Gabler had been 'a shade more conservative'.

These reservations had all been mentioned in a letter from Clive Hart to Peter du Sautoy of 12 June 1985, which reported on the Monaco Conference. A copy was then sent by Peter du Sautoy to Richard Ellmann. Though the question of delaying the trade edition dominated the summer exchanges the correspondence itself spread out over the months of June, July and August. When he did reply it was to say to Clive Hart that he thought they all had to face the fact of a trade edition with Gabler's text and that text, moreover, not very much altered. It would appear, he said, the following year. He told Ellmann the same thing, though his argument to him was that, whether they postponed the edition or not, they would always be in the middle of controversy over it.

That Peter du Sautoy did not himself wish to get involved in the controversy is clear from the response made to Clive Hart's observations about John Kidd. Du Sautoy did not wish to get involved with Kidd, even though he was emerging as the principal critic of everything that had been done. In the light of Peter du Sautoy's general handling of his responsibilities as principal Trustee of the James Joyce Estate, this is understandable. After all, what were the advisers there for? But it is hardly commendable and does suggest quite clearly that any idea of a two-year period of serious, scholarly, open-minded digestion of the criticisms of the three-volume edition had been abandoned in the most curious circumstances, where no attempts were made to assess the problems, and where the main decision-making was based on a wish to get out of the dilemma of error and misjudgment with as little embarrassment as possible, achieving the new copyright as a kind of salvage operation.

If Peter du Sautoy had no wish to have anything to do with John Kidd, he seems also to have become circumspect in his dealings with Hans Walter Gabler. He wanted Gabler to have as little as possible to say in the trade edition. He wanted the focus to be on Richard Ellmann. He wanted Ellmann's essay at the front of the book. He wanted Gabler's to be at the back, as a 'note' on the edition, much shorter than the 20,000 words which had been appended to the 1984 edition. Of course it was Gabler with whom he had to deal, but he was the one person who, notwithstanding Gabler's toughness over all issues, still had the final say and in this essentially marginal respect Peter du Sautoy prevailed. Gabler's visible role in the commercial edition was a reduced one.

Gabler, who had his own contract in the two editions, was pressing as strongly as du Sautoy and the other Trustees, who nevertheless seemed voiceless in all of this, for as little delay as possible. He wrote to Peter du Sautoy on 29 July 1985, following the Monaco Conference, to say that he thought there should be simultaneous publication by the publishers concerned in the venture on 16 June 1986. In this letter Gabler said that typesetting of the trade edition had already been coordinated by John Ryder, a director of The Bodley Head for almost 30 years and the man responsible for typography in the firm. One would imagine that at least the typography of *Ulysses*, something in which Joyce took a more detailed interest than is normal in writers, might have been got right for this major event. Yet John Ryder, in an article entitled 'Editing *Ulysses* Typographically' and written for the issue of *Scholarly Publishing* of January 1987, found that 'the design of the 1986 edition of *Ulysses* was restricted by the typographical limitations of the author, the controls of his literary executors, and the demands of the academic editors – to the reader's disadvantage'. The letter he received then said 'please send your approval or have your designer contact me with any questions as soon as possible. Random House has already approved the design.' Ryder did advise of changes he thought necessary, but little could be done about these.

On the 1984 edition it was worse; there appear to have been delays, since Ryder only saw 'a second generation copy of one opening' of the book in June 1983, when he should have received 'first proofs'. He regarded the 1984 *Ulysses* as 'a considerable editorial achievement, by no

means matched typographically'. He had little respect for
Joyce's understanding of typography and regarded Darantiere as limited by the author's instructions, particularly
over the hyphenating of words, a limitation which he did
not think should have prevailed in the 1980s resettings.
When Ryder tried to introduce principles of typographic
legibility there was conflict and his efforts were brought
to a halt. It would be clear to anyone with professional
understanding of the problems of publishing a major literary work of such prodigious length, containing so many
strange forms, devices, treatments of languages of words
and of punctuation, and with the editorial history which
Ulysses had had, that a deal of planning was needed, and
that it did not have enough. Even so, and with all the
limitations, it must be clear that the idea of a two-year
period for scholarly criticisms had been truncated to little
more than a year, whether or not there was any willing-
ness to *listen* to the scholars.

NINE

'Is No One Awake At The Wheel?'

'But I have already swept the stakes; and with the
common good fortune of prosperous gamesters, can
be content to sit quietly; to hear my fortune curst
by some, and my faults arraigned by others, and to
suffer both without reply.'

*Hans Walter Gabler, quoting Dryden
when answering John Kidd in April 1985*

*U*LYSSES: The Corrected Text was published on 16
June 1986 to wide critical acclaim. The praise
and endorsement of the edition, which had
crowned the earlier achievements of the critical and synoptic version, were repeated for the single-volume work.
Advertising in the British press was unequivocal in claiming that the book, as now presented, offered a unique
experience. 'For the first time in its history *ULYSSES* is
published as Joyce conceived it and meant it to be read.'
Three distinct versions were offered. The main Bodley
Head hardback edition was priced at £18. There was a
Penguin student edition at £10.95 and a Penguin standard
edition at £7.50. All carried the same additional slogan
in the title, 'The Corrected Text'. All were identical in
content. The student edition, which was printed on
thicker paper, making it almost fifty per cent wider than

the ordinary paperback, had exactly the same number of pages, with the same number of words on them. For the extra £3.45, students acquired the privilege of carrying around in their limousines a much heavier volume which had the single additional advantage of line numbers in the margins of each page, for easy reference to the tide of critical works, which carried cross-references to the line numbers introduced by Gabler in the 1984 edition. The impact of this had been such that many of the older critical works, on *Ulysses* in particular but on Joyce generally, had been or were being revised or re-edited in order to relate them to the new edition. An early example, understandably since he was an enthusiast for the new version, was Hugh Kenner, whose book, *Ulysses*, an introduction and study of the novel first published in 1980, appeared in a revised edition in 1987 with the message on the cover: 'a masterful introduction to James Joyce's *Ulysses* – now keyed to the new, definitive edition of the novel'. In the computer age the change between the keyed edition and the unkeyed paperback 'ordinary' edition can have cost little, since it was already part of the 1984 right-hand page text and was also standard in the 1986 hardback edition. But it has cost countless students since then money they could ill-afford and it emphasises their importance as a segment of the book-buying public, at least where James Joyce's works are concerned.

The advertising carried a quotation from Anthony Burgess: 'This is a great literary event . . . Now the greatness – the brilliance, the humour, the humanity – shine out. Rejoyce!' Not every writer, however, was quite so ecstatic. Anthony Powell, who reviewed it on the Friday after publication, 20 June 1986, for *The Daily Telegraph*, adopted a typically Powellian stance in his final judgment about Joyce the writer: 'Joyce can reasonably be claimed as a "great" novelist, if not one – in my opinion – in the very top flight. There is too much boredom, even if all great novelists have their longueurs. Those who want to read what he actually intended to write in *Ulysses* now have it all laid out for them. Some of the novel is splendid.' Some is clearly not. He cited 70 pages of 'inspissated tedium' in the penultimate 'Ithaca' episode, which he thought too hard on the reader and which Powell believed Joyce committed in this experimental form simply because he could not maintain the more direct narrative style, 'at which he can show himself so accomplished'. He made an interesting judgment about the 'Penelope' episode, firstly, that he has heard women say it made them uncomfortable, secondly, that to him it seems more a remarkable *tour de force* than writing that carries conviction.

Powell himself, who as a young man had bought the ninth edition of the book in Paris in 1927 and smuggled it back into England, found the new text somewhat sanitary. It did not evoke for him the nostalgia of his first reading of Joyce: 'Somehow one needs the grey paper, the French compositors, the under-the-counter transaction.' But Powell did accept at face value the editorial restructuring by Gabler and quoted in his review the explanation by Ellmann of 'the most significant of the small changes' dealing with the 'word known to all men' passage. He also made reference to 'more than 5,000 mistakes' in earlier editions, 'all of which are corrected as far as possible, sometimes with considerable ingenuity'.

Powell's critical approach was not untypical. Writers, lead reviewers, academics – though not necessarily Joyce scholars – and literary critics provided similar essays in virtually every serious literary page and paper, worldwide. They dealt with the book, the writer, his place in twentieth-century fiction and their own broad views, taking more or less on trust the claims about the unique experience offered. They could not do otherwise. Apart from the essential problem of space in which to deal with even a tiny proportion of the 5,000 changes, there was the simple difficulty of having some kind of critical apparatus. The edition was offered with Ellmann's 'new' Foreword at the beginning and with Hans Walter Gabler's greatly reduced Afterword at the end. With the exception of the few chosen examples of change offered by Ellmann and the simplified justification of the critical approach by Gabler, there was no scope for analysis or detailed judgment, except among those who owned the 1984 edition and were reasonably familiar with its detailed changes; and even they were not necessarily able to cope with the complexities of the critical apparatus. It was a hermetically sealed package. What the advertising and publicity claimed, what Ellmann endorsed and what Gabler explained was effectively all the generalist could go on. Unless he or she was well-informed about Joyce scholarship, intrepid in taking on a most powerful literary specialist establishment and aware of current controversy about the edition itself, the scope simply was not there for any comprehensive assessment of it in the only terms that were really relevant: how effectively it had been changed and what overall reliance could be placed on the changes.

Any pretence that the 1984 *Ulysses* had been published in an atmosphere conducive to a sober and careful scholarly consideration of its merits and defects is absurd; and the same is true of the 1986 *Ulysses*. Each time, the book was launched with a degree of pre-judgment and orchestrated critical acclaim that totally distorted the debate which followed. That this was done deliberately has been one of the main arguments of this book. The premeditation stretches over a wide range of actions or misrepresentations. Some of these involve figures, such as Richard Ellmann, who are regarded with such sanctity – a sanctity greatly enhanced by his tragic death in 1987 and deserved for a career of essentially dedicated scholarship – that their actions remain, to this day, somehow protected. Even saints commit sins.

The very act, for example, of sending out for review the three-volume text of the book was a travesty of the critical function in the literary field of popular journalism. It would inevitably go to one of a small group of potential reviewers whose qualifications to review it were, almost by definition, prejudiced in advance. By this is not simply meant the key Joyceans. Their role was potentially compromised in a number of different ways. Some of them were involved, directly or indirectly, in the scholarly investigation of the text of *Ulysses*, in some context or other. Those who were actually engaged in the vast project itself were in no sense embarrassed by the idea of judging upon their own work and judging quite frequently in direct contradiction with their private views. Those who were not quite so close, an obvious example being Hugh Kenner, who had no formal relationship with the project, were still close enough to be at best blinkered. For years before its appearance, Kenner had been an apostle for the computerised editing of *Ulysses*. More widely, the potential critics who were Joyceans were in the difficult position of being faced with a project controlled and organised by the central praesidium of Joyce interests. A formidable concentration of power was behind the project. Since that power, through its principals, concealed all of its own misgivings, the word coming from this central praesidium was powerfully persuasive and almost entirely united.

Where the reviewing function moved out from the Joyce scholars to more general literary reviewers, the dice were also loaded. It would also be a brave and a foolish general reader who embarked on a critical assessment of the textual matter involved in the three-volume version – indeed, in the single-volume version as well – and the temptation, clearly conceded to in reviews such as those of Brenda Maddox in *The Economist* or Paul Gray in *Time* magazine, was to take largely on trust the claims about errors put right, new passages correctly inserted for the first time and a finished product which offered to the reading public Joyce as never read before.

Almost a year before the publication of *Ulysses: The Corrected Text* the chief figures involved in bringing it about had entertained very serious doubts about the direction and reliability of the project. For three years there had been misgivings about the fundamental theory on which the edition was based. All three advisers had resigned from the project because of differences between themselves and the editor-in-chief, Hans Walter Gabler; and not one single principal figure in that inner circle was happy about what had been done.

If we consider them in turn, the position of the senior Trustee for the James Joyce Estate, Peter du Sautoy, must come first. As far as all the others involved in the *Ulysses* project were concerned, his was the ultimate position of power and decision-making. He controlled the contracts. He dealt with the publishers. He had the say about whether or not to go ahead with the commercial or trade edition. He had set the programme, which included the two-year period for assessing the critical and synoptic work done on *Ulysses*. He was in receipt of letters and reports from all the senior members of the project team, and therefore aware of the feelings and judgments they had about each other. No one else was in quite that position of knowledge. If there was another dimension of knowledge of which we are ignorant, involving other Trustees, the Society of Authors or the beneficiaries of the James Joyce Estate, then the others involved in the project knew little or nothing about it.

From the correspondence we know that Peter du Sautoy was uncertain about the degree of editorial change required to renew copyright, but that he had come to view the new edition mainly in that light. Really very surprisingly, he seems to have been uncertain about copyright law itself and to have sought advice, on at least one occasion, from a non-lawyer, Clive Hart. At a very late stage, August 1985, and based on tangential information, including the essay by Jerome McGann sent to him before its publication, he came to the conclusion that 'the editorial text that led up to the reading text seems to be what matters', and on this basis put forward the opinion that perhaps Gabler's text should not be published at all on its own. He then decided that it was probably too late to go back and so went on. There is an almost Beckettian doom about this.

The positions of Clive Hart and Philip Gaskell are extremely difficult ones on which to judge. Following the exchanges during 1983, and the decision first to resign from the project and then to come back to it, they both had a role limited to doing nothing other than advising on the developing situation. This fell principally on Clive Hart's shoulders, since he was more directly concerned with Joyce as a writer and maintained a reasonably close watch on developments within the Joyce industry. It was therefore up to him to report to Peter du Sautoy on the debates and discussions about *Ulysses* at various venues, in the academic journals and at the Monaco Conference. He assessed more generally the trend of critical reaction in the crucial aftermath of the appearance of the 1984 edition, and his misgivings are on record. But he was not in a position to take any action more dynamic than that. He was simply able to set down the broad range of comment and leave to the Trustee the job of deciding what to do. Philip Gaskell appears to have accepted that Clive Hart would perform this role on his behalf as well, since he made little direct contribution himself during the two-year period. Both men remained in agreement with each other, from the academic point of view, in respect of Gabler's now completed *Ulysses*. In particular this referred to the 1986 edition, rather than the 1984 edition. They were later to put this on record, in the Introduction to their *Ulysses: A Review of Three Texts* (published in 1989) where they refer to 'sometimes' disagreeing with

Gabler's readings and of dissatisfaction with a small number of Gabler's errors in reporting bibliographical facts. What was much more serious was the fundamental disagreement they felt with his handling of the evidence. For Gabler was taking the prescriptions for change, which appeared on the left-hand pages of the 1984 edition where they could be compared with the finished result, and now transferring them to the new edition, at the same time setting aside the evidence. Furthermore, all the minor, mainly Kidd-inspired changes between 1984 and 1986, unacknowledged, were being put in without references. They did not like the advance towards something that was going to be seen as 'definitive', though it was not claimed as such. The right-hand page, turned into a 'corrected' edition of the book, was a finite act and it jarred. It did so on three counts. The first was a decided preference for Joyce's first thoughts, in spite of the case being arguably stronger for later versions. The second was the normalisation of errors, even when they could possibly be presented as deliberate changes, though 'wrong' in the technical sense. The third, which they regarded also as the most important, was the taking of readings from material which was not in the 'direct line of descent' of the final text. Here, we are dealing with occasions where Joyce may have produced alternatives, which may, in the judgment of others, appear preferable, but which were set aside, abandoned, overlooked and did not contribute to the actual version of *Ulysses* as published in 1922. In the agreed, joint view of Hart and Gaskell, not inconsiderable scholars in their broad collective field, such alternative material suggests an alternative *Ulysses*, slightly different, inherently interesting, but never written, and not to be confused with what Joyce actually did write and eventually published in February 1922.

Richard Ellmann occupied a different position. He was not, as we have seen, a textual scholar. Throughout the whole period, in so far as can be judged from the correspondence, he approached the problems from a literary and critical point of view, dealing with the questions, wherever possible, in terms of his deep understanding of Joyce's character, as a writer and a man. A lifetime's work and experience in Joyce scholarship had made him quite extraordinarily powerful in the field. Quite accurately, he likened himself to God and joked about speaking from 'the Holy Seat' which circumstance had made indisputably his. One word from him and he could have delayed the whole project. He could have ensured a detailed reconsideration of the changes, brought in other scholars, actually ordered the involvement of John Kidd, had he so wished. That was the measure of his standing. He attempted none of this. He was perhaps not well enough at the time, suffering as he was from amnyotrophic lateral sclerosis, a form of motor-neuron disease. Because of this, he was working against time on his final and highly important literary project, the life of Oscar Wilde. But these are reasons rather than excuses. The fact is that he simply allowed the misgivings and difficulties faced by the others to pass him by.

The tone in his letters continued to be neutral, at least as far as taking any action was concerned. In one letter, of 22 August 1985, already quoted, he was able to deplore the fact that they were all publishing Joyce as written, rather than Joyce as Joyce intended readers to read him, and at the same time talk calmly of sending off his new preface to Penguin and pointing out that The Bodley Head was likely also to use it. He even put in a remark to the effect that Clive Hart's 'disquietudes seem sensible'! But he was not prepared to do anything, nor to suggest that the man in the ultimate position of power, Peter du Sautoy, should do so either. In the minds of all of them, the situation is a *fait accompli*.

Tendentious or not, Hans Walter Gabler was determined to achieve his objectives and to brush aside all attempts to contain him. His view of the two-year period for consideration of the 1984 edition seems, on the face of it, cavalier, since by the spring of 1985 he had dismissed in virtually absolute terms his main critic, John Kidd, and by the summer was working directly with The Bodley Head on the prospective typesetting programme for the edition, and incorporating the relatively limited changes which were made between 1984 and the late summer of 1985. Once this work was set in motion, very little more was possible, in terms of changing the shape established by the 1984 edition. It is truly extraordinary how many people seemed to think otherwise, among them the scholars themselves, believing that the printing and publishing of a truly major and massive book could be achieved almost instantaneously and who referred to the gap between the editions, regarding corrections, as two years. It was barely one.

Hans Walter Gabler's comments on this period and its fruits are interesting for an insight into how he viewed the programme for absorbing corrections. They do not form part of the edition. Just one brief paragraph at the end of his 1986 Afterword mentions 'a small number of minor amendments' made for *Ulysses: The Corrected Text*. They are not detailed. For that, readers are referred to the second impression of the critical text. This is even less of a concession to readers than had been made by the editors of the new copyright editions of *Dubliners* and *A Portrait* in the 1960s. There is no discussion of the possible contributions, written or spoken, made by Joyce scholars or commentators. There is no mention of the Monaco Conference and no mention of Kidd.

Hans Walter Gabler had swept the field. Criticisms, reservations, attacks, defences, the continuing debate about the method and execution of the whole project, went on. But the book itself, in its newly edited form, flourished. When supplies of the earlier version of *Ulysses* – essentially the 1936 edition, reprinted in 1961 and thereafter – ran out during the late 1980s, no effort was made to reprint. *Ulysses: The Corrected Text* became the only edition of the work available to the general and scholarly public. It was the version recommended for students, used by teachers, read by new followers of Joyce. This situation prevailed. The very fact that the world of Joyce studies had gone through *two* critical cycles about *Ulysses* left everyone exhausted. It also took the sting out of any public curiosity. The 1984 *Ulysses* had received publicity and acclaim vastly in excess of what the occasion merited – the publication of a virtually unread-able critical apparatus, with an adjacent new version of the book. The whole process was then repeated, if any-thing with even greater excess, when the edition was more suited to the general reader. In one way or another the process of judgment, not of the work, but of the essen-tially specialist area of the editing of the work, had gone on for two years. Into the period between the two editions had been concentrated much of the critical reaction. As a measure of this we need look no further than Professor Charles Rossman's detailed if selective bibliography of 'Gabler's *Ulysses*' which appeared in summer 1990. Taken together with the critical articles about the 1986 edition, three-quarters of the essays were associated with one or other edition and belong chronologically to what could be called the Gabler Era, as opposed to the Kidd Era.

It is an over-simplification to divide them thus. The reality, as we have all too plainly seen from the private correspondence, was that John Kidd was a force to be reckoned with from 1985 onward and that his position was also publicly established by then, mainly as a result of the important *Washington Post* article by David Remnick of April 1985. But in broad terms, Gabler domi-nated the field throughout the 1980s, until well after the appearance of *Ulysses: The Corrected Text*; and part of the reason for the continuation of this after 16 June 1986 was the sheer volume of critical acclaim given to his work.

Did the main protagonists think that the Joyce Wars were over? Did they simply intend to keep quiet and allow the huge machinery of the new edition to make its stately progress through the world, altering works of literary criticism, changing teaching practice in English faculties, persuading teachers in their turn to persuade or ordain that their students acquire the new version? Did the Trustees believe they had done the right thing on behalf of the James Joyce Estate and that nothing more needed to be said? Did Gabler believe he had demolished Kidd? Did Ellmann vacate the Holy Seat? Were the vast array of Joycean scholars, the participants at international symposia, the directors of intellectual controversy literally worldwide, entirely silenced by the bitter but total dismissal of the main critic by Hans Walter Gabler, well before the cycle for debate had run even half its two-year course?

The situation was breathtaking. 1987 introduced a static, stagnant period, with the opposing groups balefully eyeing each other, waiting for movement, anticipating and preparing for some vigorous assault, but uncertain about what they themselves should do. From time to time there were heavy bombardments. But, like all such assaults, and in spite of prodigious intellectual accomplishment and years of Joyce-studying experience, relatively little was achieved. The situation remained unchanged. The positions held by the two armies were unaffected. Gabler held the stronger position. He had control of the books and saw them being steadily sold. Kidd's position, more elusive, freer in its movements, had still not gathered sufficient force to launch any kind of decisive attack on the edition. Whenever he had attacked up to then, his success had been substantial. Really punishing treatment had been meted out and the casualties were extensive. But the literary forces which

Kidd was ranged against were formidable in their size and strength. Somewhat like Lawrence of Arabia, romantic precisely because he was essentially a solo performer inspiring rather than leading a ragged entourage made up often enough of journalists and commentators rather than the all-important 'Joyce experts', Kidd's position remained precarious.

Then, in the summer of 1988, that all changed. In an article in *The New York Review of Books*, John Kidd launched his major attack, which for some time to come would be seen as the pivot for critical judgment in the *Ulysses* affair. He must have felt a good deal of pent-up fury. For three years his criticisms had been largely ignored. The book, in all its versions, had become the standard reading text and the *only* reading text as well, since all earlier versions had, by the middle of 1988, disappeared from wholesale book suppliers and had taken on the status of rare versions where they were still available. It had taken over in the universities and schools. Rank upon rank of copies of *Ulysses: The Corrected Text* tramped their way inexorably across every literary battlefield in sight.

But John Kidd had been studying strategy and tactics. Outraged by the unfair treatment his academic paper had received at Hans Walter Gabler's hands in New York in April 1985, he now determined on a response that would be comprehensive, and chose a field of combat which lay halfway between the academic and the popular. *The New York Review of Books* is the most highly regarded literary newspaper in the world. It carries powerful essays by some of the more considerable minds of the late 20th century and they range over subjects which are really in the realm of current affairs, international politics and human rights, often unconnected with books as such. But the main thrust is literature and writing, and it is a journal with the courage to allow long, well-argued essays in its pages.

John Kidd's article, 'The Scandal of *Ulysses*', re-launched the Joyce Wars with a vengeance which seemed altogether justified. If it is a strict tenet of journalism to pick on some heightened specific item with which to begin a piece of serious verbal attack, then Kidd chose well. When this writer arrived first in Dublin, in the early autumn of 1957 to study at Trinity College, the name of Harry Thrift, though not on every lip, was known to students. The man, a fellow of the College, was admired for his sporting prowess, his great age and his abiding, lifelong love of the College. When, at the very beginning of the following year, Dublin University Players embarked on a production of *Exiles* – the first full-length production in Joyce's own city since the play appeared in 1918 – it was a matter of regret that Harry Thrift was unable to attend the first night as an honoured associative Joycean figure within the College walls, because he had died, appropriately perhaps, on the 35th anniversary of Joyce's birthday while rehearsals were going on and just a couple of weeks before the play was due to open. His honorary guest appearance would have been because he features in *Ulysses*. At least, he *did* feature in *Ulysses* until Hans Walter Gabler expunged him by changing his name to H. Shrift, lines 1258–9 on page 209 of *Ulysses: The Corrected Text*.

John Kidd may have been stretching a point when he claimed that Harry Thrift was 'known around Dublin' as the man listed in *Ulysses* as a participant in the bicycle race and mentioned in that kaleidoscope of movements and of people, real and imagined, with which Joyce concludes 'The Wandering Rocks' episode. Yet anyone who knows the city will appreciate the point. If one wants to survive as a man of letters in Dublin, it is the sort of information, marginal and throwaway, without which one is likely to be treated dismissively. When Harry Thrift became the lead example of a Hans Walter Gabler gaffe in John Kidd's essay, suddenly personal and folklore recollections of Harry Thrift became the stuff of pub gossip and literary argument from Eccles Street to Sandycove. A raw nerve had been touched which no professor of literature outside Ireland, no matter how well-versed in the subject of James Joyce, could possibly understand. There is no doubt that the blinding logic of John Kidd's case, presented as it was, acquired a following in the city of the novel straightaway.

It was just a beginning. The disappearance of Harry Thrift, Kidd claimed, was just one of thousands of unfortunate errors in the edition. He added, with a bluntness which represented total war, that the new *Ulysses* was at least in part designed by the Joyce Estate, acting through the Society of Authors in London, to acquire for itself new copyright which would run for 'seventy-five years from 1985'.* In order to do this, he claimed, an entirely new work had been accomplished, and the people responsible had gone on to attempt to persuade the world of academic study and the general public that 'all previous editions were unusable'. He demonstrated in passing that critics and commentators were making large and false claims about changes which restored 'for the first time' matter or words which in reality had been there all along, and he asked: 'Is no one awake at the wheel?'

Kidd then bedded himself down into detail. Firstly, this concerned actual words, minor in themselves, beginning at page one, where four word-changes were challenged as being not corrections, but unjustified alterations to what Joyce had seen and approved, and presumably 'meant'. No evidence to the contrary, according to Kidd, was given. He then addressed the issue of the manuscript sources, particularly the Rosenbach, and *The Joyce Archive*, a 16-volume published source of Joyce material,

* This time-span for new copyright is correct, but see earlier details of this question in Chapter Four.

drawn from many institutions and edited by Michael Groden, of the University of Western Ontario, who was one of two 'assistants' to the academic advisory committee to the 1984 *Ulysses*. John Kidd said that these sources were mainly consulted in their facsimile form, with alternative versions and prospective changes decided on in Munich and not checked against the originals. This has remained an unrefuted charge ever since. Because the material went through photographic processes to produce what were essentially 'high-contrast' printings of documents which, in their original state, varied considerably in strength and definition, and through age were often low-contrast, the need to refer back to originals, really on all points, was self-evident – so John Kidd believed. Yet this was not done. Later researches by Kidd, which he referred to in an article in the 1990 summer issue of *Studies in the Novel*, revealed that 'Librarians at the major Joyce archives volunteered that they had seen precious little of the editor during the years preceding publication'; and, though Hans Walter Gabler was asked at the Miami Conference in 1989, and before that date, to provide an itinerary of his 'three lengthy trips' to American libraries, this has never been produced.

Kidd repeated the drama created by his diatribe on Harry Thrift. He did this by erecting a complicated interrelationship between the opening references in 'The Lotus Eaters' episode, contained in Bloom's interior monologue, and referring to 'Flowers of Idleness', an allusion generally taken to relate to Byron and the poet's first book, *Hours of Idleness*. But it went much further, on to the end of the episode, and to the references to Captain Buller, who hit a cricket ball through a window of the Kildare Street Club with a slog to square leg. Anyone consulting *Thom's Directory*, used extensively by Joyce, would discover that the only Buller in 1904 who was also a captain lived at 'Byron Lodge'. This, Kidd claimed, is a typical piece of James Joyce subtlety, to lie there for discovery or not, and of course Kidd, an inveterate reader of *Thom's Directory*, and with a numerologist's sensitivity for repeats and echoes, followed up the author's prediction that he would keep the academics busy for decades and discovered the linkage. However, Hans Walter Gabler expunged Captain Buller entirely from the new edition and substituted 'Captain Culler'. There was no Culler in Dublin at the time, of any rank, but on the manuscript page there was the letter 'c' in a circle and whatever the quality of the facsimile reproduction of this symbol, it seems to have been taken as an instruction to spell 'Buller' as 'Culler'.

A third example was offered: the changing of Conolly Norman's Christian name to 'Connolly'. The real individual was the medical superintendent of the Richmond District Lunatic Asylum in North Brunswick Street, referred to as Dottyville by Buck Mulligan, who also refers to the man in question. Again, it is *Thom's Directory* that provides the detail.

No racier opening section to a broadside attack on the scholarly work of the editors of *Ulysses: The Corrected Text* could have been devised. It went to the heart of Dublin and Dubliners, it alerted real people to an academic travesty and it whetted appetites for a further three 'chapters' in Kidd's essay.

Having proved by example his point on the use of facsimiles, Kidd asserted that the whole reliability of *Ulysses: A Critical and Synoptic Edition* and, by association, *Ulysses: The Corrected Text* must crumble. Joyce scholars, if they could not rely on such lively academic ammunition as the names of the basic characters in the book, so many of whom everyone knows to have been real, must really go back into the armoury and check all stores. No one could point a gun any more in the war with certainty that it would not misfire, or explode in the face of its infantrymen.

John Kidd has a lively eye for the right example. He indicated that Bloom employs the phrase, '*crème de la crème*', but possibly misspelling it, in his own mind, as '*crême de la crême*'. Joyce, an outstanding linguist, put in the incorrect circumflex; a blue-pencil printer's or compositor's correction gives the *grave* accent. But the blue pencil, in facsimile, turns black and obscures the circumflex altogether. So it is not mentioned and the point is lost. Did Joyce give Bloom a minor misuse of French, in keeping with his highly intelligent, exploring mind, but his lack of language ability? Denser concentrations of gunfire were needed, however, and they came in the form of summaries of errors involving capitalising of letters which Joyce did not favour, punctuation, the famous dashes and whether they should be indented – as Kidd says Joyce wanted – or put out to the margin – as Gabler does – spellings (already indicated), the use of italics, the compounding of words, the alteration of abbreviations and the changing of factual detail, such as sums of money, dates and numbers.

Really major errors, from an editing point of view, were identified in the claim by Hans Walter Gabler that the 1984 *Ulysses* is the 11th edition of the book and the 1986 therefore the 12th. Kidd demonstrated that in fact the 1984 edition was the 18th and that seven separate typesettings of the book (the most general of all definitions of what an edition is) were ignored. Most of them were, and are, available in one or other of the three major research libraries in the world, in New York, Washington and London. If the editions were not even recorded, what could one say about the comprehensiveness of the collation of all printed versions? After all, as Kidd demonstrated, the Matisse-illustrated edition had changes ordained by Joyce and passed on to Stuart Gilbert. This edition was ignored by Gabler.

In the final section of John Kidd's essay he dealt with Richard Ellmann. At the time, of course, he knew nothing of what Chuck Rossman was to discover at Tulsa later that year. Had he known he might not have been as generously disposed to Ellmann, who might, had he lived, 'have quickly cut short the textual travesty of *Ulysses: The Corrected Text*'. Indeed, well he might, and should have and did not. John Kidd traced Ellmann's change of heart over the word known to all men and then addressed the question posed by quotations in the advertising for *Ulysses: The Corrected Text*, in which Ellmann's endorsement is given thus: '"AN ABSOLUTELY STUNNING SCHOLARLY ACHIEVEMENT" – Richard Ellmann'. But Ellmann denied, in a letter to Kidd, that he had used the word stunning at all and told him, 'I was approbatory'. Kidd's opinion was that the advertising would have been excessive in the light of Elmann's subsequent views, even if it had stuck to the truth and put in '"I AM APPRO-BATORY" – Richard Ellmann'.

Worse was to follow. Not only did Ellmann review the book on which he had been advising for seven years in 1984, when it first came out, in *The New York Review of Books*, but he also used his 1984 review, amended in content, as the Foreword to *Ulysses: The Corrected Text*, when it appeared in 1986. So Richard Ellmann, adviser, commentator, judge, jury, advertising promoter and unsuccessful Dean of Studies over Hans Walter Gabler turned out to be the book's main United States critic at the first of its two greatly orchestrated appearances, and the main introducer of the work for its second. Similarly inbred things occurred in *The Times Literary Supplement*, in London, with Hugh Kenner, a long-time promoter of the book and its method, reviewing it at length, and in the *James Joyce Quarterly*, where Michael Groden, one of the assistants to the advisory committee and the editor of much of the source material, was the book's reviewer. John Kidd's comment on all this showed the kind of restraint of a General Schwarzkopf: 'And so it fell out that the players reviewed the play and found it pleasing'!

John Kidd had a solution. It was simple. Withdraw the 1986 edition and go back to the 1961 version, which could be made readily available and was much to be preferred. Nothing like it happened, of course. The shops remain to this day serviced with the editions which came out in 1986. The 1984 Garland edition, in both hardback and paperback, is out of print and will not be reprinted. The only change remotely servicing Kidd's proposal was the reissue by Vintage Paperbacks in 1990 of the 1961 *Ulysses*. The keen young general in the field, having delivered his broadside and issued his ultimatum, sat back to await developments. The counter-attack in the Joyce Wars had started. The James Joyce Estate and the edition with all those involved in it, including the publishers, had been challenged and confronted by formidable weaponry. How would they respond?

TEN

The Committee That Never Met

'We're going to leave it to . . . a group of experts to
advise us. But I'm inclined to think that the edition
we're publishing now is seriously flawed.'
Jason Epstein, vice-president of Random House,
announcing the setting up of the Tanselle Committee

I MMEDIATELY AFTER John Kidd's piece in *The New
York Review of Books*, the confrontation shifted to
London and to the pages of the *Times Literary Supplement*. Throughout 1988 and into 1989, the Joyce Wars
were essentially fought through the pages of the world's
two leading literary magazines, by way of articles, but
principally in the letters columns.

The issue of Hans Walter Gabler's edition was raised
tangentially, in the *TLS*, in reviews by Roger Shattuck
and Douglas Alden of recent French editions of Marcel
Proust. Passing references, by the two reviewers, to the
1986 *Ulysses: The Corrected Text* suggested that its
editorial work was shoddy and its motivation was essentially the wish to obtain fresh copyright. Hans Walter
Gabler took up the charges levelled against the edition
in New York, in a letter which appeared in the *TLS* of
1–7 July 1988. He claimed that the copyright motive was

'ludicrously misrepresented', but then went on to deal with the criticisms of editorial standards in his work. The main burden of his argument was that the reading text published for general consumption was simply to fulfil a demand for the transfer of scholarly editions into affordable versions. He claimed that his own work on the 1984 double-sided, or two-toned, version of *Ulysses* had shown that an 'edited reading text' was neither stable nor definitive. It was a burdensome necessity to have the simpler version, but it did not fulfil the primary aim of his mammoth work on the text of Joyce's novel, and he was even surprised that Shattuck and Alden did not mention the earlier, three-volume version at all in their attacks on his performance as Joyce's editor.

The serious content of his letter was directed at the two reviewers. John Kidd's 'Scandal of *Ulysses*' article, on which their remarks are based, was referred to as 'a journalistic piece of writing' which had caused 'commotion'. Kidd's views, Gabler claimed, were deeply flawed, his perspectives narrowly confined, his method for disseminating them 'a journalism of allegations and insinuations', and his work was based on false assertions, unsupported by evidence. He had, said Gabler, avoided scholarly publication. Gabler did admit error, and cited the changing of 'one or two' names, the insertion of an indefinite article and the removal of a comma. He also denied that the comparisons had been made against facsimiles and claimed that all the basic bibliographical work had been done.

Hans Walter Gabler was followed the next week, in the same publication, by Peter du Sautoy, who wrote as Trustee of the James Joyce Estate, and rapped the two Proust experts over the knuckles for their use of 'unscholarly' words such as 'bamboozled' and 'puffery'. This, however, was only a preamble to his assertion that the Trustees had a simple objective: to put right the corruption of the existing text of *Ulysses*. They did not authorise

Ulysses: The Corrected Text in order to obtain new copyright and further royalties. The statement was categorical, as was the additional point, that the initiative came from Gabler. The Trustees, he said in his letter, had accepted the fact that the comprehensive editing would bestow a copyright status. The Trustees and Gabler had acted, he said, in good faith, 'and were always completely open in what they did'. Peter du Sautoy then explained the timescale for the edition. Two years were to elapse between the two editions of *Ulysses*, giving the scholars time to assess the work of editing. He then claimed that the reaction was so favourable that the trade publishers pressed for earlier release of the text for a commercial edition, an approach which the Trustees resisted and they did not release it 'till two years after publication of the critical edition'. Finally he gave an account of the advisory structure, claiming that at no time did the advisers say that the edition should not be published, though they did occasionally have 'reservations'. The edition, du Sautoy fairly claimed, 'is in general the best there is'.

The following week it was John Kidd's turn to fire off another salvo from across the Atlantic. He was annoyed at the references by Gabler to his not having published scholarly criticisms and he cited his paper to the Society for Textual Scholarship in New York. What was particularly galling was the fact that Gabler, according to Kidd, had taken corrections from this article and from the *Washington Post* article, and used them in reprints of the 1984 Garland edition and in the 1986 edition, but unacknowledged. Kidd then gave a detailed and lengthy outline of the scholarly work he had done and of the scholarly responses to it from a variety of different sources, including George Sandulescu's contribution to the Monaco book of essays, in which Sandulescu 'puts Gabler on notice' that he could not brush aside Kidd's work.

John Kidd also referred to the Tanselle Committee, in an entirely formal way, at the end of his long letter,

stating simply that 'Letters of support or criticism may be sent to the chair of the Random House investigative committee, G. Thomas Tanselle, Vice-President, John Simon Guggenheim Foundation, 90 Park Avenue, New York 10016, USA'. The committee had been set up in the summer of 1988. The purpose of that committee was to advise Random House as to whether the Gabler edition should remain in print or be withdrawn. It was as simple as that. Jason Epstein, Random House vice-president and the man directly responsible for *Ulysses*, said that he was leaving it to a group of experts to advise them. 'But I'm inclined to think that the edition we're publishing now is seriously flawed.'

The Tanselle Committee, appointed on 7 July 1988 was only named by its chairman on 1 November. Its members, in addition to G. Thomas Tanselle, were distinguished indeed: Denis Donoghue, the Henry James Professor of English and American Letters at New York University; Herbert Cahoon, the Curator of Manuscripts at the Pierpoint Morgan Library, who was also the joint author, with John J. Slocum, of *A Bibliography of James Joyce (1882–1941)*; and Jo Ann Boydston, President of the Society for Textual Scholarship; Tanselle was himself a former president of the same society, as well as being an adjunct professor of English at Columbia University and vice-president of the John Simon Guggenheim Memorial Foundation. In sympathy, perhaps, with everything else that had happened, the committee ran into trouble at such an early stage – through differences between Jason Epstein and Tanselle, unconnected with the *Ulysses* controversy – that it never actually met. But it did play a significant role, to which we will come in due course. Its actual life, stillborn as far as debate goes, went on until March 1990, when it was finally disbanded.

In Hans Walter Gabler's next letter, which appeared in the *TLS* of 12–18 August, he accepted that the retouching of the edited text involved 'thirty modest changes'. They were unacknowledged individually. None of them was fresh or original; they merely sharpened perceptions which were already there. As to the 1985 scholarly paper delivered in New York by Kidd, Gabler had 'dealt with' that in his own contribution from the floor. When it was actually published his own would follow.

Kidd came swiftly back the following week. What kind of an acknowledgement was that, to name neither the person, nor the extract used, nor advice taken, and yet to claim that an acknowledgement had been made? He then quoted extensively Gabler's personal references to himself.

None of this could really be described as 'war'. It was skirmishing, perhaps of a dramatic order, and certainly inflicting wounds and casualties, but of a minor kind. It was unsatisfactory stuff, tending to drive the whole controversy into areas of arcane theorising and vindictive semantics. Something more fundamental was needed. It came from Charles Rossman, of the Department of English at the University of Texas in Austin. Returning from a summer examination of the Richard Ellmann papers at the University of Tulsa in Oklahoma, he presented a report on what he had found. Far from being a minor consideration, the evidence was suddenly presented of the James Joyce Estate's keen interest in the renewal of copyright as far back as 5 May 1983 and also of the serious divisions among the advisers over fundamental questions of editing policy. Rossman declared that he was prevented by the very copyright laws which are involved from quoting as fully as he might from the papers. He had been given clearances, as far as Ellmann's own letters were concerned, by Ellmann's brother. But he was unable to get similar clearances from other correspondents and had to paraphrase the contents of their letters. He claimed that 'a rather commercial urgency' was evident in the planning and debate about the publication of the 1986 trade edition, and that Peter du Sautoy's presentation of the contractual and scholarly arrangements, given in his letter to the *TLS* of 8–14 July, was 'significantly' different from the version contained in the letter of 13 August 1985, already extensively dealt with in an earlier chapter. In short, the speed with which the 1986 edition was agreed and set in train was quite unnecessary, and was made much earlier – indeed, by the early summer of 1985 – for reasons which Rossman suggested were in no way compatible with Peter du Sautoy's claim that the principal concern of the James Joyce Estate was an edition which had been carefully assessed by scholars and was being got right if it possibly could. Peter du Sautoy was quoted as saying that it was too late to go back, despite his feeling of doubt about publishing Gabler's text at all! 'It is simply not the case,' Rossman wrote, 'that the Gabler edition of *Ulysses* was motivated without economic interests in mind, and was completed without profound disagreement among the editorial advisers themselves.'

The following week's issue carried a reply from Peter du Sautoy, denying that economic considerations were uppermost, in the minds of the Trustees, and repeating his earlier statements about 'reservations' among the advisers and the fact that the advisers had not actually advised against publication. The pressure for early release of agreement to the commercial edition was, he claimed, because the publishers *needed to reprint*. This raises an altogether new reason for the unseemly haste, at odds with what Peter du Sautoy had said privately in correspondence with his advisers, where the fact that the controversy would not go away was offered as reason to proceed, pre-emptively, with the trade edition. The questions raised in Rossman's letter were finally referred to as a 'side-issue', on which 'there is really very little to say'.

In that same issue of the *TLS* a new voice was heard. James Joyce's grandson, Stephen James Joyce, waded in.

He was not, he said, seeking to immerse himself in what he described as an 'unseemly, undignified "scholarly" brawl'. He simply wanted to direct readers back to the enjoyment of the book, in either the 1961 or the 'Corrected Text' version. His concern was to remain true to the spirit and letter of his grandfather's writing. Then, in a brief digression from the main direction of the correspondence over the previous three months, he suggested that it might be time 'for one or two scholars to sit down and write the turbulent history of *Ulysses* and of its various editions'!

Charles Rossman did not publish his findings among the Ellmann papers in the United States until December 1988. But exchanges did go on during the intervening months, between publication of 'The Scandal of *Ulysses*' article in June of that year and Christmas. They did not have the rat-tat-tat imperative of the *TLS*, a weekly. During the summer months *The New York Review of Books* goes on a more spaced-out publishing schedule. To some extent this gives the impression of John Kidd as a somewhat isolated figure, whose major bombardment of 16 June 1988 had had the curious effect of sparking off the war in an English rather than an American literary journal. The midsummer was important for another reason. John Kidd's own status changed. Throughout the period of publication of the two editions he had been a research scholar working at the University of Virginia, at its Center for Advanced Studies. But in 1988 Boston University invited him to head up its newly formed James Joyce Research Center and this was established in July 1988 in modest basement rooms at 725 Commonwealth Avenue. Their furnishings were spartan; their technology the usual computer station; but their glory was John Kidd's collection of Joyceana. He happily boasts of his buying marathons. He is perpetually collecting Joyce material wherever he goes, including apparently identical copies of *Ulysses*, in every language, every type of printing, from the richly impressive Matisse edition, down to *Ulysses – James Joyce – Complete and Unexpurgated – First American Printing – Collectors Publications* – at $5.00 – 933 small, thrill-packed pages, with advertisements at the end for similar exciting publications such as *Four Way Swappers, The Whipping Post*, Frank Harris's *My Secret Life, Bottoms Up* and *The Bawdy Tales of Firenzuola*.

John Kidd's interest in what Joyce wrote, and how he did it, largely confined to *Ulysses*, though his knowledge of the other works is extensive also, is the interest of a genuine enthusiast. In a curious way, he lapses, as a person, into a passive mode when other, non-Joycean issues are being debated. But he comes electrically to life on his principal subject and can be devastating in debate. A steely, ruthless quality of argument, logical and scholarly in its method and direction, is applied when he is confronted, as is increasingly the case, by Gabler's protagonists. His motive for all that he has done, and it constitutes a vast undermining of an even vaster critical project of huge implications, is love of Joyce. In the abstract you soon come to love what you know; and the controversy has galvanised Kidd into the creation of a huge milling mechanism, grinding down to verbal powder the whole structure of the work.

A distinct advantage of John Kidd's shift to Boston University was that he now had behind him the weight of a university which valued the publicity advantages of having on its staff a figure whose controversial impact was of world dimensions. Boston University knew how to handle this. Its Office of Public Relations is an active organisation and was soon to have press kits available on everything Joycean. It took over responsibility for a great deal, even Kidd's personal collection, and backed his offers to readers of the literary journals in which the controversy was pursued that if they wanted material update on what had gone before, they were just to write and it would be sent.

Instantaneously, as it were, Boston University joined the universities which had been in the Joyce business for decades; it did so with a young but accomplished scholar who had snatched the limelight from all the others. The riches of the Boston University James Joyce Research Center were listed in a background note: a library of 2,000 books by and about Joyce, in 25 different languages; rare editions; even rarer ephemera; the world's most comprehensive *Ulysses* collection (of this claim there could be little doubt – indeed, Kidd is unique in his knowledge of, and searches for, apparently repeat editions or impressions which in fact reveal differences); first-rate holdings in translations; a workshop; a team of graduate students; 'Boston University has become a center for the study of the most influential writer of the century', and its biggest treasure, by far, was John Kidd himself.

'The New *Ulysses*: The Hidden Controversy' was Charles Rossman's more considered delivery on his findings at Tulsa, and it appeared in *The New York Review of Books* on 8 December 1988, extending substantially the material in his letter to the *TLS* in September. There, he had entered a correspondence, replying to points made, notably by Hans Walter Gabler and Peter du Sautoy, and correcting their representation of the facts. In *The New York Review of Books* he delivered a much more magisterial essay, which quoted at length from the Ellmann letters and paraphrased the other documents and letters, where permission to quote was denied. From being a relatively unknown scholar, joining in with a letter which added important new material but was limited in the way it could be used, he shifted now to being an arbiter of some substance. In my own judgment, at the time – and I had published articles in Ireland about the controversy, commenting on John Kidd's criticisms and on his dilemma – Rossman clinched a situation and confirmed that the whole organisation of the two editions of *Ulysses* was seriously flawed, and required full and open examination. It was not that Rossman was in a position to give it that full and open examination himself. Key figures in the drama denied him permission. But he was able to deliver sufficient inside detail to paint a distressing picture in his reconstructed chronology of events, stretching from 1981 to the setting up of the Tanselle Committee. Principally, he showed that the main figures involved had either remained silent over serious disagreements and reservations, or when they had spoken out had misrepresented seriously the facts.

Rossman opened his essay by asserting that the forces behind the two new editions of *Ulysses* were unequivocally 'money, copyright law, critical ideology, strength of will'. He then gave one of the most lucid explanations throughout the whole controversy of the complicated concept of copytext and the departure made from the tradition of editing in this way by Gabler, in his attempt to create a 'genetic' or 'conflated' text. He made the point that, technically anyway, such a text, created or amalgamated out of manuscript and other material, was not amenable to the term 'corrected', since there was no entity there in the first place to be corrected.

Rossman, having referred only in general terms to the internal controversy covered by the letters, began with a summary of the story which the public already knew, starting with John Kidd's paper given to the Society for Textual Scholarship in New York in April 1985 and Gabler's reply. This, together with the evidence which emerged at the Monaco Conference, also briefly summarised by Rossman, was offered as sufficient indication of a hidden agenda. The rest of Rossman's article – apart from its concluding paragraphs – presented as detailed an analysis of that hidden agenda as the laws of copyright permitted him. They have already been summarised in an earlier chapter. Here, it is worth outlining the following further observations contained in Rossman's article.

Textually, it is clear that the disagreements among the

advisers depended often upon the credentials of the material used to construct the genetic text. In the cases where this descended simply from the Rosenbach Manuscript there was less likelihood of Philip Gaskell or Clive Hart disagreeing, whereas an episode like 'Lestrygonians', which derived from working draft and typescript in a more complicated way, provoked greater disagreement. To this Rossman attributed the fluctuations in such disagreement. The reality was that the episode was edited from a 'hypothetically reconstructed' copytext. Though they were slow to react, this kind of approach did give the advisers cause for reservation.

The second area of difference to emerge, according to Rossman's researches, concerns Hans Walter Gabler's idiomatic command of English. Richard Ellmann twice made the point 'privately' in a letter to Peter du Sautoy, that his (Gabler's) command of English idiom was a little less firm than that of someone born in an English-speaking country. This point was made even more strongly in another letter quoted by Rossman: 'Unfortunately he doesn't have a sufficiently native command of English, in spite of his high intelligence, and so he makes wrong choices based ultimately, I think, upon a deficient sense of the nuances.' The distinction between 'English-speaking' and other countries is misleadingly simple. It is a mere threshold of departure. The important idiom is that of Dublin, then of Ireland. Only after that can the modest advantage of the English from an 'English-speaking country' have a relevance and an advantage. The fact is that Hans Walter Gabler speaks a clear and precise English, studied and faintly mannered, only occasionally uncertain about the choice of word. Idiomatically, many American Joyceans seem as far as German scholars from idiomatic Dublin English as it might have been spoken in 1904.

The third point concerns control and was raised in a letter sent to Hans Walter Gabler by Richard Ellmann, following a meeting in Oxford – where Ellmann was then living and at work on *Oscar Wilde* – on 4 June 1983 at New College. The meeting was a disaster, mainly as a result of Gabler's intransigence, and immediately after it Ellmann wrote to Gabler, expressing his concern and referring to a discussion he had held with Fredson Bowers, the leading textual scholar and expert in editorial approaches, whose views were presented by Ellmann as being at odds with Gabler's approach. Ellmann appealed to Gabler to concede, referring to his appeal as a 'last ditch' one, and couching his remarks in an emotional way, with phrases like 'we have been friends for many years' and 'in our personal dealings I have never felt that you were unwilling to take other views into consideration', and finally 'I believe you will be true to your own nature if you show yourself willing to make the rather minor withdrawals from a doctrinaire position that would be necessary'. The key revelation, however, was almost an aside at the beginning of the letter, where Ellmann said: 'Although the Estate has decided to proceed with the edition regardless, I am sure that the result, which calls the enterprise into question, cannot be gratifying to you.' Quite the opposite was the true picture. Gabler knew, once the Estate had decided to proceed, that his position was essentially impregnable. He replied to Ellmann in uncompromising terms which made no concessions. In addition, he announced in that letter that he had taken on additional advisers himself, A. Walton Litz and Michael Groden, 'to support me inofficially [*sic*] with their advice'.

We are looking into the revelations which turn an encounter into a drama and which demonstrate the significance, even in arcane scholarly exchanges over details about editing a complicated text, of the strength of will and personal judgment about power. Gabler, in that respect, was the strongest of them all. Wrong and confused he demonstrably was, in both principle and practice on the book. Worse still, he was headstrong about having his way, whatever the criticisms. But when it came to confrontations he outwitted his critics and opponents, as well as those who were on his side but should have been controlling him, and the edition appeared on Bloomsday 1986, as he wanted it.

At the time of Rossman's article, 8 December 1988, the situation remained unstable. By then all other editions of *Ulysses* had been replaced on the market by Gabler's *Ulysses: The Corrected Text*. Even the Garland three-volume edition was soon to go out of print. The impact of the article was immense; far greater, as it turned out, than his earlier letter to the *TLS*, though that letter contained most of the essentials. What the article clearly established was firstly a high degree of uncertainty and disagreement, going back over a period of years, with confidence undermined in a substantial and comprehensive way; secondly, a cover-up, designed to conceal the misgivings and doubts and present a united and confident public front to *Ulysses*, not just in 1986 but back to the 1984 edition as well; and thirdly, a selective presentation of the true background to the events revealed John Kidd's criticisms were endorsed and supported, at least partially, by the very people who had been publicly assembled on the Gabler side in the Joyce Wars. Philip Gaskell and Clive Hart emerged as a kind of pro-Kidd Fifth Column, aware that he was right on matters both of principle and practice, but unable or unwilling to come out and say so. Richard Ellmann demonstrably had led a confused existence as far as *Ulysses* was concerned. Peter du Sautoy was revealed as having not known clearly what he was up to and of having been influenced very definitely by the James Joyce Estate's interest in renewal of copyright, to the point where he ordained the publication of a work over which he had quite serious misgivings.

By the time Rossman published his article, Richard Ellmann had been dead for a year and a half; but the other

advisers and Trustees – by the beginning of 1989 Clive
Hart had joined Peter du Sautoy as a Trustee of the Estate
– all wrote to the editor of *The New York Review of
Books*, as did Roma Woodnutt, on behalf of the Society
of Authors acting in its administrative capacity over the
affairs of the James Joyce Estate. This, perhaps, was one
of the most curious of all the letters published at this
time. Roma Woodnutt seemed to be giving cautionary
advice to potential applicants who wished for permission
to quote James Joyce, advice which had little or nothing
to do with the controversy, though of course it would
have sounded cautionary to a multitude of Joyce scholars
around the world. They knew that, without the kind of
permission she was outlining, they would be unable to
do their work, at least to the point of publishing it with
adequate quotation from Joyce's own writing. She told
readers of the *Review* that those wishing for permission
would need to give adequate time to allow for assessment
of the use on two grounds. The first of these is the relatively normal one, of the use of copyright material in
such a way that the writer and his work are treated 'faith-
fully'. The second is the slightly less normal use, which
is to allow the Trustees to 'satisfy themselves that family
views are respected'. Since Stephen James Joyce, the principal beneficiary under the James Joyce will and the only
surviving direct descendant of the writer, is frequently
on record about privacy and the preservation of respect
about his grandfather and the Joyce family generally, and
is not the easiest of men from whom to obtain permissions
and agreements, this clause in Roma Woodnutt's letter
carried a burden of meaning not immediately apparent
in its statement. She then advised that permission would
in no sense be guaranteed. All applications could be considered; not all of them could be granted. Her third point
repeated her first, about allowing adequate time, and her
fourth was simply to indicate that all requests should be
through the Society of Authors.

What was the purpose of her letter? To warn the army of Joyce scholars not to side with the 'enemy'? To give notice that 'adequate time' was a euphemism for time to assess a person's standing in the Joyce Wars? Those intelligent enough to grasp the full implications of the letter would have been immediately aware that a huge body of Joyce material important to many present and future Joyce scholars was under quite different copyright constraints from those governing the various editions of Joyce's works. They would also have been aware of the different copyright time-scales in America and elsewhere, the more vulnerable territories – as far as copyright constraint was concerned – being those with by far the greatest concentration of formal Joyce scholarship. While the majority of Joyce's works, either very shortly or in a matter of a few years, would go out of copyright in 1992 – with the exception of versions for which renewed copyright had been obtained – many of the letters, the manuscripts and other documents either had quite different copyright timetables, or had not even started the countdown from publication, because they were as yet unpublished. For many decades, stretching into the 21st century, the James Joyce Estate would continue to have a role and function. The letter from Roma Woodnutt appeared to underline this.

Clive Hart now appeared as joint Trustee, with Peter du Sautoy, signing a brief and clipped letter to the effect that the James Joyce Estate had agreed to work with the advisory group set up by Random House, in other words the Tanselle Committee, and set rules for this investigation. They were that a 'full statement' of John Kidd's criticisms would first be 'received'; Gabler would then be given 'an opportunity to comment'; and after that the group would consider both statements and prepare a report. At that stage the Trustees would become involved. There was no guarantee that the committee's findings would be accepted. 'Any changes to the text of

Ulysses will require the specific approval of the Estate.' The letter then concluded: 'Until the process of consultation is complete, neither the Estate nor the publishers intend to make any further public statement on the matter.'

Perhaps because of the separation in the status of Clive Hart from Philip Gaskell, by the former becoming a Trustee, the latter had a letter of his own in the same issue of the *Review*, clarifying what withdrawing from the project meant and what it meant to rejoin it. He said that he and Clive Hart had not 'rejoined', in the sense of further work on *Ulysses*, on further meetings of the advisory committee. What they had done was to decide on reflection not to make their disagreement public and risk prejudicing an edition which 'would still have considerable value'. Gaskell then demonstrated that value by referring to the book he and Clive Hart had written, proposing changes to three editions – Gabler's, the 1961 and the 1922 first edition – and pointing out that while the alterations in the two earlier versions, at least as far as Hart and Gaskell were concerned, run to a total of more than 3,000, those to the Gabler text number only (*only?*) 484.

The pace of publication of *The New York Review of Books* allows for letters in any correspondence on a particular theme to be circulated to those directly involved, who may then reply in the *same* issue, rather than serially, as in the *TLS*. This was a convenience of some value on this occasion, since Charles Rossman was in the position to write about all three letters at the one time, in response to Clive Hart and Peter du Sautoy's points, Philip Gaskell's separate letter and the implication of the points made by Roma Woodnutt of the Society of Authors, keeping a quite complex set of issues clearly before the *Review*'s keen and stimulated readers. Rossman dealt with what it meant to 'withdraw' and 'rejoin' first, and was able to point out that Philip Gaskell's memory seemed faulty, since there is, in the Ellmann collection at the University of Tulsa, a letter of November 1983, in which Hart and Gaskell accepted the text for publication, agreed to do more work on it if this was needed, railed against it on theoretical grounds, praised it for the high level of expertise in preparing it, gave a rough count of the number of disagreements on textual points ('fewer than 100 readings') and, it emerged, they had begun their own separate scholarly work analysing the errors in it, along with the errors in the two earlier editions already cited. At this stage – of working on the new analysis – the number of disputed readings had risen to 484, which, it was implied in Gaskell's letter, represented some kind of accolade when set beside the larger numbers for the two earlier versions of the book! It is hardly surprising that Rossman expressed a degree of confusion.

The point which Charles Rossman then deduced, from the other letters published in that issue of the *Review*, was that the interests of the James Joyce Estate were increasingly and demonstrably in conflict with the interests of scholarship and of the general reader. At the heart of that conflict lay the issue of copyright. It was there before the publication of the scholarly edition; it remained there during the appearance of both editions; and in the letter from the Society of Authors it was reinforced in more general terms when Roma Woodnutt placed 'family views' in the forefront of readers' minds. No matter what way one interprets 'family views', if money is concerned, then money is an issue. If a family owns a property from which an assured income of unknown but very substantial proportions derives, and this is about to be terminated, yet can be renewed and protected for a further half-century or so, then it is not unreasonable to infer that the Trustees responsible for that income, together with the administrators of the Estate – who also must benefit – as well as the publishers, would at the very least lean towards the preservation of the heritage involved. Roma Woodnutt spread a wide copyright net, involving, in addition to James Joyce, the copyrights created by his wife, his son, his daughter, his daughter-in-law, his grandson and his brother. We all know, however, that her letter was principally concerned with a single person's copyright – that of the great writer himself. But were public and scholarly interests served when Stephen James Joyce, through the Estate, destroyed Lucia's letters? Was this interest served when the Estate suppressed the epilogue in Brenda Maddox's life of Nora Joyce? Rossman cited these examples to demonstrate the potential if not actual conflicts which were implicit in the developments contained in the letters to which he wrote his careful and lengthy answer.

There was a ray of hope on the horizon, however. On the anniversary both of the first publication of *Ulysses* and of James Joyce's birthday, 2 February 1989, a conference had been called at the University of Miami. It would devote itself exclusively to the new edition of *Ulysses* and the problems which had arisen. Participants each deserve a drumroll: Hans Walter Gabler would be there. John Kidd would be there. Michael Groden, newly recruited to the Gabler team, would be there also. Philip Gaskell and Clive Hart would attend. That balanced Joycean, Fritz Senn, would offer to pour oil on troubled waters. Thomas Staley, editor of the *James Joyce Quarterly*, would be there. And the new knight who had brought such sustenance to John Kidd's lonely assault, Charles Rossman, would also be there.

ELEVEN

'What Sort of a Kip ·is This?'

'– When I makes tea I makes tea, as old mother
Grogan said. And when I makes water I makes
water . . .
– *So I do, Mrs Cahill,* says she. *Begob, ma'am,* says
Mrs Cahill, *God send you don't make them in the
one pot.*'

Buck Mulligan to Haines and Stephen

T HE CONFERENCE on *Ulysses* at the University of
Miami took place and was characterised above
all by Hans Walter Gabler's reluctance to answer
questions. While this led to criticism of him in literary
journals, it effectively stifled debate. One of his major
defences against John Kidd had been in the form of an
attack on Kidd's method of conducting what Gabler quite
correctly saw as a campaign against himself and his editions of *Ulysses.* Kidd had resorted to journalism. He had
taken the Joyce Wars out of the realms of scholarship,
and placed them firmly in the theatre of newspapers and
magazines. Though these were not exactly the popular
press as we understand the term, they were not the
scholarly journals either.

Kidd had not been shy of journalism and had used it
side by side with scholarly papers; but his limited publishing record, as a Joyce expert, allowed Gabler to con-
duct a defence which was not really a defence at all, at

least on the issues, but rather one on the personal level. Indeed, Kidd's persistent weakness as a critic of Gabler was in his failure to publish or to bring forward the basic documentation on his criticisms of Gabler's work. Kidd had gone so far as to offer, during the controversial correspondence which took place in the *TLS* and *The New York Review of Books* in the summer and autumn of 1988, to supply those newly arrived in the controversy with a Kidd-kit, a portfolio of articles and background material. Though of considerable interest, it did not amount to much. The main document, indeed virtually all the documents, could at a pinch be dismissed as journalism. Pride of place was given to 'The Scandal of *Ulysses*', published in June 1988. Then there was the David Remnick piece from *The Washington Post*, of April 1985, and Edwin McDowell's article from *The New York Times* responding to 'The Scandal of *Ulysses*' piece. Some of the material in the Kidd-kit challenged the very basis of Gabler's attacks on Kidd's methods and on his supposed reliance on 'journalism'. Where is the dividing line? Is the informed judgment of the editor of the *TLS*, Jeremy Treglown, reporting on the April 1985 meeting in New York, scholarly or not, journalism or not? Who is to decide?

The truth is that Kidd had no other effective platform. He had delivered his opening scholarly critique in his paper to the New York third annual conference of the Society for Textual Scholarship in April 1985; and he was committed to the substantive document which would spell out the details. This had to be comprehensive and he still had no clear idea what this might mean, in terms of work. In *The Irish Literary Supplement*, in the autumn of 1985, he had published an important 'scholarly' essay, 'Gaelic in the New *Ulysses*', which contains fairly fundamental fault-finding, not just concerned with Irish but with other languages as well. In September 1986 Kidd was reviewing in the pages of the *TLS* a clutch of ripeness from the autumn harvest of Joyce studies and it permitted him a brief aside on textual matters – and of course on the Gabler edition – when he dealt with the alternative 'Penelope' episode reading, based on James Van Dyck Card's *An Anatomy of 'Penelope'*. In the autumn of 1987 he was writing on genetic studies in an article in the *James Joyce Literary Supplement* called 'The Genetic Joyce'; and in February 1988, in the *James Joyce Broadsheet*, in a piece entitled 'Proof Fever', a review of *Assessing the 1984 'Ulysses'*, the book of essays from the Monaco Conference, edited by Sandulescu and Hart, Kidd was warming up for the summer big one: 'The Scandal of *Ulysses*'.

After that the Kidd-kit runs a bit thin. Kidd faltered on his undertakings. He gave his first critical paper in April 1985 and it was later published. The fuller critique was promised, though initially with no doubt. Three years passed. In July 1988, in his long letter to the *TLS*, Kidd told readers that it had been agreed between himself and the editors of *Papers of the Bibliographical Society of America* that his monograph in its final form would be with them by 1 September. In February 1989 he reported in *The New York Review of Books* that his report would be available and 'released' at the Miami Conference. This did not occur. There was justification for the growing scepticism.

When it had suited him, Hans Walter Gabler, together with the publishers, the Estate and the advisers, had used journalism in one of its least attractive forms, that of the orchestrated 'puff', as shamelessly as anyone in the business of late 20th-century media exploitation. But when journalism became a vehicle for adversarial combat against the edition, the view of it changed totally. Used for comment and criticism on Gabler's work with *Ulysses*, used moreover to fill in the background to the project laying bare a good deal that was at the very least confused and contradictory, it became reprehensible and 'unscholarly'. The journalism as such became suspect and the word itself actually turned into a term of abuse. That journalism, however, would continue to be the battlefield was ordained by the positions adopted at the beginning of 1989. In advance of the conference at the University of Miami, as a result of the positions adopted by the main parties, with the exception of John Kidd, the only route for sustaining pressure by means of comment was through journals and other publications.

Certain individuals or institutions kept out. The stated attitude of the James Joyce Estate was that no further comment would be made until the process of consultation set up with Random House was completed. There was some hope that this would move forward in an agreed form, with John Kidd supplying his detailed criticisms in a published form, Hans Walter Gabler replying to them and the Tanselle Committee making its judgment. John Kidd did indeed produce his definitive critique, though not in time for it to be 'released' at the University of Miami conference. The conference, by its very inconclusiveness, no doubt stimulated his desire to produce publicly the long-awaited critique, which was already in the hands of the Tanselle Committee chairman and the *Papers of the Bibliographical Society of America* editors, who were proposing further changes.

The Miami Conference had been originally organised to cover more general Joyce studies, but this programme was abandoned in favour of a simple title for the three-day event: '*Ulysses*: The Text'. Bernard Benstock, the organiser, personally invited Charles Rossman, John Kidd, Hans Walter Gabler, Clive Hart, Philip Gaskell, Michael Groden, A. Walton Litz and Peter du Sautoy to attend. Peter du Sautoy declined. So did Walton Litz. A further group of the usual suspects rounded themselves up in order to enjoy the fun. Eventually some 90 participants turned up, together with dreaded Grub Street hacks from newspapers in Miami, New York and London.

The format was straightforward enough. On the first

day the first two sessions were given to Gabler and Kidd successively, each presenting a paper, and being followed by a more general discussion involving other panellists and members of the audience. Charles Rossman then presented his own findings, in the Ellmann papers at Tulsa, and the remaining sessions, not just for that day, but for the next as well, were general debating encounters without further major speakers. This made possible a good deal of general discussion about the edition, all of which was recorded and subsequently published in a double number of the *James Joyce Literary Supplement*. The final day of the conference was given up to related but separate issues, including the whole question of copyright law, with lawyers explaining this in relation to Joyce and *Ulysses*. The edited version did excise certain sharp criticisms of the edition, but in general a clear and comprehensive picture was given of the proceedings. A report of the conference by Charles Rossman was also contained in that autumn's issue of *Studies in the Novel*, in an article entitled 'The Critical Reception of the Gabler *Ulysses*: or, Gabler's *Ulysses* Kidd-napped: Part Two', which covered a good deal more than just the Miami Conference.

Rossman dealt with the intractability of Gabler, who neither responded to the suggested set of questions proposed at the outset of the proceedings by Arnold Goldman, the author of an excellent study, *The Joyce Paradox*, nor addressed any of the charges made by John Kidd, with the exception of criticisms that he had relied too much on facsimiles. He simply denied this. Gabler's presentation was in the form of a lecture on editorial theory and a restatement of the 'continuous manuscript text' approach to the editing of the book. Gabler's basic strength lay in Kidd's manifest weakness: that the Boston scholar had not furnished his criticisms in a full and scholarly form. It could be clearly shown that *all* his criticisms had been through the medium of journals and magazines, letters columns, private letters and lectures or talks. John Kidd had weakened his position still further by giving the undertakings about when he would be publishing the substantive paper. By this he played into the hands of the other side.

Kidd read a letter to the Miami Conference confirming that he had already submitted his paper to the Tanselle Committee's chairman and to the editors of the *Papers of the Bibliographical Society of America*, by whom it had been accepted for publication after substantial revision. Entitled 'An Inquiry into *Ulysses: The Corrected Text*', it was due to be published in Volume 82 of the *Papers of the Bibliographical Society of America* in the issue of December 1988, that is, two months *before* the University of Miami conference. Though ostensibly this is the issue in which publication took place, the issue itself, so dated, did not in fact appear until the following summer, in June 1989. Copies by then had already been circulated on behalf of the Tanselle Committee and comments invited, though in reality the only commentator who was formally involved was Hans Walter Gabler. The 'Inquiry' had taken John Kidd four years to prepare and during that time he had worked closely with the editors of the *Papers of the Bibliographical Society of America*.

The 'Inquiry' is a 173-page paper, 75 pages of which are appendices in the form of comparative tables and lists of variants. The main part of the paper is a scholarly work of assessment and criticism. The style is both lively and dense. John Kidd, throughout the whole controversy, has been very readable, very provocative and often very entertaining. But here he comes to the very centre of his argument and opens virtually the whole of his armoury in the Joyce Wars for public judgment, the summary of which offered here is a brief and general one. In its broad outline the points are already familiar, though John Kidd offers them in what is undeniably 'scholarly' language and certainly not in tones which approach the 'polemical' attitude so often attacked by Hans Walter Gabler. Having established, in direct quotation from Gabler's Foreword of 1984, the objectives and the achievement, Kidd writes that, after his own investigations, he can report that the scholarship 'is not as thorough and accurate as once thought'. But almost immediately he goes on to assert that what has been done has become a major distraction from the real work needed, which is to edit *Ulysses* all over again.

The essential errors are, firstly, that the apparatus is faulty and that Gabler uses a jargon to explain his method which makes it extremely difficult for others to understand him. Secondly, for a 'critical' and 'synoptic' text, too many variants are omitted. Kidd numbers them in 'thousands'. Thirdly, the transcription of the Rosenbach Manuscript is seriously flawed because of too much reliance on facsimiles. Fourthly, without precedent, Gabler has invented 'levels' of text and a series of symbols to indicate them, 'in contrast with the usual way of recording what the documents actually say'. The symbols, according to Kidd, are so confusing that they repeatedly indicate two opposite situations surrounding the identical textual issue. Fifthly, the printing history of *Ulysses* followed by Gabler is incomplete and inaccurate. Sixthly, as a result of the use of a computer for the whole project, an entirely new level of computer-generated error has been introduced, compounded by imperfect proofreading of what was put into the computer in the first place. (How does one proofread a computer?) He concludes this preamble of errors by suggesting that, before anything else is attempted, the inconsistencies and contradictions listed in his paper, together with others still to be discovered, would have to be addressed. Even if the Gabler approach can be defended – and the point of Kidd's own paper was essentially to fulfil *half* a bargain, that the main opponents in the dispute submit criticisms and replies to the Tanselle Committee – it would leave a vast array of unanswered problems. Kidd then demonstrates his perspective as being well beyond the 'life' of *Ulysses: The Corrected Text* by offering readers to the paper an alternative tabulation of points, linked to the 1922 first edition, by page and line, so that the argument over an eventual re-editing of *Ulysses* can be related to alternative sources, 'whatever the fate of *The Corrected Text*'.

Kidd then deals with a major issue of claim and does so in a stimulating manner. Hans Walter Gabler had claimed, in the Foreword to the 1984 edition, that it was the first critical edition, not just of Ulysses, but of *any* Joyce work. This immediately raises doubts about the definition of the word 'critical' used by Gabler, since supposedly critical editions of *Dubliners*, *A Portrait*, *Chamber Music*, *Exiles* and indeed *Ulysses* itself had all been prepared during the previous two decades, and four of the five had been published. Is Gabler therefore saying that a critical edition is only really critical if it conforms to his own definition? And what is that definition? If it is completeness, then his own *Ulysses*, set against Kidd's list of errors, falls down. But no definition of a 'critical' edition is offered; and if anyone tried to edit *Ulysses* from the first edition, according to Gabler this would not, in any full sense, attain 'the quality or scope of a critical edition'.

Kidd recognises that this is aimed directly at himself, since his own view had increasingly moved towards the idea of using the 1922 *Ulysses* as copytext and in the interim bringing back the 1961 edition. This was his conclusion in the article which appeared in June 1988 in *The New York Review of Books*. He cites in support of this view in favour of the 1922 edition the considered judgments of Philip Gaskell, no less, and of Jerome McGann, both of whom are widely experienced in editorial theory and practice, in analytical bibliography and in literary history. Because of the losses of typescript and

manuscript material, as well as Joyce's known disposition for providing versions and fresh texts for friends or
for money, or for both, Kidd argues that the grounds for
displacing the 1922 edition are shaky.

In summary, Hans Walter Gabler is required by Kidd
to answer a substantial range of specific queries, but also
certain major points of principle or of categorical
assertion, including the dismissal of past editions of
Joyce's work and the ruling out of any possible future
alternative editions to the work which he has completed.
It is perhaps not altogether surprising that we still await
the reply to Kidd's paper.

This is but a start on the savage chronology that is
to follow in Kidd's paper in the form of argument after
argument against the thinking behind Gabler's editions
of *Ulysses*. Kidd next takes up the supposed deference of
Gabler to W. W. Greg, the great editorial theorist, whose
paper, 'The Rationale of Copy-Text', published by
another great authority in editing, Fredson Bowers, in
the 1950–51 issue of *Studies in Bibliography*, is the *only*
work on the theory of textual criticism cited by Gabler
in the 1984 *Ulysses*. From it Gabler deduces the idea of a
document text 'of highest overall authority'. Kidd then
shows that the phrase, though it sounds well, is actually
the opposite of what Greg argued, which is that there
can never be such a text of 'overall authority' and that
copytext work, by its very nature, requires the acceptance of a theory of divided authority among different
texts, some having ultimate 'authority' or approaching
it, in one specific area, others having it elsewhere. This
is particularly the case in the more mundane realm of
'accidentals', because editing deals with these often
minor variables, such as commas, exclamation marks,
the use of capitals, the use of italics, spellings, word-
elisions and the like, which are constantly changing from
edition to edition. This means, and is so argued by Greg,
that the copytext is really just a device against which

the variants from any number of editions can be compared and then edited in or not, as the case may be. The critical edition is about making the judgments as to whether a single 'accidental' (such as a comma or a particular spelling) should or should not be incorporated into the final edited version. The copytext is a starting point, a basic text, and obviously it is desirable that it should enjoy some status of value, that it be either the last version approved by the author, or indeed the first such approved version, as the 1922 edition of *Ulysses* undoubtedly was, with all its errors. But its status cannot be allowed to assume disproportionate strength. What Greg argued and what Gabler either appears to ignore or to suppress in his pursuit of the concept of 'highest overall authority' is the danger of what he (Greg) calls 'the tyranny of the copytext'. Gabler, in seeking the overall authority, seems to be running into precisely that danger and to be using a misrepresentation of Greg to endorse the move.

Even worse, in Kidd's considered judgment, is the argument he puts forward for a 'continuous manuscript text'. The concept is one of many 'novelties' in the 1984 edition. It derives, or appears to derive, from one of the more obscure and largely discredited textual theories applied to Shakespeare's works, a writer who is among the most difficult to edit. John Dover Wilson, once famous among university students for his book *What Happens in 'Hamlet'?*, put forward the belief that Shakespeare, as a result of changes, prompter's notes and emendations for specific situations or actors, created a kind of running text; E. K. Chambers then coined the expression 'continuous copy' to characterise what Wilson meant. Wilson disowned the idea, but it had currency for a time and seems to be the source for Gabler's own coinage of a 'continuous manuscript text' for *Ulysses*. The argument runs in circles and these then become convoluted into ellipses as Gabler himself, after the publication of the 1984 *Ulysses*, told

McGann that he would like to designate his base texts 'assembly texts' for the 'continuous manuscript text'! In summary, the use of the term copytext to describe a continuous manuscript text, which only exists in a computer, is to redefine the concept of copytext as editors had understood it since the editing principles of Greg and Bowers were adumbrated in the 1950s.

It would seem, above all, that the logical ordering of the work of editing *Ulysses*, not inappropriately perhaps, has been turned on its head. Where one would expect the logical sequence to be in accordance with some kind of textbook approach – first select your copytext, then edit the work – the editing process itself becomes part of the selection of the method of doing the work. Although the descriptions of how this operates become very dense indeed when there are several options to choose from, they border on the incomprehensible when the options need to be inferred. There are occasions, Gabler claims, and is so quoted by Kidd, where 'the elements of the continuous manuscript text pertaining to the missing documents must be established by inference, and thus critically, from the extant ones'. Then, in working on this inferred version, different 'levels' of revision are applied with heavy dependence on the editor's critical judgment or powers of deduction in doing the work.

If this sounds complicated, the giving of examples which further undermine its working capacities as a system is even more so. Kidd offers two, both in verse, the first being Lenehan's limerick from the 'Aeolus' episode, about the ponderous pundit, McHugh, the second being the more subtle blank verse of Stephen Dedalus in the 'Scylla and Charybdis' episode. The first pivots upon substituting 'As' for 'Since', the second upon 'But that' for 'That', both changes coming at the beginning of lines two and three respectively in the verse passages. Both raise questions about how the editor worked out his priorities, since no evidence is given and since the copytext, at this point, is open to inference and not secure. This relates to one of John Kidd's basic objections to Hans Walter Gabler's judgment over the chronology of corrections, as between the Rosenbach and other typescript sources. Differences cannot be given an order in time, unless the differences are in the form of alterations to the Rosenbach, which imply later correction than do other typescripts. However, unless the typescripts are 'clearly in error' or 'incomplete', no conjecture about Rosenbach revisions taking precedence is reliable.

Kidd is not condemning, out of hand, the approach adopted by Gabler, in attempting to create a 'continuous manuscript text'. He is fully aware of the extreme complexity of the editing challenge of the work and is prepared – as every scholar has to be in the circumstances – to accept the theory and pursue it to as clear an understanding as possible. This is done. Kidd does enter the ruined city from which the work itself has been extracted, and considers all the actions and engagements. But straightaway he raises fundamental scholarly questions about evidence. In a situation fraught with so many alternatives, the evidence becomes crucial. Once it is missing, the debate is opened up and has to be pursued. From the start it was Kidd's argument that, far from the debate taking place, the very need for it was denied, strenuously and forcefully, and those with control over the project went ahead with Gabler's conclusions. This meant that the unpicking inevitably became a process of profound confrontation, since the finished work, in its final trade form, for mass, worldwide sales, with all the investment costs involved, together with the potential humiliation and discrediting, was at stake.

The other issue of lasting controversy, already mentioned in general terms, concerns the use of facsimile as against direct reference on all changes to the original. We are face to face here with the fruits and the penalties of avid collecting of Joyce material in the 1940s and earlier, by Joyce scholars and enthusiasts, and their deposit – with some notable exceptions – in American libraries. Imagine 5,000 equivalents of the *crème de la crème*, or *crème de la crème*, issue, which have surfaced during the process of creating a continuous manuscript text and have now to be checked, not just in one place, but in several, against precious originals for the visiting of which detailed travel plans have to be made and time assigned. Five thousand is actually a modest count. Whom does one send? Is this the work of an amanuensis, a latter-day editor's equivalent of Frank Budgen? Can it be done by the computer-epoch equivalent of one of Joyce's typists? Or must it be the creator himself? Gabler was fully aware of the problem and had been since 1977, as Kidd points out, when he reviewed the Rosenbach facsimile for *Library*, the scholarly periodical dealing with bibliographical and other book-related matters. There, he said that, despite the high quality of the photography used in making the facsimile, there is undoubtedly a loss over such subtleties as the pressure of pen and pencil, and the colours of the markings. Yet, as Kidd goes on to add, the 1984 edition does not contain a record of these colours, which are important, nor of the use of pencil or pen, whichever it is.

The margin of error is actually much worse, since certain published details which depend on direct inspection of the manuscript but become illegible in the facsimile, are overlooked. We have an erasure of the word 'marmalade', the substitution of the word 'jam' and finally the choice of the word 'honey' to appear on the breakfast table, in Sandycove Tower, when Stephen, Buck Mulligan and Haines eventually sit down to their milkless tea – what sort of a kip is this? – and Haines sees the woman coming up with the precious liquid, a preamble to the book's first obscenity, about Mrs Cahill – 'Begob, ma'am, God send you don't make them in the one pot.' The 1984 edition should, in its full synoptic apparatus, have given the erased, but faintly legible alternative readings. Instead, the symbols indicate illegible readings. Thus, as Kidd declares – using italics to indicate a rare expression of emotional distaste – 'A cardinal rule of critical editing – *Check all transcriptions against originals* – was not observed.'

Kidd spent two days at the Rosenbach Museum in 1986 and came up with many errors. They are designed, he claims, simply to demonstrate the nature and range of possible mistakes. Some weeks in Philadelphia would be required to produce a full errata list. Obviously even longer was needed to create the structure of the 'continuous manuscript text' in the first place. It was not given. Kidd assembles categories of problems deriving from the use of facsimile readings rather than direct manuscript readings. There are spurious erasures and undetected erasures; there are transcription problems; there are folds in the paper, which obscure parts of words and on which Gabler was eloquently critical in originally writing about the facsimile, but which are never mentioned in the 1984 edition; there are even differently textured papers used, a leaf in the 'Sirens' episode being 'waxier' than the rest, though this is not recorded and the paper changes not analysed.

A major critical point to emerge concerns the facility with which scholars might enter the argument and make sensible contributions. Kidd points out, in the context of the Rosenbach Manuscript, that its collation by Clive Driver is not set side by side with the transcriptions made from the facsimile by his own team of workers. The obvious 'advantage', in the polemical sense, is that other scholars would have to do their own collating over a period of months, in order to be equipped to enter the debate and make any serious contribution to it. The disadvantage to Gabler, however, is that he does not have the mechanism for checking his own or Driver's annotations and collations against the original. So the differences between himself and Driver remain indeterminate as to whether they are real or a product of the facsimile. Does this mean that every word has to be checked against the original? Well, yes; that is what editing is about.

Kidd is at pains to prove that Gabler set up an extremely complex editorial theory, based on a clear perception of the myriad problems which Joyce had created for any editor, but that he then did not observe the rules which were either implicit or explicit in that theory. The practice took short cuts which are repeatedly shown to be unacceptable. Furthermore, Kidd demonstrates that Gabler's method, by definition, muddied the stream and made any attempt to unravel the faults in the system extremely difficult. In reality, there were few people in the whole world competent to undertake a detailed analysis and critique of the work. A majority of these were involved in it, in one way or another. Others were either too old, too tired, too lazy, dead, sick, or too frightened of the very serious implications which they saw in challenging something which so clearly had the Joyce establishment firmly behind it to engage in the absolutely fundamental stripping down of the machinery to all its individual parts in order to discover what was wrong with it. It is to Kidd's enormous credit that he engaged in the unscrambling processes; and it is hardly surprising that it took him until December 1988 to transform a summary of evidence against most of the claims made for the Gabler edition into a fully reasoned scholarly paper. He goes back, in fact, to his *New York Review of Books* article, taking up again the point made about it by Gabler, that it relied on only a handful of examples, and Kidd then furnishes forth 'two hundred examples of emendations' which relate to the 13 classes listed in the June 1988 article.

Kidd also deals in detail with the listing of editions of *Ulysses* at page 1855, in Volume Three of the 1984 edition, and shows Gabler to have been substantially inadequate in his provision of bibliographical information. Gabler fails to give the publisher of the Rosenbach, fails to indicate that the third volume is a reduced and annotated facsimile of the 1922 first edition of *Ulysses*, and fails to list two other important facsimile reprints, of *The Little Review* and *The Egoist* episodes, which, in December 1988 at least, were still available from the Kraus Reprint Corporation in New York. This not only means that important extant sources are not listed, but it is not made clear whether the consideration of the parts published serially was done with the fragile originals or with the Kraus reprints.

On the first edition of *Ulysses* and its early impressions, published between February 1922 and December 1925, Gabler made mistakes over the incorporation of errata and apparently relied on hearsay about the changes from errata slip to actual text. Other textual variants are not mentioned and there are misquotations. On *each* of Gabler's entries in the bibliography of editions of *Ulysses*, of which there are ten, Kidd discovers and details errors (usually in the plural), some of which are extensive and at least one is of considerable interest. This concerns the Matisse-illustrated edition of 1935, published for the Limited Editions Club, of New York, and carrying an Introduction by Stuart Gilbert, who supervised it. Since the edition was produced in Joyce's lifetime and provoked correspondence between the writer, the publisher, George Macy, Paul Léon and of course Gilbert as well, it constitutes an important document in the history of *Ulysses* and a first-hand resource for editing. Collation of it with other editions and with the correspondence reveals a number of changes, briefly outlined by Kidd. But the devastating fact about the edition is that it was not examined for the 1984 edition of *Ulysses* (according to Hans Walter Gabler's own listing of those editions that were). As Kidd concludes on this item: 'It was probably unwise of the 1984 editors to overrule Joyce's manuscripts a hundred times by adopting the 1932 readings edited by Gilbert [in the Hamburg, Odyssey Press edition] without investigating his role in the 1935 edition.'

Gabler's listing of editions concludes with the single line: 'The present edition is the eleventh edition of *Ulysses*.' This, says Kidd, is the least forgivable among the innumerable errors, from a bibliographer's point of view. Seven typesettings of the book were ignored. One of the hardest of the criticisms originally levelled at Kidd, certainly for Kidd to treat objectively, and really for all Joyceans, despite their feeling that he was somehow 'unmannerly', was that Kidd was an amateur, Gabler a professional. While bibliography is neither the beginning nor the end of editing, it occupies a crucial position in the process. Gabler's professionalism is quite evidently under serious question in this devastating analysis of factual inaccuracies over the editions of the work.

From this point to the end of 'An Inquiry into *Ulysses: The Corrected Text*', Kidd deals in table form with the different categories of error which he has already cited. With the publication of the paper, admittedly too late for the University of Miami conference, he had delivered the goods. He had placed on the table his part of the bargain, and was prepared to sit back and wait for Gabler's reply. Possibly a little smugly? John Kidd plays a hard game and his journey to this point had been uphill most of the way. Unforeseen interruptions, however, were looming ahead of him. The simple rules laid down at the time of his completion of the critique were about to be overthrown.

TWELVE

Anthony Burgess Takes Back His Words

'I mean, as an editor one owes more ultimately to
the intention of the text than the intention of the
author.'

Hans Walter Gabler to Robin Bates in interview, 1989

T HE TANSELLE COMMITTEE never met, but it did
continue in existence for well over a year. The
differences which undermined its authority were
between Thomas Tanselle, the chairman, and Jason
Epstein, head of the publishing firm of Random House.
They had nothing to do with the *Ulysses* controversy,
but derived from a series of rows between Epstein in his
capacity as a board member and treasurer of The Library
of America, and Thomas Tanselle, also a board member.
Epstein, who was replaced as treasurer, and eventually
voted off the board altogether, took exception to the role
played by Tanselle in this. The differences between the
two men led to the disbanding of the committee. There
was in fact little need for the committee to meet, even
after it had received John Kidd's substantive set of criticisms of the 1984 *Ulysses*, contained in 'An Inquiry into
Ulysses: The Corrected Text'. This paper realistically
meant a response from Gabler. Until this came the criticisms contained in it, which were an elaboration in detail

of all the general attacks Kidd had made in various forms, simply rested there as a demonstration of error unanswered.

But what if Gabler refused to answer? There was absolutely nothing that anyone could do. There were at least indications that this would be his way of tackling the insuperable problem of addressing a mass of criticism at several different levels. Many of them attacked the fundamental principles on which his editing has been based. Many demonstrated quite dreadful lapses, such as getting the editions wrong. If one goes back to the first line of Gabler's 1985 reply to Kidd, some flavour of his intellectual attitude may be perceived: 'A defence . . . is not required.' If one goes to the end of that reply, something of his stern, Miltonic disdain can be read: 'I wish I had the privilege of answering a worthier challenge.' No admission by Gabler in the intervening years had done more than modify very slightly the firm resolve against accepting the errors and trying to work out a means of incorporating them in a further revised edition – at least, *formally* incorporating them. Informally, without any agreement or discussion, many of the changes which were put forward as errors by John Kidd between the publication of the 1984 and 1986 editions appeared in the latter; but they were unacknowledged.

To admit, to accept, to agree, to resolve and to declare the help, involvement and justice of the critical case against the editions: Gabler's character did not permit of this approach. Circumstance did not require it. The reality of the situation was that *Ulysses: The Corrected Text* was selling worldwide in a variety of different editions. It was the recommended text on many university courses. It had reactivated the interest of new generations in the reading of Joyce, and particularly of *Ulysses*, and it had been tied in with the revised editions of a number of the basic critical works. Though it was not available in time for Richard Ellmann to make the necess-

ary changes to the 1982 revised edition of his biography
of Joyce, switching from the 1961 *Ulysses* to the 1984
Ulysses as his version for reference and quotation, he did
pay tribute in the new set of acknowledgements to Dr
Hans Walter Gabler, with whom at that stage he was
already involved.

Other publishing changes which bear on the controversy also took place in 1990. In the spring of that year,
Garland Publishing announced that it would allow the
critical edition to go out of print, once it had run its
course. This announcement coincided with the advent
of another figure in the drama, Robin Bates, who had
interviewed the president of Garland, Gavin Borden, the
previous September (1989), when he was working on an
article about the Joyce Wars, subsequently published in
The Smithsonian in March 1990. Borden had been quite
categorical: 'Our book has run its course,' he told Bates.
'It will not be revised. We are not going to reprint it.'
Sales at the time when he was interviewed by Bates were
running at 50 sets a year and the question of revising it
was inevitably linked to a reprint. 'You would have to
go back and change all of Gabler's programming,' Borden
said to Bates. 'It would be an exercise in madness and
stupidity.' Borden, however, soon changed his mind. In
the *New York Times* of 28 June 1990, in a story about the
reissuing by Random House of the 1961 edition of *Ulysses*
as an alternative choice to *Ulysses: The Corrected Text*,
it was also reported that the three-volume 1984 *Ulysses*
was *now* going to be *kept* in print. Robin Bates wrote to
the newspaper to point out that the 'madness and stupidity' was a matter of confusion as well, since the whole
point of the corrections which had been identified as
either needing to be done or having been done were
mainly John Kidd's proposed changes and not Hans
Walter Gabler's. So whose editions were they, anyway?

Like the present writer, Robin Bates came to the debate
at a relatively late stage, picking up on it with John

Kidd's *New York Review of Books* article of June 1988. He responded as a journalist would, by following up the story. After his *Smithsonian* piece in March 1990, he published later in the same year, in the special issue of *Studies in the Novel* devoted to *Ulysses*, a much more detailed article, 'Reflections on the Kidd Era', which included detailed records of his interviews with Hans Walter Gabler, Clive Hart, Hugh Kenner and Jason Epstein.

Bates interviewed Gabler and tackled with him the matter of the corrections made in the 1986 edition, and apparently based on Kidd's listing of errors. Initially, Gabler declined to be interviewed at all. Then he agreed in September 1989 to discuss issues up to but not including 'An Inquiry into *Ulysses: The Corrected Text*', Kidd's paper for the Bibliographical Society of America. Gabler denied that *any* of the corrections made in the 1986 edition came *solely* from John Kidd. Gabler attributed them to Charles Peake, a Joyce scholar who was then dead and unable to comment or confirm, and an unnamed member of an audience at Columbia University, who subsequently turned out to be a friend of John Kidd's who had picked up the reference to a full-stop after 'ashpit', in the Molly Bloom soliloquy, from David Remnick's *Washington Post* article, and had put it to Gabler, little knowing how it might be used, or not be credited!

Robin Bates also cross-questioned Gabler quite closely on the extent to which he honoured the requirements of the Center for Scholarly Editions, where Dr Jo Ann Boydston (a member of the Tanselle Committee and therefore one of the few people to whom Gabler was responsible in replying to Kidd's paper), had insisted to Bates that it was an editor's responsibility to look at every edition and every printing published during a writer's lifetime, and for some period after his or her death, since authorised changes might be discovered therein. Had Gabler fulfilled this requirement? He agreed that he had not, in the case of the Matisse edition. He went on, in response to further questioning, to accept that other printings had not been collated, but justified this on the grounds that *his* edition was one established from manuscript sources, rather than from a copytext source. He would, he said, be taking it up in his statement to the Tanselle Committee, in response to Kidd's criticisms.

Robin Bates dealt with three other matters in his interview with Gabler: the use of facsimiles, the checking of proper names – notably the 'Harry Thrift' error, admitted by Gabler, though perhaps in a manner that seems now a bit parsimonious – and the placing of the dashes before lines of dialogue. On facsimiles, for the first time in the whole controversy and after four years of argument, Gabler admitted that he had not collated *either* the Rosenbach Manuscript *or* the other manuscript sources fully. 'We developed an intricate system of marking things that needed checking and we were quite liberal in doing these markings and I had extended opportunities on three occasions to work in all the libraries that held the original documents and went both for those marked places and for a general check of the original documents.' Gabler admitted that he checked but did not collate. The situation was clear-cut. Dr Boydston maintained on this a standard which was exigent: while transcriptions could be made and indeed checked against facsimile, a full collation between text and original was an essential requirement. It had not been done. Gabler admitted that it had not been done. It was sufficient, according to Bates, 'to condemn the Gabler *Ulysses* in the eyes of the Tanselle Committee'.

The second category, which Bates referred to as 'a minor point', was the one covering the changing of proper names, notably Thrift into 'Shrift', which Kidd attributed to the use of facsimile and which was one of several such changes, affecting not only persons, but places as well. In the cycle race with Harry Thrift were several other riders, some of whom in the original are correctly spelled, according to the records of the race itself, but two are not. Green and Adderly, both of whom should have an extra 'e' in their names – Greene and Adderley. This has nothing to do with the records, but with the errors introduced by Frank Budgen in transcribing for James Joyce. But whereas Gabler's mistake on Thrift is obvious and stemmed from the misreading of the facsimile, because he did not check the historical record he failed to pick up the correct spelling of the other two names and the mistake made by Budgen. He defended these two additional errors in the single sentence in which, with 'Shrift', they are contained, on the grounds that the work is a work of fiction and the names, even if derived from real people, are fictional. Yet, as Bates also pointed out, Gabler corrected Joyce's misspelling of the factually correct name of Lansdowne Road (Joyce spelled it 'Landsdowne'), and justified the apparent contradiction by distinguishing between persons and places. Lansdowne Road, Gabler claimed, was 'an outside referent'.

Controversy has always surrounded Gabler's placing of the dashes which precede direct speech in *Ulysses*. In the first edition and all subsequent editions known to Joyce, the dash is indented. In Gabler's two editions it is set flush with the margin. Gabler explained this to Bates by telling him about the 'consciousness of the status of dialogue' revealed by Joyce's manuscript and how the dashes, set in the way he had ordered them to be set, made it possible for the reader to appreciate this. It was Gabler's belief that Joyce intended speech and narrative to run together, and was perhaps deflected in achieving this aim by traditional typesetting procedures, which gave an indent to the dash preceding direct speech, turning that speech effectively into a new paragraph. But it is only theoretically what Joyce may have intended. In his manuscript version, Joyce actually placed the dash in the margin. This of course would have made for massive typographical problems, even with computer-setting. In pursuing the line taken in *Ulysses: The Corrected Text*, Gabler claimed not only to be rendering a characteristic of Joycean prose, but a fundamental characteristic of Joyce's 'narrative stance'. These 'views' are set by Bates in his questioning against the fact of Joyce indenting the dashes not just in *Ulysses* but in *Finnegans Wake* as well. To which Gabler responded with a remarkable expression of priority: 'I mean, as an editor one owes more ultimately to the intention of the text than the intention of the author.' Bates was 'flabbergasted' by this single expression of an approach to the priorities of editing Joyce which put the editor above the author.

Bates interviewed Clive Hart and Hugh Kenner, and spoke with both Thomas Tanselle and Jason Epstein, in an effort to piece together the reasoning behind the decision to disband the committee. The interview with Clive Hart was 'lively', in Robin Bates's word, but frustrating as well, since Hart declined to give his side of the events revealed in Richard Ellmann's papers at the University of Tulsa, and covered by Charles Rossman in his letter to the *TLS* and his article in *The New York Review of Books*. At the same time Hart claimed that the published account was 'highly fictionalised'. On some matters Clive Hart's view could be described as bizarre; he answered Bates's outline of the somewhat odd fact that Ellmann had twice expressed reservations about Gabler's command of English, particularly the idiomatic Dublin English supposedly of 1904 as used by James Joyce in *Ulysses*, by suggesting that this limitation might be 'precisely what you need in such a case'. Clive Hart's view of the revelations made by Rossman, as expressed to Bates, was that they were 'sensationalist literary history', which he did not like or think helpful, since it would feed a prurient interest. A comparably tendentious view was taken of the interpretation of the words 'resign' and 'rejoin', in the context again of the Rossman discoveries.

Hart and Gaskell did not rejoin, but allowed their names to 'go along' and not to dissociate publicly. 'So did you *stay* resigned?' a somewhat puzzled Robin Bates asked. Having denied any 'formal' resignation (begging the question as to what an informal resignation might be), Clive Hart then said to Bates: 'I really oughtn't to go into this. What has been said in the press is probably as much as needs to be said about it. The slant is wrong in all the reports I have seen of it.'

The Kenner interview, as reported by Bates, is only of marginal interest and seems to underline quite strongly the degree to which computer technology, as Kenner knew and grasped it in April 1980 when he wrote his article in *Harper's*, 'The Computerised *Ulysses*', had advanced beyond anything Kenner understood. It seems that the details and issues of the debate had also moved beyond Hugh Kenner, and become far more contentious and bitter than suited him. But the interview with Epstein was a different matter altogether.

In fact, Epstein was not interviewed by Bates, in the accepted sense of the term. He declined, twice. Then, through the editor of *The Smithsonian*, Tim Foote, Robin Bates heard that Epstein had 'dissociated himself' from the Tanselle Committee. Bates then rang Epstein and had a telephone conversation with him, which he reported verbatim in his article. In it Epstein referred Bates to Tanselle for an explanation of the meaning of 'dissociate', since the committee, as Bates understood it, *was* Epstein's committee. Epstein, however, claimed that it was Tanselle's committee and that 'I told him I was no longer interested in the committee's findings'. This left the textual issue unresolved and many people bewildered about what to do. Epstein concluded the exchange by telling Bates: 'I no longer know what to think. I am trying to find out.'

The 'ownership' of the committee is not entirely amenable to Epstein's interpretation, when he gave it to Tanselle. It was originally a Random House committee, but, if we recall the letter written by the then Trustees of the James Joyce Estate, Clive Hart and Peter du Sautoy, to *The New York Review of Books* in January 1989, the committee was an advisory group with which the Estate had agreed to work. Moreover, the Trustees would be directly involved in the discussions, once both Kidd and Gabler had filed their arguments and responses to each other. The Trustees claimed that neither the Estate nor the publishers would comment until that work was complete. Yet here, apparently, was unilateral action in disbanding the committee and a breaching of the vows to silence made just a year earlier. Clearly, the edifice of revision was crumbling.

These circumstances – essentially a stalemate – prevailed from then on. In March 1990, the Tanselle Committee was formally disbanded. It had not received any response from Hans Walter Gabler; nor has the James Joyce Estate; nor have individuals mentioned in this book.

My own writing on the matter dates from June 1988 and concentrates mainly, though not exclusively, on the question of copyright. In an article in *The Irish Independent* headed 'The scandal of *Ulysses*: How an Irish publisher could make a fortune in 1992', I related the end of the period of copyright in James Joyce's work to the 'harmonisation' within the European Community on 1 January 1992 and suggested Irish publishers should consider bringing out *Ulysses* in a version based on an alternative to *Ulysses: The Corrected Text*. The arguments were largely based on John Kidd's article in *The New York Review of Books*, predicting that the key issue was copyright and that the 'show' encompassed by the title *The Scandal of 'Ulysses'* was likely to run to the end of the century. I reported again in December, confirming from the evidence in the Ellmann papers, as reported by Rossman, that copyright was indeed a central issue and was certainly a motivation with the James Joyce Estate. I then had occasion to follow up the work done during 1988 when, in June 1990, I was invited to cover the 12th International Symposium of the James Joyce Foundation in Monte Carlo and to make a film based on the proceedings. In the event, two films were made. The first, 'The Scandal of *Ulysses*', was shown by Radio Telefis Eireann on 2 February 1991, the anniversary of Joyce's birth. The second, 'Images of Joyce', shown in the early summer.

The conference topic, arranged by George Sandulescu, of the Princess Grace Irish Library, was itself called 'Images of Joyce'. It was a comfortable title, all-embracing, and it had a visual accompaniment, in the form of a Louis le Brocquy 'reconstructed head' of Joyce, one of a number in paint, watercolour and monochrome done by this distinguished Irish artist. Indeed, since the 1960s, when he first addressed, in the context of Samuel Beckett, the problem of Irish writers and how their images can be deployed by the painter, he had been reconstructing the heads of Yeats, Beckett and Joyce. The Symposium had a stronger than usual Irish presence, with several Dublin academics, with an Irish dramatic presentation of *Finnegans Wake* and with Anne Yeats becoming something of a star of the week, on two counts. The first had nothing directly to do with Joyce. The conference had, as one of its additional events, an exhibition of paintings by Jack Yeats, principally from the Michael Smurfit Collection. Anne Yeats's impact among participants was due to her simple, straightforward description of the character of her uncle, the painter, given as one of the plenary sessions. It was singular for the rounded and moving picture she gave of his complex and subtle personality. The second was moderately controversial: a rejection by her, to his face, of Stephen Joyce's unworthy aspersions cast on her absent brother, Michael Yeats, as someone who was in the business of selling family documents. She pointed out that, whatever may have been the monetary terms under which Joyce documents made their way into the various institutions in which they now rested, the Yeats family had given the majority of family papers, with a single notable exception, to Trinity College in Dublin. 'The Irish' at the conference – the inverted commas, like a class of error in *Ulysses*, write themselves into the sentence – were pervasive in other ways, even contributing a stimulating evening of Irish dancing from the Irish-American Trinity Dance Academy of Wisconsin.

The major speakers were advertised as Anthony Burgess, Klaus Reichert, Anne Yeats, Sandra Gilbert, Stephen James Joyce, Karen Lawrence and Claude Gaignebet. The distinguished Joyce scholars – a somewhat different listing – included Hugh Kenner, Hans Walter Gabler, Morris Beja (the then president of the foundation), Michael Groden, Bernard Benstock, Thomas Staley, Clive Hart and many, many others. John Kidd was not present. He has major reservations about such conferences. He was still waiting for a reply from Gabler to his criticisms and it might have seemed a little insensitive to have turned up as a normal paying delegate with no role other than to listen to papers on Joyce about subjects on which he was powerfully informed anyway.

Attending as a normal, fee-paying delegate was the only option he had. If there had been an invitation to come at the foundation's expense – which was the basis for the key speakers – he would undoubtedly have considered this and probably accepted, preparing a suitable paper to move things forward a bit. Even more would this have been the case had there been a single session focused upon his criticisms and the unresolved situation that still prevailed over them. It would have put him in the position of being able to further, in a formal way, his arguments about the editions of *Ulysses*, which were advancing anyway. But this option was not open to him and he did not attend. Indeed, the view of the conference organisers and the view of the hosts to the conference, the Director George Sandulescu and the staff of the Princess Grace Irish Library, backed by the administration of the Principality, was that the issue of the editing of *Ulysses* was 'closed'. This may have been true, in the aftermath, but the conference did address the problem and in one session the argument became heated. Charles Rossman organised and chaired a session on the Friday, 15 June, entitled 'Editing Joyce and Lawrence: Principles and Problems'. Rossman himself is a D. H. Lawrence scholar, but apart from him, none of the Lawrenceans turned up and the session was devoted entirely to Joyce. Three speakers attacked aspects of Gabler's edition. Rossman himself was critical of the flush-left setting of the dashes in *Ulysses*; Ira Nadel was critical of the ending of the 'Circe' episode; Susan Sutcliff Brown attacked Gabler's treatment of numbers in the text. Gabler joined the session, together with Wolfhard Steppe and Claus Melchior, and became very angry, keeping the microphone beyond the allotted time for floor speakers, in order to argue extensively against what had been said. There was also a working session presided over by George Sandulescu in the format of what is called 'a living book review', where a title is examined by a panel and by speakers from the floor. The book in question was *Ulysses: A Review of Three Texts*, by Philip Gaskell and Clive Hart, and the session was chaired by Sandulescu, who had Hans Walter Gabler on his panel, together with one of his two principal editorial assistants, Wolfhard Steppe. This was fairly pedestrian stuff: no fireworks, no aggression, no real dispute and certainly no references to John Kidd. The extraordinary contrast between institutional indifference – the *Ulysses* issue is 'closed' – and the intense interest of individuals was readily apparent in the discussions between sessions, and in the private meals and debates which included constant speculations over the *Ulysses* controversy.

The conference, as is normal for these biennial meetings, which usually involve between 300–400 people, had a programme which included special plenary sessions in the main auditorium of the new Monte Carlo Conference Centre, with all the other meetings taking place in smaller conference rooms. None of the smaller meetings conflicted with the plenary sessions, which were the occasions for the 'Major Speakers' to give their addresses.

Anthony Burgess, a richly fluent public speaker, with a great deal to say about James Joyce and a fair amount about himself, opened the proceedings with a witty introductory speech on himself and Joyce as novelists. The title was 'Joyce as Novelist'. It was given in the presence of Princess Caroline and Prince Albert. It was followed, in subsequent plenary sessions, by general papers or question-and-answer encounters, one of which had the faintly embarrassing title 'Why Are We Here? The Source of Joyce's Fascination'. No clear answer emerged.

The only plenary session which came anywhere near addressing the controversy as such was when Clive Hart and Stephen James Joyce made themselves available for questions, and did address some of the issues surrounding the *Ulysses* controversy, notably the role played by the Estate and the reasons for the short period allowed for scholarly debate between the 1984 and the 1986 editions of the book. Stephen James Joyce professed to know little of the detail about the Estate's decisions. He said that it was his understanding that the initiative for the edition came from Gabler and that the pressures to go ahead with the 1986 edition came from the publishers. He did not mention that this was because a reprint of *Ulysses* was required anyway. He alluded to none of the points which had come out in the correspondence of 1988, articles published since then, the Tanselle Committee's unfinished business or the criticisms contained in John Kidd's substantive article. There was no special reason why he should. The pressure was simply not there, in the audience, to provoke discussion or interrogation on the single most controversial event to have plagued Joyce scholarship in living memory. Yet here was the principal beneficiary of the James Joyce Estate, sitting on a platform beside the man who had recently become the Sole Trustee of that Estate and available to tell the world of Joyce scholarship what the position was.

I interviewed a number of participants. These included Hans Walter Gabler, Clive Hart, Charles Rossman, Anthony Burgess, Michael Groden, Hugh Kenner, Fritz Senn, Morris Beja, Augustine Martin and David Norris. There were background discussions with many others, with a view to forming a comprehensive picture of the current situation and the likelihood of its resolution, together with an examination of the options. The interviews all included questions about the controversy over *Ulysses*, but also dealt with broader issues of Joyce scholarship. They did not focus in detail on the conference plenary sessions for reasons which may be obvious when the titles for these are considered: 'Language of Economy and Economies of Language', 'Virginia Woolf, James Joyce, and the History of the Future'.

The programme for the conference certainly implied a hidden agenda, since it included no session directly related to the major controversy about which virtually all Joyceans in attendance expressed interest or concern. It was a key element in the majority of interviews to bring this hidden agenda to the surface. On this point, all those interviewed, including Hans Walter Gabler, spoke freely and without reservation. One of the notable things to emerge was that remarkably few of the delegates seemed to understand the copyright situation. Even fewer were familiar with, or interested in, the contractual relationships between the copyright owner and the publishers. Such matters are not, it seems, the stuff of scholarship. They are peripheral, not central. There is a faint whiff of commercialism in the expression of any interest

there, much the same as the reservation felt at different times by participants in the controversy that journalism was being used as an unfair weapon in the Joyce Wars, bringing unwarranted publicity to what should be a refined, scholarly debate, essentially private.

On the issue of copyright, there was a confused impression that somehow *Ulysses* itself had obtained a new copyright and was therefore 'secure' in the Gabler version. The problem was therefore perceived as one that had to be sorted out within that constraint. This devolved upon the James Joyce Estate and Clive Hart, who had remarkably little to say about the problem in the plenary session given by himself and Stephen James Joyce. The debate overall was seen by most scholars present in Monte Carlo as having run its course. There was no possibility of reconciliation between the conflicting parties. All that could be said had been said. Whatever needed to be done lay within the remit of the Estate, which had control for the present over the works of the writer. It seemed to register with very few participants just how short the time was before that control, under copyright law, would begin to evaporate.

Hans Walter Gabler defended his own position in a spirited way, indicating once again that, in his belief, there was really no serious case to answer. Gabler has in fact not been much interviewed in connection with the controversy, so that any indication of his position has been gauged generally from his conference papers. At the Monte Carlo symposium, in answer to questions, he outlined the development of the editing of *Ulysses*. This began with his original drafting of the project and its submission to the James Joyce Estate, together with the seeking of the agreement of the American and British publishers who had the sole right to publish the book. This was necessary, he said, because the scholarly project, from its inception, was designed to culminate in a published edition. Gabler claimed that the Estate was hesitant and that Peter du Sautoy, in an early meeting, had taken the position that an author 'entrusts his text to a publisher and a publisher has no right to change it'. Gabler's response was to point out the state of the text and put it to the Trustee that he had a duty to do something about this. Before agreeing, according to Gabler, du Sautoy took advice. That was how the project came into being.

As far as the criticisms were concerned, Gabler's view was essentially that 'we've had a conglomeration of statements, of individual and partly unconnected facts, of half-reported evidence from our edition, and of half-thought theoretical approaches to editing that we've got to work through and to respond to, or perhaps simply to include and incorporate into, what I would like to [do], a critique of our edition.' Gabler said that he believed the conference in Miami had clarified matters. 'I felt for a time that some unease had been caused by the polemical attacks we're all aware of. I feel very confident. Well, for example, an event like a two-and-a-half day conference on these issues in the University of Miami a year and a half ago contributed to setting the sight lines right again.'

In summarising the present position, Gabler felt ready to re-evaluate things: 'I was the editor. I finished the work six years ago. I feel about ready to look at it from a distance, to evaluate rather than defend it. I've been very much reassured about the principles and the solutions. People understand what the issues are. I have become aware through the spin-offs of the polemical confrontation.' He appealed to a body of support which might reasonably have been seen as somewhat depleted: 'It's up to those who defended my work in the first place to stand by it.' He concluded: 'The replies will come. They will be specific. They will be to the point, as I hope for the most part they have been. I do not feel that a disaster has occurred. I do not feel that a catastrophe has broken in upon us. On the contrary, there have been enormous increases in interest, in understanding, in communication about the basis of all literary culture, the text and the works themselves.'

Gabler was supported in his arguments by Michael Groden, who spoke of always having had 'a great deal of confidence in Gabler's achievement, and thorough faith and confidence in the methods he has used. I've always seen the controversy with some scepticism. There is a profound difference in their understanding about how the book should be edited.' His view was that *Ulysses: The Corrected Text* 'doesn't need to be rethought. It needs to be corrected in about 100 places.' Nevertheless, he did express the belief that there would be a proliferation of texts and they could be different in several ways. They would take time, because of the editing problems, but he saw them as an inevitable outcome of the controversy.

Several of those present at the conference were not directly committed to either side in the controversy and made interesting judgments about the way it had progressed. David Norris, a lecturer on Joyce and his work at Trinity College, Dublin, and one of those who had attended not only the 1985 conference in Monaco but also the University of Miami conference and several other Joyce conferences, saw irreconcilable differences between Gabler and Kidd. He rated John Kidd 'magisterial' in his presentation of the arguments and felt that Gabler 'must be embarrassed by it [the controversy] because he's been challenged by a young scholar . . . with a considerable variety of examinations of locations in the text where he takes a different view from Gabler'.

Fritz Senn expressed regret about the direction and tone of the controversy. It was strident, he said, and this attracted newspaper interest, polarising and distorting the disagreements. 'This made it difficult for any of us to join the battle because it looked like taking sides. That is how it went wrong.' Senn thought that John Kidd's character made the events more difficult to ameliorate.

'John Kidd, a young, devoted, gifted, also somewhat flamboyant, not exactly self-belittling person ... brought it out into the open, and incidentally made headlines.' But Senn also believed that too much had been changed by Gabler. 'It was only normal. It's just possible, in case of doubt, that you would probably argue for *more* changes. If anything, too many principles were applied too rigidly.'

Part of the bewilderment about the later venom in the argument resulted from the fact, revealed by Carol Shloss, who was present for the occasion, that Gabler had originally been something of a mentor to John Kidd. They had first met in Dublin during a session on numerology, where Gabler had been the only academic fully able to grasp a paper given by Kidd on sequences of numbers and their relationship to the placement of words on the page. Kidd at that time was totally unknown. Subsequently, Gabler had tried to get for Kidd an academic fellowship.

Clive Hart's position at the 1990 Monte Carlo conference was perhaps the strangest of all. By the time it took place he had not only joined Peter du Sautoy as Trustee, but had replaced him, and become *Sole* Trustee for the James Joyce Estate. He had produced, with Philip Gaskell, a book which proposed nearly 500 changes to *Ulysses: The Corrected Text*. He stood over a curious, even questionable record as adviser to the project and he was now quite clearly the dominant figure in Joyce scholarship, since he controlled, of course with advice, the business of the Estate. In spite of the differences which had arisen about editorial principle, he said, 'in the long run the best solution seemed to be to go forward despite the disagreements, since they were differences over principle rather than about whether the work had been shoddily or well done. We at no point believed that Gabler and his team were doing a bad job according to its own lights. We thought they were doing a very good job. It's just that we would have preferred them to do a slightly different job.' This had changed with Kidd's criticisms. 'His is a major critique. Gabler has undertaken to write a rebuttal. The matter is crucial. It is crucial that it be resolved some day.' But these expectations of a response and this use of the word 'crucial' in respect of achieving resolution have to be set beside Clive Hart's view that the whole question of how this should be done, or whether it will be done, had lapsed for the present with the disbanding of the Tanselle Committee. 'The Estate, therefore, is back where it was before, with a new and copyright edition which has aroused some controversy. And that controversy will no doubt continue. But until something really substantial arises for us to confront, the Estate will simply allow it [*Ulysses: The Corrected Text*] to appear.' Clive Hart did not indicate what 'something really substantial' might be. But he did express an interest in himself going down the editorial road. On the basis of his own and Philip Gaskell's book, as contained in its recommendations, he felt that there was 'a contribution to an alternative text for the book'. In answer to the question, would he undertake the editing of *Ulysses* himself, he replied: 'I could . . . I am somewhat tempted to go along that road myself. Yes.'

It is perhaps hardly surprising that Charles Rossman, who had studied more closely than anyone else the Hart–Gaskell–Ellmann–du Sautoy correspondence, should have been surprised almost to the point of alarm and astonishment at the development of Clive Hart's position, in that he was now considering himself a possible editor. 'Any future developments regarding Joyce's texts that require Joyce Estate approval now have, rather ironically, as the single voice of approval, Clive Hart, who has gone through all these permutations and shifts of attitude, and change, and now has a competing volume, and finds himself in the position of being able to accept or reject John Kidd's bid to edit a 1922 edition. I find this rather amazing.' Rossman found amazing also the vaunting ambition to change the text which had led Gabler, at an early Joyce conference, to 'become enthusiastic and get carried away by the number of changes: six, eight, or more thousand. Who *knows*? No one really knows how many changes we'll find. It was the reclaiming of a lost, rather than the correcting of an existing text.'

Anthony Burgess has been a lifelong enthusiast for James Joyce. He started, as he told the conference, with *Finnegans Wake*, which was more available when he was young than the then banned *Ulysses*. He was a natural person to be approached for the pithy quotation upon which much of the 1986 advertising and publicity campaign was based, culminating in the epithet 'Rejoyce!' When his adulation was put to him in Monte Carlo in June 1990, he replied: 'I would take back those words. That great Germanic edition was supposed to be error-free. There are just as many errors, though of a different kind, as there were in the old one.' He went on to conclude that we should 'Leave it alone. Even with the errors, I think it's time to leave it alone.'

Although John Kidd was not in Monte Carlo for the 12th International James Joyce Symposium, his views were subsequently sought in the light of what people had said in Monte Carlo. In a filmed interview, a month later, he claimed that the project had been initiated on the basis of a misrepresentation of the state of the earlier editions. There was, he said, 'a process of first condemning the book which had existed previously. The assessment of there being seven errors per page, a total of 5,000 or so errors in the book as a whole, this really wasn't a scholarly assessment, it was more of a publicity ploy and a slander on the book which Joyce had published. Most of the corrections which needed to be made had already been made in Joyce's lifetime. But there was a tendency to want to obscure and to talk absolutely impenetrable theory at certain moments, and that has certainly worked to Gabler's advantage, because he's the obscurest and most impenetrable of them all.'

John Kidd was colourfully outspoken. 'He's made bigger blunders than any other editor in history,' he said. 'He's made a hash of Joyce's *Ulysses*.' He charged: 'In a more rigorous field, a scientific field, there might be a committee right now investigating plagiarism. But this being a literary, humanities field, nobody wants to haul Gabler up.' Of course, Kidd had done just that. He claimed that his own detailed critique 'lists more factual errors than have ever been brought into print against any scholar in our time'. Kidd feels that, 'if the James Joyce Estate is serious about having accurate texts of the works of James Joyce, then they will see to it that they get the best advice and that they have a good edition. If there is a really good text of *Ulysses*, you won't have to worry. The Gabler text will just fade away.'

Afterword

THE GABLER TEXT has shown no inclination whatever to fade away. In bookshops throughout the world it flourishes in a variety of different versions. For all its faults, it is accepted as the standard version of *Ulysses*. It remains the one that is taught. There are no proposals to revise it. There are no proposals to replace it. It is currently serving the purposes of the James Joyce Estate.

The scandal of *Ulysses*, as outlined in this book, is a scandal by design. Errors and mistakes abound; there is human weakness and vacillation; there are many puzzles and uncertainties, at least some of which will never be cleared up. But the evidence at the centre shows that those responsible for the Estate of James Joyce sought to create fresh copyright in the most profitable work of fiction in the 20th century and did so without adequate regard for scholarship. They also represented their actions in a favourable light, implying harmony and agreement, prudence and good judgment, when the facts show that a quite different situation prevailed behind the scenes.

Several dates are important in teasing out what happened; but the most crucial span of all is the time between April and September of 1985. In early April David Remnick published his article in *The Washington Post*. This was a serious piece of journalism, alerting the public to the fact that there were things wrong with the edition and that a relatively unknown academic, John

Kidd, had challenged 4,000 of the supposed 5,000 'correc-tions' in the edition as unnecessary. What he was going to reveal would 'blow the whole Joyce establishment wide open'. Kidd delivered the first version of these criticisms on 26 April 1985. His charges against the edition included errors of fact, incoherent theories, principles stated but not followed and fundamental tenets of editing ignored or overruled. By any standard of judgment and notwith-standing the manner of his approach or the journalism that had preceded his scholarly paper, he merited a hear-ing. Gabler gave him none and clearly indicated that there was 'nothing' in what Kidd had charged that required answer.

Others thought differently, including the editor of *The Times Literary Supplement*, Jeremy Treglown, who had attended the confrontation and published an article sug-gesting to the James Joyce Estate that publication of the new 'standard' edition of *Ulysses*, without the scholarly apparatus, and 'assured of huge sales', should be delayed.

Kidd, in his paper, was a solitary figure, voicing criti-cisms which appeared so extreme as to suggest that his position was eccentric. This perception was not helped by his manner, which Fritz Senn describes as 'strident'. But a more substantial body of established Joycean critics assembled in late May at the Princess Grace Irish Library for the specific purpose of assessing the 1984 *Ulysses*. Seri-ous misgivings were expressed, some of which did not appear in the book of essays subsequently published. Among those that did was Richard Ellmann's address about 'Love, yes. Word known to all men.' This addition to the 1984 *Ulysses*, which quite definitely changes the emotional balance of the book, was the most substantial single editorial alteration made by Gabler and had attracted more comment than any other aspect of the editing. Ellmann recommended that it should be taken out.

The implications of much that was debated at Monaco,

together with the implications of John Kidd's criticisms, were that detailed and fairly extended scholarly consideration of the edition was needed. The same message had been coming for some time from the more informed of the advisers. At least a preliminary view of the seriousness of the challenges would have been available by the middle of June to those who controlled the project, headed by Peter du Sautoy.

In the interests of scholarship the need for delay was quite clear. For the trade edition, *Ulysses: The Corrected Text*, to appear as originally planned, on Bloomsday 1986, setting would need to start in the early autumn of 1985 and the planning of this was already in hand by the end of July. If the undertakings were to be honoured about allowing scholars to register their reservations and for Gabler to be given the opportunity to consider the criticisms comprehensively, the timetable would have had to be substantially changed.

Quite the opposite happened. The plans which were already in place, which were to go ahead with *Ulysses: The Corrected Text*, were given a new impetus by the criticisms, and appear to have been speeded up. Certainly, the urgency expressed by Hans Walter Gabler in late July of 1985 implies the complete rejection of any scholarly debate, or the public acceptance of changes. At that point typesetting was already being organised by The Bodley Head. Changes were made in the edition, but without reference to any of the scholars who had suggested them. They were incorporated piecemeal and unacknowledged. They included changes based on criticisms made by John Kidd himself and published in *The Washington Post*.

When Clive Hart wrote to Peter du Sautoy in August 1985 to give him a report on the Monaco conference and to advise him about what action was needed, the processes required to meet the 16 June 1986 *Ulysses* deadline were already advanced. Yet Hart told the Trustee for the

James Joyce Estate that Kidd's criticisms alone 'are so damaging as to need at least some consideration'.

They were given the most peculiar consideration of all: to pick some and implement them unacknowledged, and to ignore the rest. Peter du Sautoy, whose responsibilities required him to make judgments about the criticism of Kidd and of others in order to be in a position to decide on the future of the edition, relied on Hart to make those judgments for him and then ignored Hart's advice. He could have invited Kidd to meet him and then have listened to his case. He could have forced his own editor, Gabler, to answer a range of the points that had been made. He could, in short, have fulfilled the undertaking which was part of the programme for the editions – that time would be allowed for scholarly consideration of the synoptic and critical text, with a view to incorporating better readings and making the kinds of corrections which were likely to emerge from so massive an undertaking.

He did the opposite. He washed his hands of Kidd and simply went ahead in accordance with the plans to publish without any delay at all. They would adhere to the original programme. During the period from April to August 1985, all the essentials of the confrontation, with the important exception of the idea of an underlying copyright motive, were given publicity. The troubles of the next five years were set in concrete. The edition appeared. The acclamation was massive. Critical reservation was minimal. Sales were extensive. The reading public, despite no previous sense of alarm about the supposed mass of errors in earlier editions of the work, now felt reassured that they could acquire Joyce in a purified and authentic version. He had been cleaned up.

Kidd continued his criticisms. The Estate ignored him. So did Gabler. These criticisms increased in volume, but were not substantive and there is a case *for* the edition and *against* Kidd, on the grounds of his arguments about the edition, in the main, being piecemeal. This was so up to and including his article in *The New York Review of Books*. A major change emerged with Charles Rossman's findings in Tulsa, which revealed a massive amount of uncertainty and doubt, confusion and disagreement between the Trustee for the James Joyce Estate, his editor-in-chief and the advisers to the edition. They also confirmed a suspicion, voiced by John Kidd, that the main motive for the level and extent of change in the edition was to ensure a new copyright. This raised fundamental doubts about the integrity of the whole project.

The Estate denied these charges. So did Gabler. Yet the evidence is incontrovertible: Peter du Sautoy's aim appears at best to have included renewal of copyright, less so at the beginning than later, but always as a serious consideration. He lists copyright as one of the issues at stake as a result of the Trustees' meeting on 31 October 1977*. He neither understood nor cared much about the details of synoptic and critical editing. As late as August 1985, he confessed in his letter to Ellmann how disconcerting he found it, as a publisher, to be discovering that Hans Walter Gabler had produced the text of the work *as Joyce wrote it* and not the text which Joyce aimed for as the public text of *Ulysses*. In eight years, it seems, the principal figure acting on behalf of the James Joyce Estate in the project was unaware of the main difference between Hans Walter Gabler's *Ulysses* and all the previous editions of the work.

The role of the publishers has been obscure. Up to the time of the agreement between the Estate and Hans Walter Gabler to go ahead with a re-edited *Ulysses*, the book had been published in hardback in the United States by Random House and in paperback by Vintage. In Britain, the Commonwealth and elsewhere, the hardback

---

* (See 'Editing *Ulysses* A Personal Account' by Peter du Sautoy, *James Joyce Quarterly*; Vol. 27, No. 1, published autumn 1989.)

publishers had been The Bodley Head, the paperback publishers Penguin. The licence given to Garland Publishing for the 1984 *Ulysses: A Critical and Synoptic Edition* was a licence for two years. Negotiations on the contracts involved in this arrangement, according to the Ellmann papers, were completed in 1982, the James Joyce centenary year. Stephen James Joyce, in response to a question by the author from the floor during a plenary session at the 1990 Monaco conference, claimed that the pressure for publication of the revised 1986 edition of *Ulysses* came from the publishers. A later claim, also involving the motives of the publishers and made by Peter du Sautoy in a letter to *The Times Literary Supplement* in September 1988, represented the matter in the following terms: 'The Gabler edition received wide approbation from leading Joyce scholars: so much so that the trade publishers pressed for early release of the text, as they needed to reprint.' There is no evidence of this pressure in any of the Ellmann papers. Perhaps it was outside the realm of discussion between the Trustee and his advisers, though this would seem odd, since the contracts are certainly mentioned, so is the question of copyright.

The publishers have not entered the debate directly. Yet the most senior of them, Jason Epstein, vice-president of Random House, was responsible for the move to resolve the impasse created by Kidd's main critical attack and was then responsible for suspending that effort at resolution, without attempting any kind of replacement. At the time his view was that the edition was seriously flawed and he confessed to being totally confused. Yet for more than a year neither he nor any other publisher has sought to resolve the situation. Could this be deliberate? Any resolution during the present period of normal copyright on the basic text of *Ulysses*, in the form used up to the publication of the 1984 *Ulysses*, would require the permission of the Estate. After 1992, while the 1984 and 1986 Gabler editions will still be under a copyright stretching well into the next century, all other versions will be free of copyright and the publishers, both those presently responsible for Joyce's works in the main countries which read them and any other wishing to become a publisher of Joyce, will have public domain access to the works. This reality must give pause to those interested in what is still, from a commercial point of view, arguably the hottest literary property in the world today.

The James Joyce Estate presides over a mess largely of its own making. The mess is extensive and embraces more than *Ulysses*, though *Ulysses* is the most notable element in it. The Estate has achieved new copyright, but over an edition which has been shown to be deeply, fundamentally flawed and will need to be replaced. The world of publishing and of scholarship is free from 1 January 1992 to remedy the problems without having to seek the permission of the James Joyce Estate, and most certainly will so remedy the situation created by the faulty management of the interests of Joyce's heirs.

Only one of those heirs plays any kind of public role, Stephen James Joyce. He is understandably secretive about his own family affairs, meaning the affairs of his grandparents as much as those of himself and his wife. He believes that people should read the books and *only* the books without the handicap of controversy. He has little time for the scholarly debate in which he rarely engages. He is on record, in a letter to *The Times Literary Supplement* of 9–15 September 1988, calling for someone to sit down and write 'the turbulent history of *Ulysses*'. I am happy to have obliged him.

Bruce Arnold
Dublin, spring 1991

A Chronology of *Ulysses*

1906
Joyce considers adding to *Dubliners* a story entitled 'Ulysses'. This is the first emergence of the idea on which the novel was based.

1914
Joyce starts writing *Ulysses*.

1916

September
In letter to Yeats, referring to *Ulysses*, Joyce says it will not be finished for 'some years'.

November
In letter to Harriet Shaw Weaver, Joyce expresses the hope that he will finish *Ulysses* in 1918.

1918
First episode published in *The Little Review*.

1919

August
Joyce predicts, in letter to John Quinn, completion of *Ulysses* by the end of 1920.

1921

21 February
Trial takes place in New York; Margaret Anderson and Jane Heap convicted of publishing obscenity.

Publication in *The Little Review* ceases at an early point in Episode 14, 'Oxen of the Sun', almost exactly halfway through the book.

10 June
Joyce receives first galley proofs from Darantiere.

6 November
Joyce announces to Frank Budgen: '*Ulysses* is finished'.

1922

2 February (Joyce's birthday)
First edition of *Ulysses* published by Shakespeare and Company, Paris, 1,000 numbered copies.

October
Edition by Egoist Press, London, 2,000 numbered copies.

1923

January
Edition by Egoist Press, London, 500 numbered copies.

February
Joyce starts on *Finnegans Wake*.

1924

1 January
Shakespeare and Company publish an unlimited edition of *Ulysses* (reset in 1926).

16 January
Quinn's manuscripts of *Ulysses* (which becomes the Rosenbach Manuscript) sell for $1,975.

Herbert Gorman's *James Joyce: The First Forty Years* published.

1925

Translation of *Ulysses* into French.

1927

Paul Jordan Smith's *A Key to the 'Ulysses' of James Joyce* published.

1930

Stuart Gilbert's *James Joyce's 'Ulysses'* published.

1931

Joyce marries Nora in London.

5 August
Joyce signs his will in London.

1932

15 February
Stephen James Joyce born.

Charles Duff's *James Joyce and the Plain Reader* published.

December
The Odyssey Press, Paris, Hamburg, Bologna, unlimited edition of *Ulysses* published.

1933

Louis Golding's *James Joyce* published.

December
Judge Woolsey declared *Ulysses* not pornographic. Book no longer banned in USA.

Prohibition ends.

1934

January
First American unlimited edition from Random House.

Frank Budgen's *James Joyce and the Making of 'Ulysses'* published.

1935

October
Limited Editions Club, New York, 1,500 copies, illustrated and signed by Henri Matisse.

1936

October
The Bodley Head in Britain brings out limited edition of *Ulysses*, 1,000 copies.

1937

September
First unlimited English edition (The Bodley Head).

1941

13 January
James Joyce dies.

1945

Probate obtained on the Joyce estate.

1951

10 April
Nora dies.

1953

John J. Slocum and Herbert Cahoon publish *A Bibliography of James Joyce*.

1956

Richard M. Kain and Marvin Magalaner publish *Joyce: the Man, the Work, the Reputation*.

1959

Richard Ellmann publishes *James Joyce*, his biography of the writer.

1960

April
The Bodley Head *Ulysses* reset.

1961

Random House *Ulysses* reset.

1964

New copyright edition of *A Portrait of the Artist as a Young Man*.

1967

New copyright edition of *Dubliners*.

International James Joyce Symposium, Dublin.

1968

Penguin Books, London, unlimited paperback edition of *Ulysses*.

1969

International James Joyce Symposium, Dublin.

1971

International James Joyce Symposium, Trieste.

1973

International James Joyce Symposium, Dublin.

1975

International James Joyce Symposium, Paris.

1976

12 June
Giorgio Joyce dies.

Franklin Library, New York, issue between 1976 and 1979 three illustrated editions in special bindings.

1977

Hans Walter Gabler begins the editing of *Ulysses*. He is backed by a $300,000 grant from a German Government agency.

June
International James Joyce Symposium, Dublin.

1979

June
International James Joyce Symposium, Zurich.

1980

April
Hugh Kenner publishes 'The Computerized *Ulysses*' in *Harper's*. The article hails the edition and begins the process of debate.

1981

Between May and September, in correpondence between the Trustee for the James Joyce Estate, Peter du Sautoy, the editor, Hans Gabler, and the advisers, Clive Hart, Philip Gaskell and Richard Ellmann, serious differences over what is being done emerge. They are resolved in favour of the advisers having 'the last word'.

1982

International James Joyce Symposium, Dublin.

Lucia Joyce dies at St Andrew's Hospital, Northampton.

1983

Throughout 1983, in correspondence between the editor, his advisers and the Trustee, a crisis develops. In June Hart and Gaskell resign; Ellmann attempts reconciliation; Litz and Groden join the project to advise Gabler. Then, at the end of the year, differences are cleared up sufficiently to allow the former advisers to rejoin.

1984

John Kidd working as a post-doctoral fellow at the University of Virginia, at its Center for Advanced Studies.

16 June
International James Joyce Symposium, Frankfurt.

Ulysses: A Critical and Synoptic Edition is published by Garland Publishing, New York.

25 June
Ellmann reports to Peter du Sautoy on a conversation with Stephen James Joyce at Frankfurt in which the author's grandson says he is going to assert himself with the Estate.

1985

2 April
'Jolting the Joyceans': article by David Remnick on John Kidd for *The Washington Post*.

26 April
John Kidd delivers paper, 'Errors of Execution in the 1984 *Ulysses*', to the Society for Textual Scholarship, in New York.

10 May
The editor of the *TLS*, Jeremy Treglown, in a report on the Kidd paper, urges the Joyce Estate to delay publication of *Ulysses: The Corrected Text*.

Late May
Monaco Conference on *Ulysses*.

From June, an extended correspondence takes place, beginning with Clive Hart's letter to Peter du Sautoy on the Monaco Conference and on the criticisms of the Gabler edition. A meeting of the Trustees takes decision to publish in June 1986. In a letter from Peter du Sautoy to Richard Ellmann is mentioned the possibility of postponing trade edition. Hans Walter Gabler, in letter to Richard Ellmann, defends all his decisions, refuses to change. Later, a letter from Ellmann to du Sautoy explains the differences with which they were all dealing, between what Joyce wrote and what he saw into print.

Autumn issue, *Irish Literary Supplement*, 'Gaelic in the new *Ulysses*'.

1986

16 June
International James Joyce Symposium, Copenhagen.

Ulysses: The Corrected Text published in London and New York.

All other editions of *Ulysses* either go out of print or are withdrawn.

1987

Autumn
'The Genetic Joyce': article by John Kidd in the *James Joyce Literary Supplement*.

1988

Boston University sets up James Joyce Research Center with John Kidd as its Director.

15 June
Article in *New York Times*: 'Corrected *Ulysses* sparks scholarly row', by Edwin McDowell, reporting on the next day's issue of *NYROB*, with Kidd's 'The Scandal of *Ulysses*' in it.

16 June (Bloomsday)
Kidd article appears in *NYROB*.

International James Joyce Symposium, Venice.

September
Extensive correspondence begins in the *TLS* on Kidd's challenges to Gabler's version of *Ulysses*. Among those who write are Peter du Sautoy, Hans Walter Gabler, John Kidd, Charles Rossman, Michael Groden and Clive Hart (in review form).

1989

February
University of Miami Conference dedicated to a debate on the *Ulysses* controversy.

June
Publication by the Bibliographical Society of America of John Kidd's 'An Inquiry into *Ulysses: The Corrected Text*'.

Autumn issue of *James Joyce Quarterly* publishes 'Editing *Ulysses*: A Personal Account' by Peter du Sautoy in which he writes that, having gone through his files, it is beyond him to give 'even a moderately detailed account' and he offers instead selected points of interest.

1990

16 June
International James Joyce Symposium, Monaco.

Vintage International reissue the pre-Gabler version of *Ulysses*.

Summer
Special issue of *Studies in the Novel* is entirely devoted to 'Editing *Ulysses*'. Among other things, it publishes, in the form of their two papers, with postscripts, details of the Gabler–Kidd exchange in New York in 1985.

Autumn
James Joyce Quarterly publishes Michael Groden's: 'A Response to John Kidd's "An Inquiry Into *Ulysses: The Corrected Text*"', together with John Kidd's reply to it, 'Gabler's Errors in Context: A Reply to Michael Groden on editing *Ulysses*'.

Index

'Adderley', 232
Aldeburgh Festival, 107
Alden, Douglas, 192–3
Aldington, Richard, 45, 60
Anderson, Chester G., 96–7
Anderson, Margaret, 5, 10, 15, 45, 84
Aquinas, St Thomas, 151
Asquith, Herbert Henry, 65

Bates, Robin, 108; interviews Gabler, 227–33
Beach, Sylvia, 1, 11–12, 15, 17–21, 26–27, 33–9, 47–9, 76, 135, 136
Beckett, Samuel, 55, 236
Beja, Morris, 93, 237, interviewed by author, 240
Bennett, Arnold, 47, 60
Benoît-Méchin, Jacques, 24–5
Benstock, Bernard, 94, 213, 237
Berlin Convention on Copyright, 81
Berne Convention on Copyright, 80–2
'Best', 144
Bibliographical Society of America, 230
'Bloom, Leopold', 1–2, 4, 7–10, 22, 55, 110, 144, 146, 163, 189
'Bloom, Molly', 2, 4, 22–3, 146, 230
'Bloomsday', 53
'Boardman, Baby', 9
'Boardman, Edie', 9
Bodleian Library, 80
Bodley Head, 62, 76, 141, 162, 166–7, 170, 172, 180, 251, 254
Bodley, John, 125
Boheeman, Christine van, 94
Boland, Harry, 28
Boni & Liveright, 48

Borden, Gavin, 112, 121, 125, 146, 229
Bosinelli, Rosa, 155
Boston University, 198–200
Bowers, Fredson, 218, 220
Boydston, Jo Ann, 195, 230–1
Brady, Terence, 76
Brentano's (bookshop in Paris), 39
British Library, 75
British Museum, 75, 77, 106
Brocquy, Louis le, 236
Brown, Susan Sutcliff, 238
'Bryher' (pseud. of Sir J. Ellerman's daughter), 21
Budgen, Frank, 8–9, 49, 66, 221, 232
Buller, Captain, 187
Burgess, Anthony, 78, 91; hails 'Corrected Text', 173, 237, 239; interviewed by author, 240, 246
Byron, Gordon, Lord, 187

'Caffrey, Cissie', 9
Cahiers des Amis des Livres, 18
'Cahill, Mrs', 210, 222
Cahoon, Herbert, 195
Cambridge University Library, 80
Cape, Jonathan, 46, 96, 97
Card, James Van Dyck, 212
Center for Scholarly Editions, 230
Cerf, Bennett, 11, 60, 61
Chambers, E.K., 219
'Chester, Earl of' (pseud. for Edward VIII, King), see Edward VIII
Clongowes Wood College, 66
Congrès Mondial Irlandais, see: World Congress of the Irish Race
Columbia University, 195, 230
Colum, Padraic, 46, 76

'Conroy, Gabriel'
Corrigan, J.E., 10
Crane, Harte, 45
Criterion, The, 52, 57
'Culler, Captain', 188

Daily Express, The, 98
Daily Telegraph, The, 173
Dalton, Jack, 112–3, 124, 137, 159
Darantiere, Maurice, 18, 26–7, 29,
    32–4, 39, 49, 134, 135, 163, 171
Deane, Seamus, 104
'Dedalus, Simon', 91
'Dedalus, Stephen', 22, 134–5, 144,
    145–5, 149
Derwent, Lord, 65
Deutscheforschungsgemeineschaft, 104
de Valera, Eamon, 28
Donoghue, Denis, 195
Driver, Clive, 221–2
Dublin University, 107
Dublin University Library, 80
Duff, Charles, 53
Dujardin, 58
du Sautoy, Peter, 73, 97, 102, 105–6, 107,
    111, 112–125, 146, 152, 161, 163–70,
    his ultimate position of authority,
    177–8, 180, 193, 196–7, 200, 205,
    206, 213, 235, 242, 244, 251–4
Economist, The, 145, 176
Edinburgh University Library, 80
Edward VIII, King, 50
Egoist, The, 4–5, 18, 135, 136, 162, 225
Egoist Press, 29–30, 38, 45
Eliot, T.S., 45, 46, 56–7, 59, 63
Ellerman, Sir John, 21
Ellmann, Richard, 20, 27, 53, 73, 90–3,
    96, 103, 104, 106–7, 108, 113–15,
    120–6, 146–7, 148–50, 151–3, 165,
    167, 168, 174, 179, 183, 189, 196, 200,
    202–3, 204, 214, 233, 235, 245, 250,
    254
Emory University, Atlanta, 164
Envoy, 88, 140
Epstein, Jason, 192, 195, 227, 230, 233,
    254
Ernst, Maurice L., 62

Faber and Faber, 105
Faulkner, William, 87
Fendant de Sion (Swiss white

wine), 55
FitzGerald, Desmond, 27–8
FitzGerald, Garret, 27
Foote, Tim, 234
Forster, E.M., 60
Franfurter Zeitung, 72
Friis-Moller, Kai, 63
Fry, Roger, 5

Gabler, Hans Walter, 85, 102, 103, 104,
    108; early exchanges on editing
    process, 109–12; and Jack Dalton,
    112; 113–26; and his editing
    procedure, 127–39, 141, 142, 145,
    147, 148–9, 151–70; encounter with
    Kidd in New York, 158–61; 162–9,
    172–4, 180, 181, 182–3, 184–9;
    exchanges in *Times Literary
    Supplement*, 192–6, 197, 200;
    206–7, command of English, 202;
    208, 209; at Miami Conference,
    210–11, 213, 215–6; extensively
    criticised by Kidd, 217–26; failure
    to answer, 227–33; 237–8;
    interviewed by author, 240–3; 244,
    247, 249–55
Gaignebet, Claude, 237
Galignani (bookshop in Paris), 31, 39
Galsworthy, John, 46
Garland Publishing, 112, 121, 145, 146,
    164, 166–7, 191, 204, 229
Gaskell, Philip, 102, 107, 113–22, 125,
    133, 147, 152–3, 168, 178, 179, 204,
    209; at Miami Conference, 213;
    217, 234, 238, 244
Georgia Review, The, 151, 202, 207
Gide, André, 19
Giedion-Welcker, Mrs., 67
Gilbert, Sandra, 237
Gilbert, Stuart, 53–55, 56, 85, 159, 163,
    189, 225
Gogarty, Oliver St. John, 91, 142
Golding, Louis, 53
Goldman, Arnold, 214
Gorman, Herbert, 52–3, 88
Gray, Paul, 143–4, 176
'Greene', 232
Greg, W.W., 218–20
Gregory, Lady Augusta, 35
Groden, Michael, 106, 108, 120, 122, 123,
    125, 187, 190, 203, 209; at Miami

Conference, 213; 237; interviewed by author, 240–3

'Haines', 222
Harper's, 110, 141, 234
Harrison, Samuel, 72
Harris, Frank, 199
Hart, Clive, 73, 77–8, 107–8, 112, 113–20, 122, 125, 133, 147, 152–3, 161, 165, 167, 168–9, 177, 178, 179, 180, 202, 204, 205, 206–7, 208, 209, 212; at Miami Conference, 213; 230; interviewed by Bates, 233–4; 235, 237, 238; interviewed by author, 240–1; 244–5, 251–2
Harvard University, 74, 88
Heap, Jane, 5, 11, 15
Hemingway, Ernest, 19
Henchy, Patrick, 91
Henke, Suzette, 165
Hogarth House, 6
Hogarth Press, 6
Hours of Idleness, 187
Housman, A.E., 47
Huebsch, B.W., 48, 60
Humanities Research Centre (Texas), 94, 157
'Images of James Joyce' (film), 236
International James Joyce Symposium, 93, 109, 145, 246
Irish-American Trinity Dance Academy of Wisconsin, 237
Irish Independent, 235
Irish Literary Supplement, The, 162–3, 211
'Ivors, Miss', 98

Jackson (bookseller in Paris), 31
James Joyce Broadsheet, 94, 212
James Joyce Estate, 72–3, 78, 96, 97, 104, 106; trusts of, 105–7; 109; rows over Gabler's editing, 109–112; copyright question, 113–26; 137, 147, 151; publication of 'Corrected Text' and, 169; 177, 183, 186, 192, 196, 204–6, 208, 209, 213, 235–6, 244–5, 249, 252–5
James Joyce Foundation, 93, 145, 236, 241
James Joyce Literary Supplement, The, 94, 212, 214

James Joyce Museum (Sandycove), 94
James Joyce Quarterly, 94, 190
James Joyce Research Centre (Boston), 198
John Simon Guggenheim Foundation, 195
Johnston, Denis, 88, 89
Joyce Archives, The, 186
Joyce, Giorgio, 39, 64, 66, 68, 70–1, 74
Joyce, James: gives copy of Chamber Music to Nora, 74; makes his will, 67–8; marriage to Nora, 68; renewal of copyright, 97–101
Joyce, James, works by
  Chamber Music, 44, 48, 74, 82; critical edition of, 217
  'Clay', 98
  Dubliners, 13, 44, 48, 60, 65, 82, 83, 92, 96, new copyright edition, 97–101; and the origins of Ulysses, 130; critical edition of, 217
  Exiles, 8, 48, 75–6, 77; Dublin University Players' production, 76, 185; critical edition of, 217
  Finnegans Wake, 41, 44, 50, 55, 56, 75, 77, 88, 104, 112, 163, 246
  Portrait of the Artist as a Young Man, A, 44, 48, 60, 82, 83, 92, 96; publication, 4; proof sheets bought by Quinn, 8; Anderson's copyright edition, 96–7, 100; critical edition of, 217
  'The Dead', 98
  Ulysses
    Academic advisers to edition, 106–7
    'A Critical and Synoptic Edition', 102, 105; initiation of edition, 106–7; 1984 publication confirmed, 123; critical reception, 140–51
    agreement with Sylvia Beach, 17–18
    appearance, 27; Joyce's views on, 34–5
    argument over editorial approaches, 218–23
    attitude of Joyce in early in years, 31–2
    bibliography of controversy, 110
    bookshop sales in Paris, 39–40

'continuous manuscript text', 221
control over edition, 202–5
'*Corrected Text, The*' (Gabler), 85,
  96, 102–5; errors in, 155–67;
  publication of, 161–8, 172–3;
  critical reception of, 173–5;
  New York Review of Books
  attack by Kidd, 184–90;
  mistakes over editions, 189
copyright (in U.S.A.), 59–60,
  77–86
critical reception, 42–50; Ezra
  Pound and, 43; in post-war
  period, 87–
Dalton, Jack, corrections to, 112–3
details of early printings, 31
editorial confrontations, 110–126
Ellmann's role in editing, 92,
  102–110; his Preface to
  'Corrected Text', 147–8
explanations of text, 51–4
final word decided, 24–5
first American edition, 61–2; first
  English edition, 62–3
first parody of, 24
initiation of Gabler edition,
  239–40
late corrections, 22–23
listing of editions by Gabler, 224–6
loses interest in textual errors, 50
love passage in, 143–4
Miami Conference debate, 210–11
mockery of Joyce over, 59
obscene book, 1–3
ownership of rights, 59
pirating of (in U.S.A.), 59–60
printing and design of, 20–21
publication, 4, 26–8; in serial
  form, 5, 8–9, 15–16, 51
sale and disposal of mss., 34–8,
  67–69
sales compared with *Seven Pillars
  of Wisdom*, 46
seized by Customs, 30–1
Sylvia Beach and, 1, 11–12, 15;
  offers to publish, 17; sells ms
  material, 37–8; and critical
  reception, 42
time taken to write, 19
translation into French, 51
use of facsimiles, 221–4

view on corrections, 24, 28–9,
  32–3, 34
writing of, 13, methods of
  transcription, 14–15
Joyce, Lucia, 67, 68, 70, 209
Joyce, Nora, 6, 27, 58, 64, 66–7, 68,
  70–1, 74, 91–2, 145
Joyce, Stephen James, 68, 71, 73, 78, 126,
  197–8, 205, 209, 236, 237; on the
  initiation of the edition, 239–40;
  241, 255
Joyce Studies Annual, 94
Jung, Carl, 7

Kain, Richard M., 45, 52, 93, 165
Kavanagh, Patrick, 87, 88–9
Kenner, Hugh, 92, 108, 110, 122, 127;
  reviews 1984 *Ulysses*, 140–6, 148,
  161, 172, 176, 230; interviewed by
  Bates, 233–4; 237; interviewed by
  author, 240
Kidd, John, 102–3, 148, 152; and
  Washington Post article, 155–8;
  blowing open Joyce
  establishment, 156; supporters of,
  157; Society of Textual
  Scholarship meeting, 158–61; 172,
  179, 180, 181, 182–3; article in *New
  York Review of Books*, 184–90; 192,
  195, 198; moves to Boston
  University, 198–9; 200–4, 209; at
  Miami Conference, 210–12; reads
  paper at, 215; extensive criticisms
  of Gabler's editing, 216–26; 229,
  230, 237; interviewed by author,
  246–7; 249–50, 252
Kildare Street Club, 187
King's College, Cambridge, 107
Kraus Reprint Corporation, 225
Kristensen, Tom, 63

Lane, John, 62
Larbaud, Valérie, 23, 52, 53
Lawrence, D.H., 47, 238
Lawrence, Karen, 93, 237
Lawrence, T.E., 46, 63
Léon, Paul, 53, 66, 75, 225
Leslie, Shane, 35, 47
Levin, Ira, 88
Lewis, Wyndham, 60
Librairie la Hune, 74

Library of America, 227
Limited Editions Club, 225
Little Review, The, 4–5, 8–10, 15–16, 19,
 45, 84–5, 129, 135, 136, 162, 225
Litz, A. Walton, 106, 108, 119, 122, 123,
 125, 203, 213
Lowerey, Robert G., 162–4
Lyttleton, Humphrey, 107

Macy, George, 225
McAlmon, Robert, 21–22, 28
MacCarthy, Desmond, 58
McCormick, Mrs Harold, 6–8
McDowell, Edwin, 211
'McDowell, Gertie', 2, 9
McGann, Jerome, 157, 178, 217, 219–20
MacNicholas, Jack, 113
Maddox, Brenda, 71, 74, 145–6, 176, 209
Magalaner, Marvin, 45, 52
Maison des Amis des Livres, La, 11, 18
Mansfield, Katherine, 47
Manton, Judge, 62
'Maria' (in 'Clay'), 99
Martin, Augstine, interviewed by
 author, 240
Matisse, Henri, 189, 225, 230
Melchior, Claus, 105, 238
Meredith, George, 36
Meyerbeer, 142
Miami Conference (1989), 187, 209, 212,
 213, 242–3
Miami University, 94
Michael Smurfit Collection, 236
'Misses Morkans, The', 98
Monaco Conference (1985), 132,
 149–50, 152–4, 167, 170, 178, 201, 212
Monnier, Adrienne, 11–12, 18, 24, 51
Monroe, Harriet, 5
Monte Carlo Conference (1990),
 235–47
Montgomery, Niall, 88, 89, 140
Moore, George, 65
Moore, Thomas, 110
Morel, Auguste, 51, 53
Moschos, Myrsine, 18
'Mulligan, Buck', 91, 188, 210, 222
Munich University, 104
Munro, David, 72, 73, 125
Munro, Fred, 72
Munro, Lionel, 73, 125
Munro, Pennefeather (Joyce's

solicitors), 72
Munro-Kerr, Anne, 73

Nadel, Ira, 238
National Library (Dublin), 66, 75
National University of Ireland, 104
New College (Oxford), 203
New York Herald, 24
New York Review of Books, The, 102,
 103, 147, 151; Kidd article in,
 184–90, 192, 198, 200, 205, 207, 211,
 212, 217, 224, 230, 233, 235, 253
New York Society for the Prevention of
 Vice, 9, 41
New York Times, The, 211, 229
New York University, 195
Nicolson, Harold, 58
Nobel Prize, 28
'Norman, Connolly', 188
Norman, Conolly, 188
Norris, David, interviewed by author,
 240, 243
Nouvelle revue francaise, la, 51–2
Noyes, Alfred, 46
Nutting, Myron, 23

O'Connor, Judge Sandra Day, 100
O'Connor, Ulick, 91
Odyssey Press, 226
O'Faolain, Sean, 87, 89, 95
O'Kelly, Count, 66
O'Kelly, Sean T., 28
'Old Mother Grogan', 210
Ott, Wilhelm, 109
Oundle School, 107

Papers of the Bibliographical Society of
 America, 212, 213, 215
Peake, Charles, 164–5, 230
Penguin Books, 172
Phillips Andover Academy, 71
Pierpoint Morgan Library, 195
Poetry, 5
Pound, Ezra, 4–6, 13–15, 19, and his
 promotion of Joyce, 43–4, 46, 56,
 82–3, 95
Powell, Anthony, 173–4
Power, Arthur, 27
Prescott, Joseph, 73
Prince Albert of Monaco, 239
Princess Caroline of Monaco, 239

Princess Grace Irish Library (Monaco), 94, 236, 238, 250
Proust, Marcel, 19–20, 127, 192

Quinn, John, 8–12, 35–8, 48, 50, 83, 131, 135

Radio-Telefis Eireann, 117
Random House, 11, 60, 61, 76, 85, 113, 129, 137, 166–7, 170, 192, 195, 213, 235, 254
Reagan, Ronald, 86
Reichert, Klaus, 237
Reith, Lord, 58
Remnick, David, 155, 158, 182, 230, 249
Richards, Grant, 98, 99
Richmond District Lunatic Asylum, 188
Rockefeller, John D., 6
Rodgers, W.R., 88
Rodker, John, 29–31, 38, 40
Rosenbach, A.S.W., 36–7, 76
Rosenbach Institute, 76
Rosenbach Manuscript, 130, 133–4, 149, 152, 186, 202, 221, 223, 231
Rosenbach Museum, 76, 120, 223
Rossman, Charles, 103, 110, 151, 182, 190, 196, 197, 198, 200–1, 204, 207–8, 209; at Miami Conference, 213–4; 233, 235; chairs Monte Carlo debate on Joyce editing, 238; interviewed by author, 240; 245, 253
Roth, Samuel, 59–60, 83, 85
'Rowan, Bertha', 76
'Rowan, Richard', 76
Royal Air Force, 106
Royal Artillery, 107
Russell, George, 35
Ryder, John, 162, 170, 171
Sackville-West, Vita, 58
Saintsbury, George, 43
Sandulescu, George, 152, 194, 212, 238
Sauermann, Charlotte, 7
Scandal of Ulysses, The (film), 236
Schalke, Kuno, 109
Scholarly Publishing, 170
Scholes, Robert, 97
Schwarzkopf, General, 190
Senn, Fritz, 94, 108–9, 164, 209; interviewed by author, 240, 243–4

Shakespeare and Company, 11, 27, 46, 49, 59
Shattuck, Roger, 192–3
Shaw, G.B., 19
Shloss, Carol, 244
'Shrift, Harry', 185
Slocum, John J., 29–30, 74, 195
Smith, Paul Jordan, 53
Smithsonian, The, 229–30, 234
Smythe, Colin, 94
Society for Textual Scholarship, 103, 158, 161–2, 194, 195, 201, 211
Society of Authors, 72, 112, 162, 186, 205
Spoo, Robert, 94
Sporting Times, The, 47–8
Staley, Thomas, 209, 237
Stephens, James, 35, 60
Steppe, Wolfhard, 105, 112, 238
Straumann, Heinrich, 64
Studies in Bibliography, 218
Studies in the Novel, 110, 187, 214, 230
Sumner, John, 9
Sykes, Claud W., 14, 134, 159

'Tallboys, Mrs Mervyn', 7
Tanselle Committee, 103, 192, 194–5, 201, 206, 213, 215, 227, 230–1, 234–5, 244
Tanselle, G. Thomas, 195, 227, 233
Tatlow, Juliet, 76
Terquem (Bookshop in Paris), 39
Thom's Directory, 187–8
Thrift, Harry, 185, 187, 231–2
Time Magazine, 143–5, 176
Times, The, 27
Times Literary Supplement, The, 103, 140, 161–2, 190, 192, 198, 211, 250, 254, 255
Treglown, Jeremy, 161–2, 211, 250
Trinity College, Cambridge, 107
Trinity College (Dublin), 76, 185, 237, 243
Turner, Decherd, 158

University of Bologna, 155
University of Buffalo, 74
University of Connecticut, 73–4
University of Miami, 209, 226, 242
University of South Carolina, 112–3
University of Texas at Austin, 94, 103, 158, 196

University of Tubingen, 109
University of Tulsa (Oklahoma), 94,
103, 165, 190, 196, 208, 233
University of Virginia, 155, 164, 198
University of Western Ontario, 187
Uppingham School, 106

Verene, Donald Phillip, 164
Vintage Paperbacks, 191

Washington Post, The, 155–8, 182, 211,
230, 249, 251
Weaver, Harriet Shaw, 4–6, 13–15,
18–19, 23–5, 27, 29–32, 38, 40,
44–5, 48–9, 50–1, 56, 68, 69,
involvement in Joyce's affairs
after his death, 69–71; 72, 74–5,
77, 82–3, 135
Weiss, Ottacaro, 55–6
West, Rebecca, 55, 57–8, 60
Wilde, Oscar, 92, 107, 203

Willard Gallery, 38, 76
Willard, Marion, 38
Williams, William Carlos, 27
Wilson, John Dover, 219
Woodnutt, Roma, 112, 125, 205–6, 207–9
Woolf, Leonard, 5
Woolf, Virginia, 5–6, 45, 60, 89
Woolsey, Judge John M., 2–3, 60, 61–2
World Congress of the Irish Race, 28

Yale University, 88, 107
Yale University Library, 38
Yeats, Anne, 236–7
Yeats, George, 92
Yeats, Jack, 236
Yeats, John Butler, 35
Yeats, Michael, 236
Yeats, W.B., 13, 19, 65, 75, 107, 236

Zurich James Joyce Foundation, 94, 109